Document Formatting and Typesetting on the UNIX™ System – Volume II

AT&T

AT&T

Document Formatting and Typesetting on the UNIX System – Volume II

grap, mv, ms & troff

Narain Gehani
&
Steven Lally

AT&T Bell Laboratories

Silicon Press
25 Beverly Road
Summit, N. J. 07901

Silicon Press
25 Beverly Road
Summit, NJ 07901

First Edition
Printing 9 8 7 6 5 4 3   Year 93 92 91

UNIX is a registered trademark of UNIX System Laboratories, Inc.

Library of Congress Cataloging in Publication Data
(Revised for Vol. 2)

Gehani, Narain, 1947-
  Document Formatting and Typesetting on the UNIX System.

  Vol. 2: grap, mv, ms & troff.
  Vol. 2 by: Narain Gehani & Steven Lally
  Bibliography: v. [1], p. 341-345; v .2, p.
  Includes Indexes.
  1. Word Processing. 2. UNIX (Computer Operating System)
  I. Lally, Steven. II. Title.

252.5.U54G43 1986   652'.5   85-61997
ISBN 0-9615336-2-5 (v. 1)
ISBN 0-9615336-3-3 (v. 2)

To
Terri & Kate
and
Indu, Neel & Varun

Contents

Contents

Preface

This book is strictly a sequel to the book titled *Document Formatting & Typesetting on the UNIX System* [Gehani 1986]. We assume that the reader is familiar with the material discussed in the first book; specifically, the reader should be familiar with typesetting terminology, basic formatting concepts and UNIX system document preparation facilities such as `tbl`, `pic` and `eqn`. The goal of this book is to discuss important UNIX system document preparation facilities that were either not discussed or were only discussed briefly in the first book; i.e., the facilities we will discuss in this book are `grap`, `mv`, `ms` and `troff`.

`grap` is a `pic` preprocessor for drawing graphs. `mv` is a macro package for specifying viewgraphs and slides. `ms` is a page-layout macro package that provides high-level formatting facilities similar to those provided by the more elaborate `mm`. `troff` is the UNIX system formatter that forms the basis of the UNIX system document preparation facilities.

There were several reasons why these facilities were not discussed in the first book. `grap` was not discussed because it had been just designed and it was in an evolutionary stage. The `mm` package for specifying the document format was selected in preference to its counterpart `ms`, because it is more comprehensive than `ms`. A strong motivation for discussing `ms` in this book is that `ms`, like `mm`, is also widely used. `troff` was not discussed in detail because it is a hard to use low-level, but powerful, facility that in general should not be used for specifying the document format directly. Higher level facilities, such as `mm` or `ms`, along with the preprocessors, should normally be used in preference to `troff`. The average user will probably not want to (or, should not) use `troff` directly. However, the sophisticated user may prefer to use `troff` directly because of its powerful capabilities, for extending existing macro packages such as `mm` or `ms`, or for writing new macro packages.

1. Organization of the Book

One chapter each is devoted to `grap`, `mv`, `ms` and `troff`. Each of these chapters is followed by detailed examples and exercises that complement the material presented in the chapter. To make the `mv` and `ms` chapters complete by themselves, we have discussed the `troff` facilities used with `mv` and `ms` in these chapters even though the `troff` facilities are discussed in detail in the chapter on `troff`.

In addition to the above chapters, the final chapter contains `ms` templates for the common types of documents. There is also an appendix that describes the commands for using the UNIX system formatting facilities discussed in this book and an annotated bibliography.

The input used to produce the examples, when given, is printed in constant-width font and enclosed in a box. For ease of reference, line numbers are given just outside the left edge of this box.

2. Contributions of the Authors

Steven Lally wrote the chapter on `troff` while Narain Gehani wrote the remaining material in this book.

Murray Hill, NJ   Narain Gehani
Middletown, NJ   Steven Lally
August 1987

Acknowledgment

We are grateful to many of our colleagues at AT&T Bell Laboratories who have helped us improve the quality of this book by giving us numerous comments and suggestions. Specifically, we greatly appreciate the help of R. F. Cmelik, R. Drechsler, D. Gay, C. L'Hommedieu, J. Joyce, J. P. Linderman, R. A. Lippman, J. Nowlin, M. Plotnick, M. E. Quinn, C. L. Simonds and T. L. Vaden.

Chapter 1

Specifying Graphs

A *graph* is a series of points, a line, a curve or an area that represents the variation of a variable in comparison with that of one or more other variables. Graphs are visual representations of data. They are often the most effective mechanism for summarizing, describing and exploring large amounts of data. Well-designed graphs *reveal* data [Tufte 1983]; that is, they

- show and summarize large amounts of data,
- illustrate the differences and similarities between large sets of data,
- highlight the meaning of the data (instead of the graphical display) and
- avoid distorting the data.

grap [DWB 1986a; Bentley & Kernighan 1984] is a pic preprocessor for specifying graphs. It provides a wide range of facilities for making customized graphs. For example, it provides facilities such as those for

- plotting data,
- connecting the data points,
- explicitly specifying axis ranges,
- logarithmic scaling,
- labeling axes,
- drawing grid lines,
- drawing lines, arrows and circles,
- placing text at arbitrary points on the graph,
- explicitly specifying the frame size and
- including data (and instructions) stored in files.

For most straightforward applications, grap is an easy to use tool. For example, a scatter graph,[1] was specified by supplying only the data points. grap draws the axes, puts tick marks on the axes and prints the ranges for the x- and y-axes. Before we discuss grap's facilities in detail, here is an example of a graph, its specification and an explanation of the specification.

---

1. A *scatter graph* is a graph consisting of points whose coordinates represent values of variables under study. A scatter graph is also known as a scatter diagram, a scatter plot or a scatter gram.

1. An Example of a `grap` Specification

Consider the following graph that shows the past, current and (projected) future expenses and revenues of Transcendental Transportation Inc. (TTI):

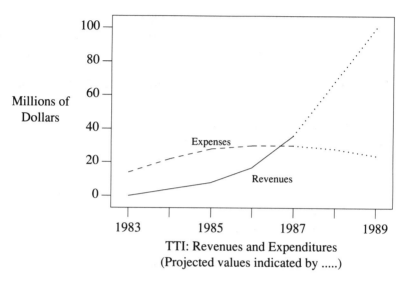

TTI: Revenues and Expenditures
(Projected values indicated by .....)

The box surrounding the graph is called the *frame*. The short vertical and horizontal lines on the bottom and left sides of the frame (the x- and y-axes) are called *ticks*. The numbers next to the ticks are the *tick labels*. The text on the left and at the bottom of the frame are the *axis labels*.

This graph was specified as

```
    .G1
    label left "Millions of" "Dollars" left .2
    label bot "TTI: Revenues and Expenditures"\
            "(Projected values indicated by .....)"
 5  ticks left out from 0 to 100 by 20
    ticks bot out from 1983 to 1989 by 2
    ticks bot out from 1984 to 1988 by 2 ""
    "Revenues" size -2 ljust at 1986, 10
    "Expenses" size -2 at 1985, 32
10  draw solid; copy "ttrev.data"
    draw dotted; copy "ttrev.fcast"
    new dashed; copy "ttexp.data"
    draw dotted; copy "ttexp.fcast"
    .G2
```

Graph specifications begin with the graph-begin instruction `.G1` and end with the graph-end instruction `.G2`. The frame is automatically printed by `grap`. However, the axis labels must be explicitly specified with `label` instructions (lines 2-4). Note that the second `label` instruction, on line 3, is continued onto line 4 by ending line 3 with a backslash. The `ticks` instructions (lines 5-6) print tick marks on the left and bottom sides of the frame (i.e., the x- and y-axes). The default tick labels used for the x- and y-axes are the x- and y-coordinates, respectively, of the tick locations. The tick label can be suppressed by specifying that the null label (the string `""`) be printed (see line 7).

Instructions on lines 8-9 specify labels for the graph lines (the exact position of these labels was determined experimentally by trial and error).

Line 10 contains two instructions: `draw`, which specifies that the data is to be plotted as a solid line, and the `copy` instruction, [2] which specifies that data values are to be read from the file `ttrev.data`. Note that multiple instructions can be given on the same line provided they are separated by semicolons. Line 11 specifies that additional data values are to be plotted as a dotted line and that they are to be read from the file `ttrev.fcast`.

The instructions on lines 12-13 are similar to those on lines 10-11 with one exception: the `new` instruction is like the `draw` instruction except that it plots new data points on a separate line. A `new` instruction indicates that a new set of data points is to be plotted while a `draw` instruction indicates continued plotting, usually with different characteristics, of the current or an existing set of data points. Had a `draw` instruction been used instead of the `new` instruction on line 12, then the "Expenses" line would have been drawn as a continuation of the "Revenues" line. Note that a `new` instruction could have been used in place of the `draw` instruction on line 10 but not in place of the `draw` instructions on lines 11 and 13.

Here is the data that was used for drawing the solid line marked "Revenue" (copied from the file `ttrev.data`):

```
1981  0
1982  4
1983  8
1984  17
1985  36
```

The data items stored in files `ttrev.fcast`, `ttexp.data` and `ttexp.fcast` are similar to those in file `ttrev.data`.

---

2. The `copy` instruction is similar to the `pic` instruction with the same name [Gehani 1987].

2. Format of a Graph Specification

A graph specification has the form

```
.G1
macro definitions
variable assignments
other grap instructions
.G2
```

where .G1 and .G2 are the graph-start and graph-end instructions.

Comments begin with the character # and continue up to the end of the line. Multiple instructions can be given on a single line provided they are separated by semicolons. Instructions can be continued across lines by ending the unfinished lines with a backslash.

3. Basics

By default, grap takes a set of x- and y-coordinate pairs, one coordinate pair per line, and produces a scatter graph. If each line contains a single number, then grap assumes that it is a y-coordinate and it uses i as the x-coordinate for the ith y-coordinate. If a data line contains two or more numbers, then grap takes the first number to be the x-coordinate and the remaining numbers to be corresponding y-coordinates all with the same x-coordinate.

The graph produced by grap consists of three major components: the frame surrounding the graph (which includes the axes), the data points or lines, and objects such as text and circles. grap provides facilities for refining or customizing these components to suit individual tastes. Before we discuss these facilities, we will first show you the default graph produced by grap.

3.1 The Default Graph

As an example of the default graph produced by grap, consider the following scatter graph, which plots the grades received by the students in one class:

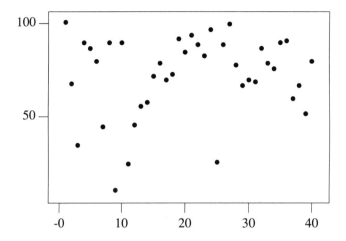

`grap` automatically puts the graph in a 2" × 3" frame and prints the ranges for the x- and y-axes. A bullet is plotted at the coordinates specified by each data point.

The specification of this graph is very simple:

```
.G1
copy  "rawgrades"
.G2
```

The `copy` instruction reads in the contents of the file `rawgrades`, which are the grades received by the students. Here are sample data values from the file `rawgrades`, which are used to draw the graph shown above:[3]

```
100
67
34
89
86
. . .
79
```

Instead of using the `copy` instruction to include the data from a file, the data could also be given directly within the graph specification:

---

3. We shall show the first five data lines and the last data line; the missing data lines are indicated by ". . .". This conforms with the convention used by Bentley and Kernighan [1984] to show graph data.

```
.G1
100
67
34
89
86
...
79
.G2
```

Let us now take a closer look at the scatter graph. This graph is not very meaningful because it does not show any interesting relationship between the x- and y-variables (the x-coordinate values are supplied by `grap`). The graph just shows the grades received by students 1, 2, 3, and so on. It does not, for example, show at a glance the number of students with grades in the ranges 0-9, 10-19, 20-29, ..., 80-89, and 90-100. Such information can be computed within the `grap` specification and then plotted. We will show you how to do this later; for the moment, assume that this information is available in a file named `grades`:

```
5  0
15 1
25 2
35 1
45 2
...
95 6
```

The first number in each line represents the midpoint of the corresponding range, e.g., 15 represents the range 10-19. The second number represents the number of students who received a grade within this range.

Using the data in file `grades`, i.e.,

```
.G1
copy "grades"
.G2
```

the graph produced is

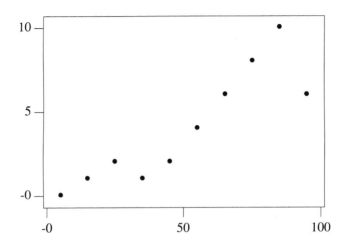

Now the number of students in a particular grade range can be easily determined from the graph. The data points can also be connected by a line:

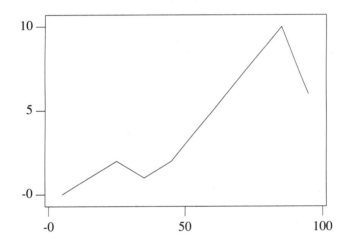

The line connecting the data points was specified with the draw instruction:

```
.G1
draw solid
copy "grades"
.G2
```

grap connects the data points in the order in which they appear in the data. Therefore, the data points must be given in order of increasing (or decreasing) x-values; otherwise, the graph produced may not be the one expected. For example, the following useless graph is drawn using the same data values as before, but this time these values are not sorted with respect to the x-values:

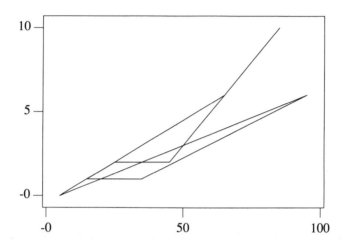

3.2 Variables, Expressions and Built-in Functions

`grap` provides facilities for defining floating-point variables and for floating-point arithmetic. Variables are not declared explicitly. The first assignment to a variable in a graph specification also serves as the declaration of the variable. Here are some examples of variable assignments:

```
h = 2.0; dx = 0.1
depth = 2.25
```

Within a single document containing several graphs, `grap` variable definitions carry over from the graph specification containing them to all successive graph specifications.

Floating-point expressions are constructed by using variables, floating-point and integer literals, the operators +, −, * and /, parentheses and built-in functions. The following assignment statements contain examples of floating-point expressions:

```
pi = 3.14159265; pi2 = pi * 2
```

A *coordinate expression* (i.e., a coordinate pair) consists of a pair of floating-point expressions; it is used to denote a specific point on a graph. Coordinate expressions have the form

$$(x, y) \quad \text{or just} \quad x, y$$

where x and y are floating-point expressions.

`grap` provides the following built-in functions:

function	description/comments
sin (e)	sine of e (e in radians)
cos (e)	cosine of e (e in radians)
atan2 (e_1, e_2)	the arctangent of e_1/e_2
log (e)	logarithm base 10 of e
exp (e)	10^e
sqrt (e)	square root of e
max (e_1, e_2)	maximum of e_1 and e_2
min (e_1, e_2)	minimum of e_1 and e_2
int (e)	integer part of e
rand ()	yields a random number r such that $0 \leq r < 1$.

3.3 Predefined Plotting Symbols

Predefined symbols that can be used for plotting data points are[4]

symbol	denotation	symbol	denotation
•	bullet	+	plus
■	box	*	star
·	dot	×	times
–	htick	|	vtick
□	square	Δ	delta

---

4. `grap` automatically reads the definitions of the plotting symbols from the file
   `/usr/lib/grap.defines`.

These symbols can be explicitly placed at a point "(x, y)" by using an instruction of the form[5]

sym at [*coord-system-name*] (x, y)

where *sym* specifies the symbol to be plotted. The optional *coord-system-name* refers to an explicitly specified coordinate system (see Section 4.1.1). The parentheses around "x, y" are optional.

Here is an example of the above instruction:

```
bullet at (25, 50)
```

The symbols shown above have been tailored for plotting data points. For instance, their sizes have been reduced and their printing positions have been changed to make them coincide with their plotting positions. However, any arbitrary character c, such as \ (12 which prints as ½, can also be plotted by using the string "c" instead of *sym* in the above instruction.

4. Frame

By default, grap draws a 2" by 3" frame using solid lines. Alternative frame styles can be specified using the frame instruction. For example, the following instruction

```
frame ht 3.0 wid 2.0 top invis right invis
```

specifies a 3" by 2" frame whose top and right sides are not printed. Using this instruction to specify the frame of the student grades graph explicitly, we get the following graph:

---

5. In describing instruction syntax, we will use square brackets ([and]) and the vertical bar (|) as follows:

    • [a] specifies the optional occurrence of item a.

    • a | b specifies either item a or item b.

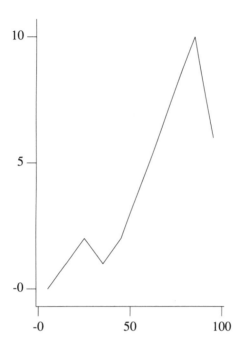

The `frame` instruction has the general form

frame [ht *h*] [wid *w*] [[*side₁*] *side-desc₁*] [[*side₂*] *side-desc₂*] ...

where *h* and *w* are expressions specifying, in inches, the frame height and width. *side_i* is one of the keywords `top`, `bot` (bottom), `left` and `right` specifying a frame side. Each *side-desc_i* consists of one of the keywords `solid`, `invis` (invisible), `dotted` or `dashed`, which describes the type of line that is to be used for drawing the frame side. If *side_i* is omitted, then the side characteristic *side-desc_i* applies to the whole frame.

The order in which the side descriptions are given is significant. For example, if the top side is first specified to be invisible and after that the whole frame is specified to be solid, then the result will be a solid frame. Alternatively, if a solid frame is specified first and after that the top side is specified to be invisible, then the result will be a solid frame with the top side missing (invisible).

Here are some examples of frames:

`grap` produces the solid frame by default; the other frames were specified with the following instructions:

```
frame dotted ...
frame dashed ...
frame top invis right invis ...
frame top invis ...
```

4.1 Coordinate Ranges

grap automatically computes the coordinate ranges from the data values; it uses this information for plotting the points and marking the axes. If the ranges computed by grap are not satisfactory, then alternative ranges can be specified with the coord instruction; this instruction has the form

coord [*coord-system-name*] [x l_x,u_x], [y l_y,u_y]

[log x | log y | log log]

coord-system-name is the name given to the coordinate system whose axis ranges are being specified. Each coord instruction defines a new coordinate system. l_x and u_x are the lower and upper limits of the x-axis coordinates, and l_y and u_y are the lower and upper limits of the y-axis coordinates. Clauses log x and log y specify logarithmic scaling for the x- and y-axes; clause log log specifies logarithmic scaling for both axes. Note that x and y are reserved names that cannot be used as variable names.

Unless explicitly specified, a point is considered to belong to the default (unnamed) coordinate system.

As an example of the coord instruction, we will explicitly specify the range for the y-axis to be 0 through 25 in the student grade graph:

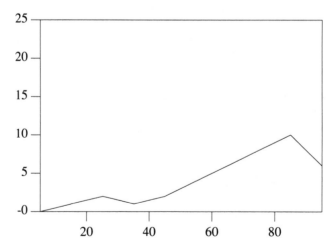

The `coord` instruction used for the above graph is

```
coord y 0, 25
```

4.1.1 Multiple Coordinate Systems: Suppose you want to plot points belonging to multiple coordinate systems in a single graph. Each coordinate system may have different x- and y-axis ranges and/or different axis scales. To do this, the different coordinate systems must first be specified with the `coord` instruction. Each system is referred to by the name given in the `coord` instruction (one of the systems can be unnamed). This name is then used for specifying points belonging to named coordinate systems:

[*coord-system-name*]   (*x*, *y*)

If the coordinate system name is not specified, then the point is assumed to belong to the unnamed coordinate system.

As an example, consider the following graph that shows the average monthly temperatures and rainfall in Shangrilla:

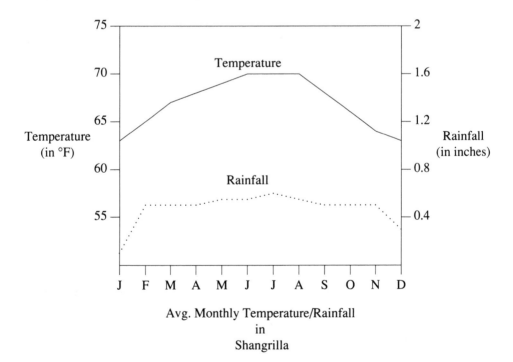

Avg. Monthly Temperature/Rainfall
in
Shangrilla

Here are some sample data values from the data file `weather-data`, which was used for drawing the above graph:

```
1  63  0.1
2  65  0.5
3  67  0.5
4  68  0.5
5  69  0.55
...
12  63  0.3
```

The first column specifies the month, and columns two and three specify the corresponding temperature and rainfall.

The graph shown above was specified as

```
    .G1
    frame solid  ht 2.5 wid 3.0
    label bot "Avg. Monthly Temperature/Rainfall"\
                     "in" " Shangrilla" down 0.1
5   label left "Temperature" "(in \(deF)" left 0.1
    label right "Rainfall" "(in inches)" right 0.1
    coord T x 1, 12 y 50, 75
    coord R x 1, 12 y 0, 2.0
    draw T solid
10  draw R dotted
    ticks bot out at 1 "J", 2 "F", 3 "M", 4 "A",\
             5 "M", 6 "J", 7 "J", 8 "A", 9 "S",\
             10 "O", 11 "N", 12 "D"
    ticks left out from T 55 to 75 by 5
15  ticks right out from R 0.4 to 2.0 by 0.4
    copy "weather-data" thru {
        next T at T 1,2
        next R at R 1,3
    }
20  "Temperature" at T 6, 71
    "Rainfall" at R 6, 0.7
    .G2
```

Notice that the name T is used for specifying both the temperature coordinate system and the temperature graph line (lines 7, 9 and 17). The name R is used similarly for the rainfall coordinate system and the rainfall graph line. The weather data is read with the copy thru instruction[6] (lines 16-19). Within the body of the

---

6. The copy thru instruction is similar to the pic instruction with the same name [Gehani 1987].

`copy thru` instruction, which is delimited by curly braces, a variable of the form $\$i$ denotes the ith element on a data line. The two `next` instructions (lines 17 and 18) are used explicitly for specifying the graph line associated with the next point to be plotted. For example, the `next` instruction on line 17 plots the next data point (from the next line of the data file `weather-data`) to be part of the temperature graph line T.

The `next` and `copy thru` instructions are discussed in detail in Sections 5.4 and 10.2.

4.1.2 Logarithmic Scaling: Logarithmic graphs are graphs in which the logarithms of the coordinates are plotted. One or both the axes can be logarithmic. Coordinates corresponding to a logarithmic axis must be neither less than nor equal to zero. Logarithmic graphs are useful for displaying data values that span several orders of magnitude. Logarithmic graphs are sometimes preferred to ordinary graphs, if data values can be logarithmically plotted as a straight line. This is because linear graphs can be easier to read than non-linear ones.

Semi-log graphs (graphs with exactly one logarithmic axis) are used when small changes in one variable (generally x) lead to large changes in the other variable. Log-log graphs (graphs with both axes scaled logarithmically) are used when both variables change in large quanta.

As an example, suppose that the y-axis is to be scaled logarithmically; i.e., a tick at coordinate y is to be printed at a distance $log(y)$ on the y-axis and data points (x, y) are to be plotted at coordinates $(x, log(y))$. `grap` will do this scaling automatically if the `log` clause is given for the y-axis in the `coord` statement.

The only automatic scaling supported by `grap` is logarithmic scaling. Other kinds of scaling must be done explicitly using `grap` arithmetic.

4.1.3 Example of Logarithmic Scaling: We will now show you three graphs that plot the equation $y = x^2$. In the first graph no scaling is used (normal axes); in the second logarithmic scaling is used for the y-axis; finally in the third logarithmic scaling is used for both axes.

First, here is the normal axes version:

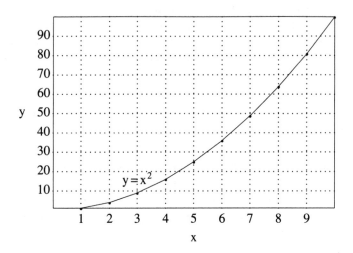

Now here is a semi-log version of the above graph:

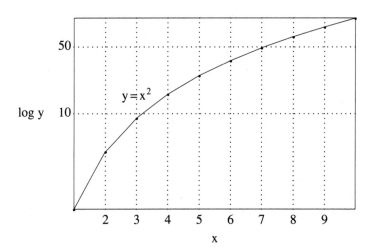

This graph was specified as

```
    .G1
    coord x 1, 10 y 1, 100 log y
    grid bot dotted from 2 to 9
    grid left dotted at 10 "10", 50 "50"
5   draw solid bullet
    label left "log y" left 0.1
    label bot "x" up 0.1
    "$y = x sup 2$" at 3, 15
    for i = 1 to 10 do
10  {
        next at i, i*i
    }
    .G2
```

Here are some interesting points about this graph specification:

- The coord instruction (line 2) contains the clause log y, which causes the y-axis to be scaled logarithmically.
- The grid instruction (lines 3 and 4) draws grid lines instead of ticks.
- Instead of reading the data points from a file, the data points for this graph were generated internally by using the for instruction (see Section 8.2).
- An eqn expression (delimited by the $ characters) is used to label the plotted line. For more details about eqn, see the chapter on specifying equations in the companion UNIX system typesetting book [Gehani 1987].

Changing the clause log y to log log in the above specification produces a log-log version of the above graph:

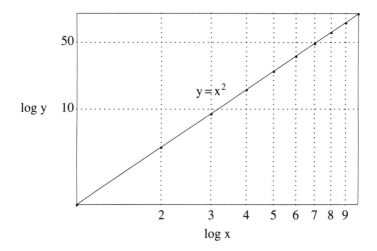

4.1.4 Example of Logarithmic and Other Axis Scaling: Here is another example of a log-log graph [Meyer 1970] that plots the sales volume versus the unit sales price:

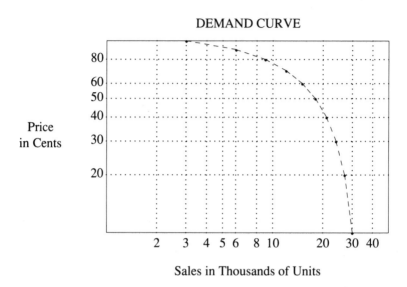

The data used for this graph (contents of the file `sales`) consists of pairs of values, one per line, of the form

price-in-cents no-of-units

Before the above pairs of data values were plotted, each of these pairs was transformed to the pair

no-of-units/1000 *price-in-cents*

The number of units is scaled to thousands of units (by dividing it by 1000), and the data value pairs are transposed (vis-a-vis the input order). This transformation was done in the graph specification itself.

The above graph was specified as

```
   .G1
   coord x 1, 50 y 10, 100 log log
   draw dashed bullet
   grid left dotted from 20 to 50 by 10
5  grid left dotted from 60 to 80 by 20
   grid bot dotted from 2 to 5
   grid bot dotted from 6 to 10 by 2
   grid bot dotted from 20 to 40 by 10
   label bot "Sales in Thousands of Units"
10 label left "Price" "in Cents" left 0.25
   label top "DEMAND CURVE" down 0.25
   copy "sales" thru {
       next at $2/1000, $1
   }
   .G2
```

As mentioned earlier, aside from logarithmic scaling, any other kind of scaling must be done explicitly by using `grap` arithmetic. In this example, the scaling of the number of units to thousands of units was done by using the `copy thru` and `next` instructions. The `copy thru` instruction reads in the contents of file `sales`; each data line read is processed by the `next` instruction, which is used to do the data scaling (and the transposition of each pair of values).

Note that multiple `grid` instructions (lines 4-8) were used to print grid lines at different intervals.

4.2 Labels

Each side of a frame can be labeled. The labels are written horizontally; they cannot be written vertically. Labels are specified using the `label` instruction, which has the form

`label` *side label$_1$* ... *label$_n$* [*shift*]

where *side* is one of the keywords `top`, `bot`, `left` or `right`.

Each *label$_i$* is of the form

"*text*" [*alignment*] [`size` ± *exp*]

where *alignment* is one of the keywords `rjust`, `ljust`, `above` or `below` specifying the alignment of the text string and the `size` clause specifies the change in point size for the label.

The *shift* clause in the `label` instruction specifies the extra amount (relative to its default placement) the label is to be shifted with respect to the axis. The *shift* clause has the form [left *e* | right *e*] [up *e* | down *e*]

where expression *e* specifies the desired shift in inches.

As an example, consider the labeled version of the student grade graph:

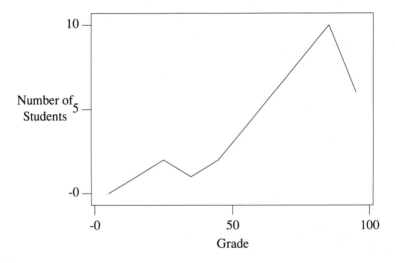

This graph was specified as

```
.G1
draw solid
label bot "Grade"
label left "Number of" "Students"
copy "grades"
.G2
```

Because the left label is too close to the tick label ''5'', we will left shift it by 0.4 inches (using the shift clause). At the same time, we will increase its point size by 3 (using the size clause). We will also move the bottom label down a bit and increase its point size:

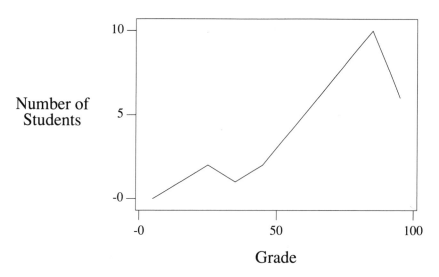

This graph was specified as

```
.G1
draw solid
label bot "Grade" size +3 down 0.1
label left "Number of" size +3\
        "Students" size +3 left 0.4
copy "grades"
.G2
```

4.3 Ticks: Marks on the Axes

Ticks are automatically printed on the left and bottom sides of the frame. By default, the x- and y-coordinates of the tick locations are used as the tick labels for the x- and y-axes, respectively. When printing automatic ticks, grap leaves a margin of 7 percent on each axis, which is the default value of the special variable margin; the margin can be changed by assigning an appropriate value to margin. As an example of default ticks, consider the following graph:

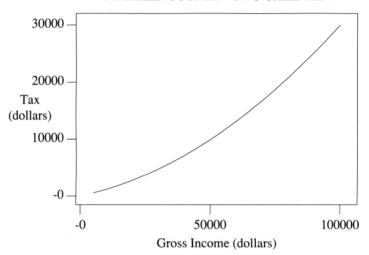

Notice the margins on the axes. The margin is set to 0 if the `coord` instruction is used. The margin can also be eliminated by setting `margin` to 0:

Setting the margin to 0 also leads `grap` to generate a different set of default ticks. One of the tick labels is now printed on top of the y-axis label. The axis label can be left shifted by using the `left` clause in the `label` instruction.

The preceding graph was specified as

```
 .G1
 margin = 0
 label top "MARRIED COUPLE\(emTWO CHILDREN"\
                                 down 0.25
 label bot "Gross Income (dollars)"
 label left "Tax" "(dollars)"
 draw solid
 copy "tax"
 .G2
```

4.3.1 Stopping Ticks: Ticks are automatically printed on the left and bottom axes. Automatic tick printing is stopped by using the `ticks` instruction with the `off` clause:

`ticks [ left | bot ] off`

If no frame side is specified, then no ticks are printed.

4.3.2 User-Specified Ticks: Ticks can be explicitly specified, overriding the automatically generated ticks, by using the `ticks` instruction that has the form

`ticks side [ in | out [ l ] ] [ tick-locations ]`

where *side* is one of the keywords `top`, `bot`, `left` or `right`. Keywords `in` and `out` specify whether the ticks should print on the axes facing inside or outside the graph. By default, the ticks point outwards. Expression *l* specifies the length of the tick mark.

Tick locations are specified with the *tick-locations* clauses. Individual tick locations can be specified with the `at` clause:

`at [ coord-system-name ] e_1 [ s_1 ], ..., e_n [ s_n ]`

Expression e_i specifies the ith tick location and string s_i specifies the corresponding tick label.

Ticks can be placed at periodic intervals by using the `from` clause:

`from [ coord-system-name ] e_1 to e_2 [ by [ op ] e_3 ] [ s ]`

Ticks are placed at points on the axis starting from e_1 to e_2 with intervals of e_3. If the by clause is omitted, then the tick interval is assumed to be 1. If expression e_3 is preceded by the operator *op* (+, −, $\star$ or /), then the next tick interval used is p op e_3, where p is the previous tick interval; e_3 is the initial tick interval. s is the tick label. If a tick label is not given, then the appropriate coordinate of the tick location is itself used as the label. If the coordinate system is not specified, then the tick locations are assumed to belong to the default (unnamed) coordinate system.

Tick labels can contain format specifiers like %f or %g (these specifiers are similar to those used in the C printf function [Gehani 1989]). The format specifiers are replaced by the value of the tick location (in the specified format) before printing the label. The empty string " " is used to print unlabeled ticks.

The following version of the tax graph illustrates printing of user-specified ticks:

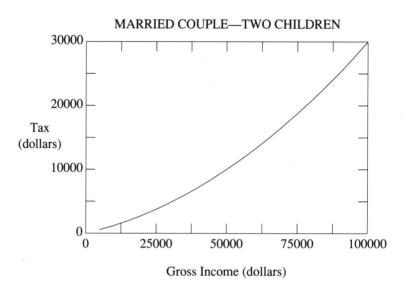

This graph was specified as

```
   .G1
   label top "MARRIED COUPLE\(emTWO CHILDREN" down 0.25
   label bot "Gross Income (dollars)"
   label left "Tax" "(dollars)"
5  ticks left in from 0 to 30000 by 10000
   ticks left in from 5000 to 25000 by 10000 ""
   ticks right in from 0 to 30000 by 5000 ""
   ticks bot in from 0 to 100000 by 25000
   ticks bot in from 12500 to 100000 by 25000 ""
10 ticks top in from 0 to 100000 by 12500 ""
   draw solid
   copy "tax"
   .G2
```

The left axis ticks were printed with 2 ticks instructions (lines 5-6). The second instruction prints ticks between the ticks printed by the first instruction. The null string in the second instruction suppresses printing of the tick labels with the ticks printed by this instruction. The bottom axis ticks were also printed using two ticks instructions.

4.4 Grid

As shown earlier, instead of printing ticks, horizontal and vertical lines, called *grid lines*, can be drawn across the graph frame. Grid lines make it easy to locate points in the graph. These lines are drawn with the `grid` instruction, which is similar to the `ticks` instruction. The `grid` instruction has the form

grid *side* [*line-desc*] [*grid-line-locations*]

Grid lines are drawn perpendicular to the specified side. The descriptor *line-desc* is one of the keywords `solid` (default), `invis`, `dotted` or `dashed` specifying the nature of the grid line. Here are two examples of `grid` instructions:

```
grid bot dotted from 0 to 10
grid left dotted from 10 to 100 by 10
```

4.5 Dynamic Specification of the Graph

All graphs shown so far have been specified with some advance knowledge of the data. Some of this knowledge (graph labels, tick intervals, coordinate ranges, etc.) has been "hard wired" in their specifications. Changes in the data may require changing the graph specification. Graph specifications can be made "data independent" by parameterizing them, i.e., by making all data-dependent items part of the data and by not including them directly within the specifications. As an example, consider the following graph [Kimble 1978]:

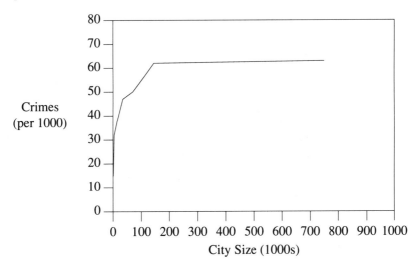

This graph was specified as

```
     .G1
     n = 0
     copy "independent" thru {
         if n == 0 then {
5            n = 1
             ticks bot from $1 to $2 by $3
             ticks left from $4 to $5 by $6
             label bot $7
             label left $8 $9 left 0.25
10       } else {
             next at $1, $2
         }
     }
     .G2
```

The `if` statement (lines 4-12) specifies conditional execution: if n is equal to zero, then lines 5-9 are executed; otherwise, line 11 is executed. See Section 8.1 for `if` instruction details.

The data file `independent` contains lines of the form

xa xb xi ya yb yi "*bottom-label*" "*left-label$_1$*" "*left-label$_2$*"
city-size$_1$ no-crimes$_1$
...
city-size$_n$ no-crimes$_n$

Items *xa*, *xb* and *xi* specify the initial and final x-axis tick locations and the x-axis tick increment; *ya*, *yb* and *yi* represent similar values for the y-axis. city-size$_i$ is the size of the city$_i$ in thousands and no-crimes$_i$ is the number of crimes per thousand in city$_i$.

The data values are read using the `copy thru` instruction within which a variable of the form $i denotes the ith element on a data line. The `if` statement ensures that the first data line is processed differently from the other data lines.

Here are some sample lines from the data file `independent`:

```
0 1000 100 0 80 10 "City Size (1000s)" "Crimes" "(per 1000)"
1    15
4.5 32
16   38
35   47
...
750 63
```

Blanks delimit data items, but only if they are not enclosed within double quotes. Consequently, the axis labels, which have embedded blanks, are enclosed in double quotes. Because of these double quotes, the `copy thru` instruction variables `$7`, `$8` and `$9` (lines 8-9) must not be enclosed in double quotes even though they represent strings.

The graph specification shown above is data independent since changes to the tick locations or to the tick labels do not require changes to the graph specification. This is because the tick locations and tick labels are not explicitly specified within the graph specification; instead they are read as data.

5. Graph Data

Graph data values can be given explicitly or they can be generated within a graph specification by using the `for` instruction. Explicitly specified data values are given as a series of lines containing x- and y-coordinate values. If each line contains

- one number, then `grap` assumes that it is a y-coordinate and it automatically uses i as the x-coordinate for line i.
- two or more numbers, then the first number is interpreted as an x-coordinate and the rest of the numbers are interpreted as y-coordinates each with the first number as the x-coordinate; for example, a line of the form

$$x \ y_1 \ y_2 \ \cdots \ y_n$$

is interpreted as the coordinate pairs $(x, y_1), (x, y_2) \ldots (x, y_n)$.

Data lines can be intermingled with `grap` instructions or they can be included in the specification with the `copy` or the `copy thru` instructions.

5.1 Data Sets (Data Partitions)

Graph data can be partitioned into sets and each of these sets plotted as a separate line. One data set, the default data set, is unnamed and is not explicitly specified. All other data sets are named, and are specified with the `draw` and `new` instructions. Unless otherwise specified, the data values are assumed to belong to the unnamed data set. Elements of the named data sets can be plotted only with the `next` instruction.

5.2 Displaying the Data

By default, the data values are plotted as a scatter graph. The `draw` instruction can be used to connect the plotted points with a line; this instruction has the form

```
draw [d]  solid|dotted e|dashed e  [mark]
```

Points belonging to the data set d (or the unnamed data set if a data set is not given) are to be plotted as specified. Keywords `solid`, `dotted` and `dashed` specify the kind of line to be used for connecting the data points. Expression e specifies distance between the dots or the length of the dashes as appropriate. Argument *mark*, which is a string of the form "*string*", is plotted at each data point if it is given.

For example, the instructions

```
draw dotted
draw A solid
draw B dashed
```

specify that the elements of the unnamed data set and the data sets A and B are to be plotted as dotted, solid and dashed lines, respectively.

The manner in which data points are plotted can be changed by using additional draw instructions. For instance, in the first graph shown in this chapter, draw instructions are used to make the tail ends of the dashed and solid lines dotted:

```
draw solid; copy "ttrev.data"
draw dotted; copy "ttrev.fcast"
new dashed; copy "ttexp.data"
draw dotted; copy "ttexp.fcast"
```

Instruction new, which is discussed below, starts a new graph.

5.3 Multiple Data Sets, i.e., Multiple-Line Graphs

Each data set can be plotted as a separate line in the graph. There are two ways of doing this:

- After plotting one set of data points, start a new line for the next data set by using the new instruction, which specifies that additional data points are to be plotted as a separate line.

- Use the new instruction to name the data sets. (Named data sets must be used if the data values are not partitioned into disjoint sets.) Specify the appropriate data set when using the next instruction to plot the point.

The new instruction is similar to the draw instruction except that it starts a new line. The new instruction has the form

new [*d*]   solid | dotted *e* | dashed *e*   [*mark*]

Points belonging to the data set *d* (or the unnamed data set if a data set is not given) are plotted as specified. Keywords solid, dotted and dashed specify the kind of line to be used for connecting the data points. Expression *e* specifies the distance between the dots or the length of the dashes as appropriate. If given, the optional argument *mark*, which is a string of the form "*string*", is plotted at each data point.

As an example of a graph with several lines, consider the following three-variable graph that plots mixtures of two fuels X and Y needed to achieve a given heat output in a furnace [Meyers 1970]:

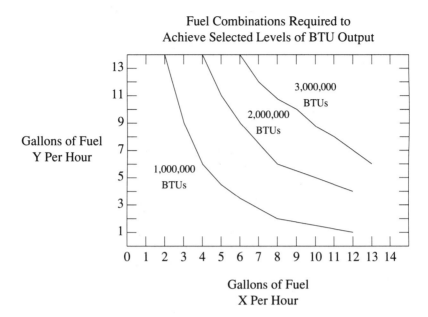

This graph was specified as

```
    .G1
    coord x 0, 15 y 0, 14
    ticks left in from 0 to 14 by 2 ""
    ticks left in from 1 to 14 by 2
5   ticks right in from 0 to 14 ""
    ticks bot in from 0 to 14
    ticks top in from 0 to 14 ""
    label top "Fuel Combinations Required to"\
        "Achieve Selected Levels of BTU Output"\
10      down 0.25
    label left "Gallons of Fuel" "Y Per Hour"
    label bot "Gallons of Fuel" "X Per Hour"
    draw solid; copy "btu1m"
    new solid; copy "btu2m"
15  new solid; copy "btu3m"
    "\s-21,000,000\s0" "\s-2BTUs\s0" at 2.5, 5
    "\s-22,000,000\s0" "\s-2BTUs\s0" at 7.5, 9
    "\s-23,000,000\s0" "\s-2BTUs\s0" at 10, 11
    .G2
```

The `draw solid` instruction (line 13) specifies that the initial data values are to be plotted as a solid line. The two `new solid` instructions (lines 14-15) specify that subsequent data values are to be plotted as separate solid lines. A new solid instruction could also have been used instead of the `draw solid` instruction (line 13).

The data values for each line drawn in the graph are read from files containing data lines of the form

X-gallons-per-hour Y-gallons-per-hour

5.4 Columnar Data: An Example Illustrating the Use of Named Data Sets

Consider a graph for which the data is stored in a file in columnar fashion. Each column of this data is to be plotted as a separate line. Because data values are read line-by-line and not column-by-column, the easiest way to plot the data is by using named data sets. First, the `new` instruction is used to create a named data set for each line. The `copy thru` instruction is then used to read the data values. Within the body of the macro associated `copy thru` instruction, these data value can be accessed with the names `$1`, `$2`, `$3`, etc. (see Section 8.2 for more details). Using these names, the `next` instruction is then used to plot the data values with the data set names explicitly specified (except in case of the unnamed data set).

The `next` instruction has the form

`next [d] at p [solid|dotted e|dashed e]`

d specifies the name of the data set (previously created using either the `new` or the `draw` instruction). If *d* is omitted, then the next instruction refers to the unnamed data set. Point *p* is plotted as part of the data set *d*. If the line description keyword (`solid`, `dotted` or `dashed`) is specified, then it overrides the current line style *just* for the line segment ending at point *p*.

Point *p* is an "*x, y*" coordinate pair, which is optionally preceded by the name of a coordinate system:

`[ coord-system-name ]  (x,  y)`

Suppose, for example, that the fuel combination experiment (discussed above) data is stored in one file named `btu` instead of three files as done before:

2	14	−1	−1
3	9	−1	−1
4	6	14	−1
5	5	11	−1
...			
12	1	4	7
13	−1	−1	6

Values in first column specify the amount of fuel X and the values in the remaining columns specify the amount of fuel Y to produce one, two and three million BTUs, respectively. A negative y-value indicates a null data point that is not to be plotted. To plot each of the three different heat outputs as separate lines, we will define three named data sets (A, B and C) with the new instruction. The copy thru instruction will be used to read the data file btu, and the next instruction will be used to plot the data points.

Using the data in file btu, the fuel combinations graph shown earlier can be specified as

```
    .G1
    coord x 0, 15 y 0, 14
    ticks left in from 0 to 14 by 2 ""
    ticks left in from 1 to 14 by 2
5   ticks right in from 0 to 14 ""
    ticks bot in from 0 to 14
    ticks top in from 0 to 14 ""
    label top "Fuel Combinations Required to"\
      "Achieve Selected Levels of BTU Output"\
10    down 0.2
    label left "Gallons of Fuel" "Y Per Hour"
    label bot "Gallons of Fuel" "X Per Hour"
    new A solid; new B solid; new C solid
    copy "btu" thru {
15  if $2 != -1 then {next A at $1, $2}
    if $3 != -1 then {next B at $1, $3}
    if $4 != -1 then {next C at $1, $4}
    }
    "\s-21,000,000\s0" "\s-2BTUs\s0" at 2.5, 5
20  "\s-22,000,000\s0" "\s-2BTUs\s0" at 7.5, 9
    "\s-23,000,000\s0" "\s-2BTUs\s0" at 10, 11
    .G2
```

The if instructions (lines 15-17) ensure that only valid data points are plotted.

5.5 Generating Data Points within a Graph Specification

Data can be generated within a graph specification with the for control instruction (discussed in Section 8.2) and plotted with the next instruction. We have used internally generated data in earlier examples. Here is another graph that uses internally generated data to plot the curve $y = \sqrt{x}$:

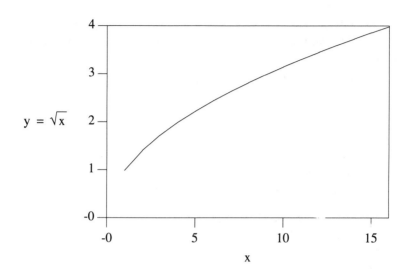

This graph was specified as

```
     .G1
     coord x 0, 16 y 0, 4
     draw solid
     label left "$y ~=~ sqrt x$"
5    label bot "x"
     for i = 1 to 16 do
     {
         next at i, sqrt(i)
     }
     .G2
```

Note that the y-axis label (line 4) is an equation (specified with eqn; $ is being used as the eqn delimiter).

The for instruction (lines 6-9) executes the next instruction within its body (line 8) 16 times, once for each value of i between 1 and 16. The for instruction essentially enumerates x-coordinate values. The corresponding y-coordinates are computed by using the built-in function sqrt.

6. Multiple Graphs

Two or more internally unrelated graphs can be plotted using one pair of .G1 and .G2 instructions. The graph instruction is used to begin a new graph and to position it relative to the other graphs. This instruction has the form

graph *pic-name* [*pic-instruction*]

where *pic-name* is a name suitable for the pic preprocessor; the first character of *pic-name* must be an upper-case letter [Gehani 1987]. The *pic-instruction* is used to specify the graph position by referring to the corners of the previous graph frames (which are like `pic` boxes). Frame corners are `.n` (north or top), `.e` (east or right), `.w` (west or left), `.s` (south or bottom), `.ne` (north-east), `.nw` (north-west), `.sw` (south-west), `.se` (south-east) and `.c` (center). The frame of the graph being specified is referenced as `.Frame`. The frame of a previously specified graph *g* is referenced as *g*`.Frame`. Note that the first graph is automatically given the name `Graph`.

One use of the `graph` instruction is to place two graphs side-by-side. As an example, consider the following two adjacent graphs, which show the same data plotted as vertical and horizontal bars:

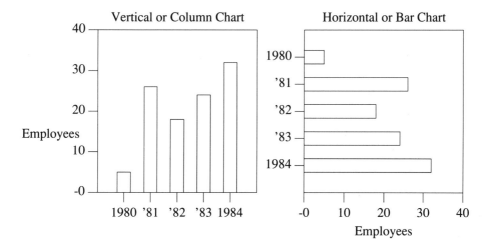

The preceding graphs are specified as

```
    .G1
    frame ht 1.7 wid 1.7
    coord x 1979, 1985 y 0, 40
    ticks bot at 1980 "1980", 1981 "'81",\
 5       1982 "'82", 1983 "'83", 1984 "1984"
    label top "Vertical or Column Chart" down .3
    label left "Employees" down 0.25
    copy "employee" thru {
        line from $1-0.25,0 to $1-0.25,$2
10      line from $1-0.25,$2 to $1+0.25,$2
        line from $1+0.25,$2 to $1+0.25,0
    }

    graph H with .Frame.w at Graph.Frame.e + (0.5,0)
15  frame ht 1.7 wid 1.7
    coord y 0, 6 x 0, 40
    ticks left at 1 "1984", 2 "'83", 3 "'82",\
        4 "'81", 5 "1980"
    label top "Horizontal or Bar Chart" down .3
20  label bot "Employees"
    copy "employee" thru {
      line from 0, 1985-$1-0.25 to $2, 1985-$1-0.25
      line from $2, 1985-$1-0.25 to $2, 1985-$1+0.25
      line from $2, 1985-$1+0.25 to 0, 1985-$1+0.25
25  }
    .G2
```

Notice how the y-coordinates of the second graph are plotted in decreasing order going up the y-axis (lines 17 and 18).

7. Printing Strings and Other Objects in a Graph

grap provides facilities for printing strings, circles, lines and arrows in a graph.

7.1 Strings

Strings can be printed at any place in a graph as follows:

"string" [rjust | ljust | above | below] [size ±*p*] at *p*

The specified string is printed centered at point *p*, which is of the form

[*coord-system-name*] (*x*, *y*)

Keywords rjust, ljust, above or below can be used to specify that the string is to be placed to the right of, to the left of, above or below point *p*, respectively. The point size used for the string can be changed with the size clause.

Numeric expressions can also be printed, but they must first be converted to a string format with the `plot` instruction, which has the form

plot *e* [*"format-string"*] at [*coord-system-name*] (*x*, *y*)

e is the expression to be printed. *format-string* contains a format specifier[7] specifying the format in which *e* is to be printed. If present, *format-string* is printed with the format specifier replaced by the value of *e* (in the specified format).

Two examples of the `plot` instruction are

```
plot  i  at  (x,  y)
plot  i  "%f"  at  (x,  y)
```

If `i` has the value 3, then these two instructions will print it as 3 and 3.000000, respectively.

7.2 Circles

Circles are drawn using the `circle` instruction, which has the form

circle at *p* [radius *r*]

p specifies a point and is of the form

[*coord-system-name*] (*x*, *y*)

The circle radius *r* is specified in inches. If the radius is not specified, then the small circle ○ is drawn by default.

In the following example, circles are used to show the distance from the city center in the following graph that plots crime locations. The difference between adjacent circles is one mile:

---

7. The format specifier is like the ones used in the C `printf` function [Gehani 1989].

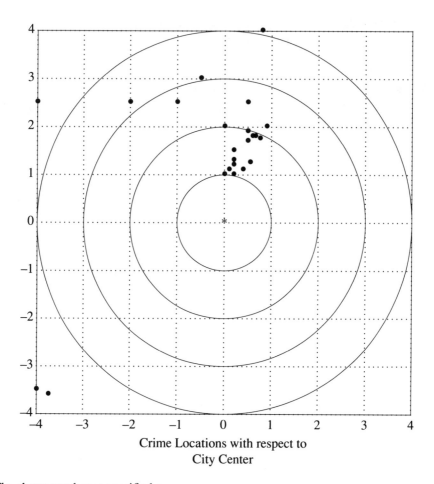

Crime Locations with respect to
City Center

The above graph was specified as

```
.G1
frame wid 4.0 ht 4.0
coord x -4, 4 y -4, 4
for i=0.5 to 2.0 by 0.5 do {circle at 0, 0 radius i}
grid dotted left from -4 to 4
grid dotted bot from -4 to 4
label bot "Crime Locations with respect to"\
            "City Center" up 0.1
star at (0, 0)
copy "crime"
.G2
```

7.3 Lines and Arrows

Lines are used to draw customized graphs (and graphic displays such as histograms). Arrows are used for pointing to items in a graph. Lines and arrows are drawn with the line and arrow instructions. These instructions have the form

[line | arrow] from p_1 to p_2 [solid | invis | dotted e | dashed e]

where p_1 and p_2 are points of the form

[*coord-system-name*] (x, y)

Expressions e given after the keywords dashed and dotted are optional and are used to specify (in inches) the length of the dashes (default is 0.05 inches) and the distance between the dots (default is 0.05 inches), respectively.

An example illustrating lines and arrows is the following graph, which shows the growth of money at an annually compounded rate of 25%:

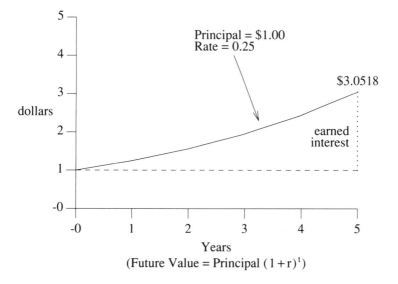

This graph was specified as

```
     .G1
     r = 0.25; p1 = 1+r; p = 1; yrs = 5
     frame top invis right invis
     coord x 0, yrs y 0, 5
  5  label bot "Years"\
             "(Future Value = Principal !(1+r) sup t!)"
     label left "dollars"
     draw solid
     0, 1
 10  for i = 1 to yrs do
     {
         p = p*p1; next at (i, p)
     }
     line dashed from (0, 1) to (yrs, 1)
 15  line dotted from (yrs, 1) to (yrs, p)
     "earned" rjust at 4.85, 2.0
     "interest" rjust at 4.85, 1.7
     plot p "$%.4f" at (yrs, p+0.25)
     arrow from (2.8, 4.0) to (3.25, 2.3)
 20  "Principal = $1.00" ljust at (2.1, 4.5)
     "Rate = 0.25" ljust at (2.1, 4.2)
     .G2
```

The first graph point "(0, 1)" was specified within the graph specification (line 10). The other points were generated using the for instruction (lines 10-13). Generated points must be explicitly plotted using the next instruction (line 12).

Note that ! is used as the eqn delimiter for the above graph.

8. Control Instructions

grap provides two control instructions: the if instruction for conditional execution and the for instruction for repeated execution. These instructions are similar to the if and for instructions in pic.

8.1 if Instruction

The if instruction has the form

if *expression* then
{ *anything*$_{true}$ }
[else { *anything*$_{false}$ }]

If *expression* evaluates to true, then alternative *anything*$_{true}$ is executed; otherwise, *anything*$_{false}$ is executed. Note that a zero value is interpreted as false and a non-zero value as true.

The following operators can be used in constructing the `if` expression:

operator	meaning
==	equal (numeric and string)
!=	not equal (numeric and string)
>	greater than (numeric)
>=	greater than or equal to (numeric)
<	less than (numeric)
<=	less than or equal to (numeric)
&&	logical *and*; the second operand is evaluated only if the first one is true
||	logical *or*; the second operand is evaluated only if the first one is false

Here are some examples of the `if` instruction:

```
if $2 != -1 then {next A at $1, $2}

if f > 0 && f < 1 then
{
    line from i-1, j to p, j
}

if 10 <= j && j < 20 then {x1 = x1 + 1}

if first then
{
    min_x = $1
    max_x = $1
    first = 0
} else {
    min_x = min($1, min_x)
    max_x = max($1, max_x)
}
```

Note that identifiers of the form $*i* represent macro parameters (see Section 9).

8.2 `for` Instruction

The `for` instruction is of the form

```
for i = l to u [by j] do
{
    instructions
}
```

where i is the loop variable. Instructions given within the `for` instruction are executed once for each value of the loop variable i which is initially assigned the value l. The value of i is then increased in steps of j (1 in the absence of the by clause) as long as it is not greater than u.

As an example of the `for` instruction, consider the following graph:

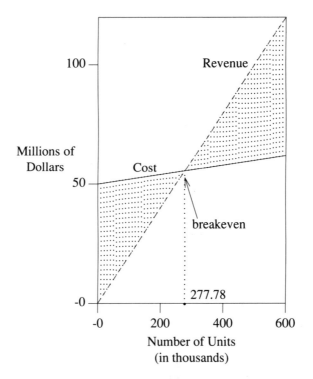

`grap` does not provide explicit facilities for shading graphs. We will therefore use the `for` instruction to draw dotted lines to produce the effect of shading.

The shaded graph was specified as

```
.G1
#cost = 50+0.02*no_units, revenue = 0.2*no_units
#at breakeven 50+0.02*no_units = 0.2*no_units
#   that is, when 50/0.18 units are produced

be_no = 50/0.18         #breakeven number of units
be_rev = 0.2 * be_no #breakeven revenue
n = 600   #graph plotted for 0 to n units

margin = 0
frame ht 3.0 wid 2.0
line from 0, 50 to n, 50+0.02*n
line dashed from 0, 0 to n, 0.2*n

#shade the area between the cost & revenue lines
#by plotting dotted lines

    for i from 10 to 590 by 10 do
    {
        cost = 50+0.02*i; revenue = 0.2*i
        line dotted from i, cost to i, revenue
    }

line dotted from be_no, 0 to be_no, be_rev
plot be_no "%.2f" at be_no+75, 3
bullet at be_no, 0
arrow from be_no+40, be_rev-20 to be_no,be_rev-3
"breakeven" ljust at be_no+23, be_rev-23

label bot "Number of Units" "(in thousands)"
label left "Millions of" "Dollars"
"Revenue  " rjust at 500, 0.2*500
"Cost" above at 150, (50+0.02*150)
.G2
```

9. Macros

Macros are used to encapsulate frequently used and/or logically related instructions in a "higher level" instruction. grap macro definitions are of the form

define *macro-name* θ *macro-body* θ

macro-name is a character sequence not containing item separators such as blanks, tabs and quotes. θ, which specifies the beginning and end of the macro body, may be any character not in the macro body. Items of the form $1, $2, ..., $n denote the parameters in the macro body. Note that `grap` macros are similar to `pic` macros.

Macros are invoked (called) as

macro-name (a_1, a_2, ..., a_n)

where a_i is the ith argument (corresponds to the parameter $\$i$). A macro call is replaced by the corresponding macro body after the parameters have been replaced by the corresponding arguments. A missing argument is replaced by the null string.

As mentioned before, within a single document that contains many graphs, variable definitions carry over from the graph specification containing them to all successive graph specifications.

9.1 Histograms: An Example of Macros

A *histogram* is a columnar graph in block form that displays the frequency with which the data values occur. As an example, consider the following histogram:

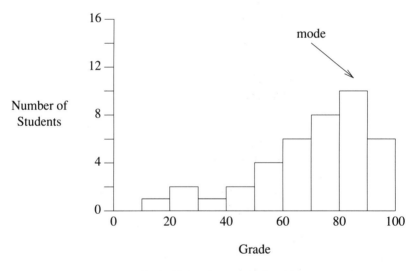

`grap` does not provide specific facilities for specifying histograms. Boxes must be constructed explicitly by drawing lines of the right length. This histogram was specified as

```
.G1
x0 = 0; x1 = 0; x2 = 0; x3 = 0; x4 = 0
x5 = 0; x6 = 0; x7 = 0; x8 = 0; x9 = 0

define hist X
a=$1*10
line from a, 0 to a, $2
line from a, $2 to a+10, $2
line from a+10, $2 to a+10, 0
X

frame right invis top invis
coord x 0, 100 y 0, 16
label left "Number of" "Students" left 0.3
label bot "Grade"
ticks bot in from 0 to 100 by 10 ""
ticks bot in from 0 to 100 by 20
ticks left out from 0 to 16 by 2 ""
ticks left out from 0 to 16 by 4
copy "rawgrades" thru {
    if $1 < 10 then {x0 = x0 + 1}
    if 10 <= $1 && $1 < 20 then {x1 = x1 + 1}
    if 20 <= $1 && $1 < 30 then {x2 = x2 + 1}
    if 30 <= $1 && $1 < 40 then {x3 = x3 + 1}
    if 40 <= $1 && $1 < 50 then {x4 = x4 + 1}
    if 50 <= $1 && $1 < 60 then {x5 = x5 + 1}
    if 60 <= $1 && $1 < 70 then {x6 = x6 + 1}
    if 70 <= $1 && $1 < 80 then {x7 = x7 + 1}
    if 80 <= $1 && $1 < 90 then {x8 = x8 + 1}
    if 90 <= $1 then {x9 = x9 + 1}
}
hist(0,x0); hist(1,x1); hist(2,x2); hist(3,x3);
hist(4,x4); hist(5,x5); hist(6,x6); hist(7,x7);
hist(8,x8); hist(9,x9)
arrow from (70, 14) to (85, 11.1)
"mode" above at (70, 14)
.G2
```

Without the use of macros, the above specification would have been much larger.
Each of the ten hist macro calls (lines 34-36) would have to be replaced by the
body of hist (lines 6-9).

10. Including and Reading Data from Files

The `copy` and `copy thru` instructions are used to include files and read data stored in files. These instructions are similar to the `pic` instructions with the same names.

10.1 `copy` Instruction

The `copy` instruction is used to include files within graph specifications and it has the form

`copy "`*file-name*`"`

All `.G1` instructions and `.G2` instructions within the included file are ignored. This allows files containing complete `grap` specifications to be included without modification.

10.2 `copy thru` Instruction

The `copy thru` instruction allows items on each line of an input file to be used as arguments for a macro call. Each sequence of non-blank characters or a sequence of characters enclosed within double quotes is interpreted as one argument. The `copy thru` instruction is particularly useful for drawing graphs based on data produced by another program or device. The `copy thru` instruction has the form

`copy "`*file-name*`" thru` *macro-name*

where *macro-name* is the macro that will be called once for each line of the file *file-name* with items on the line as arguments.

Instead of specifying the macro name, the macro body can be given directly in the `copy thru` instruction:

`copy "`*file-name*`" thru {` *macro-body* `}`

The `until` clause can be used to terminate file reading; e.g., the following `copy thru` instruction stops reading the file `flight-data` on encountering a line with `ZZZZ` as the first item:

`copy "flight-data" thru screen until "ZZZZ"`

11. Graph Size

The width of a graph can be explicitly specified as a parameter of the graph-begin instruction `.G1`:

`.G1 [` *graph-width-in-inches* `]`
graph specification
`.G2`

This explicitly specified graph width overrides the width specified in the `frame` instruction or the default width computed by `grap`. The height of the graph is adjusted proportionally.

11.1 Proportional Size of Graphs [Tufte 1983]

Visual preference for rectangular proportions has been studied by psychologists and they have found a mild preference for graphs whose relative dimensions range between

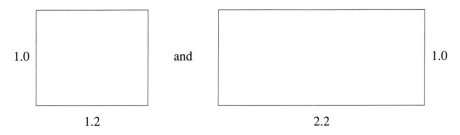

The width of a graph should be greater than its height because we are more accustomed to differentiating deviations from the horizon and because of labeling ease. More horizontal space also means that labels can be written on one line instead of on multiple lines. Of course, these are just hints. If the nature of the data suggests other proportions, then those should be used.

12. How to be a Graphic Liar

Graphs can be misused to project an incorrect impression by selecting the appropriate scale and frame size. In this section, we will show you some examples of how graphs can be (and have been) used to mislead the reader.

12.1 Government Payroll [Selby 1979]

The following graph gives the impression that the government payroll is skyrocketing:

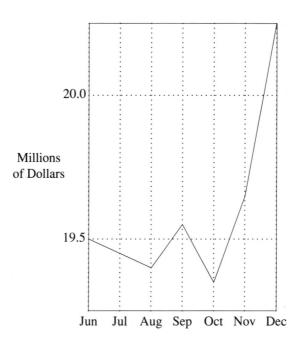

This graph was specified as

```
    .G1
    frame ht 3.0 wid 2.0
    margin = 0
    coord x 6, 12 y 19.25, 20.25
 5  label left "Millions" "of Dollars"
    grid left dotted at 19.5 "19.5", 20.0 "20.0"
    grid bot dotted at 6 "Jun", 7 "Jul",\
        8 "Aug", 9 "Sep", 10 "Oct",\
        11 "Nov", 12 "Dec"
10  draw solid
    copy "payroll"
    .G2
```

The following graph uses the same data as the above graph but uses a different scale
for the y-axis giving the impression that the government payroll is stable:

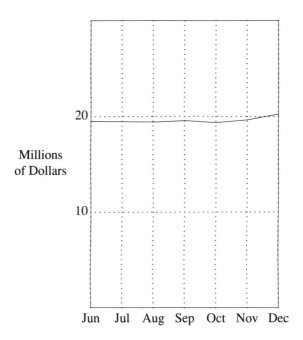

12.2 Housewife's Workweek [Kimble 1978]

The following graph shows that the average housewife's work week has remained relatively constant, at just over 50 hours, in four decades despite the introduction of the labor saving devices:

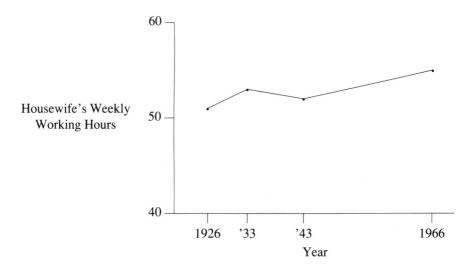

This graph was specified as

```
     .G1
     frame top invis right invis
     coord x 1920, 1970 y 40, 60
     label left "Housewife's Weekly" "Working Hours"\
  5                                          left 0.25
     label bot "Year"
     ticks left from 40 to 60 by 10
     ticks bot at 1926 "1926", 1933 "'33",\
          1943 "'43", 1966 "1966"
 10  draw solid bullet
     copy "housework"
     .G2
```

The following alternative version of the above graph exaggerates the slight increase in the working hours:

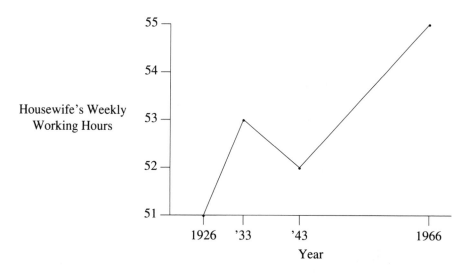

13. Interface with mm/ms, pic, tbl, eqn and troff

grap is a pic preprocessor because it generates pic instructions as output Consequently, a document containing a graph must be processed first by grap and then pic before it is processed by troff. The following figure shows the order in which the various document formatting facilities should be used to format a document containing graphs, figures, tables and equations.

Typesetting documents with graphs, figures, tables and equations

To use ms instead of mm, use the troff option −ms instead of −mm.

13.1 Interface with mm/ms

grap specifications are normally enclosed within displays for centering graphs and for ensuring that graphs are not split across pages:

```
.DS [ parameters ]
.G1
graph specification
.G2
.DE
```

Text and other items associated with a graph, but which are not part of the graph, can also be placed in the display:

```
.DS [ parameters ]
text (or other items) to be placed above the graph
.G1
graph specification
.G2
text (or other items) to be placed below the graph
.DE
```

Several graphs can be specified in one display:

```
.DS [ parameters ]
.G1
specification for graph_1
.G2
.G1
specification for graph_2
.G2
   ⋮
.G1
specification for graph_n
.G2
.DE
```

Macro and variable definitions carry over from one graph specification to another in a document.

Neither mm nor ms has an instruction for captioning graphs.[8] Fortunately, it is straightforward to implement such an instruction by defining a troff macro (see Chapter 4), say gP, as follows:

```
.nr g! 0 +1
.de gP
.sp 6p
.ce
\fBGraph \\n+(g!.\fP \\$1
..
```

The .nr instruction defines the numeric variable (register) g!, initializes it to 0 and specifies the auto-increment value; g! keeps track of the graph numbering. The .de instruction begins the definition of macro gP, the .sp instruction outputs some blank space and the .ce instruction centers the next line, which contains the graph caption. The escape sequence \\n+(g! increments the value of g!, which is then printed. $1 denotes the argument supplied when calling the macro gP. Finally, the last line terminates the definition of gP.

The instruction (i.e., the macro call) .gP can now be used to generate graph captions. For example, the instruction

.gP *caption-string*

will generate a caption of the form

Graph *n*. *caption-string*

where *n* is the graph number.

To ensure that graph and its caption are printed on the same page, both the graph specification and the associated .gP instruction should be enclosed in an mm or ms display.

13.2 Interface with pic

The grap instruction pic can be used to pass commands to the pic preprocessor. It has the form

pic *instruction*

---

8. Note that mm, unlike ms, does provide caption instruction for figures, tables and equations.

Argument *instruction* is passed directly to pic, which interprets it appropriately.

13.3 Interface with eqn

Like the eqn and pic interface [Gehani 1987, DWB 1986b], the grap and eqn interface does not work correctly when eqn outputs some extra vertical space in the equation (e.g., when an equation has fractions). If an equation given within a grap specification has items other than subscripts and superscripts, then the extra information "space 0" must be added at the beginning of each equation.

13.4 Interface with troff

troff instructions to change the font and point size may be used within graphs. troff escape sequences can be used to specify fonts and point sizes within strings; however, the original font and point size must be restored before the end of the string. Vertical spacing should not be changed nor should space be added (e.g., with the .sp instruction) within a graph specification.

14. Checking for Errors: grap

grap can be used to check for graph specification errors prior to typesetting the document. To check for grap errors, use the UNIX commands

grap *files* >/dev/null

or

grap *files* >temp

Error messages (if any) are printed on the standard error file. The first command discards the output of grap while the second command stores the output in file temp for possible later examination by the user.

To facilitate debugging, grap provides the print instruction, which has the form

print *expression-or-string*

The print instruction prints its argument on the standard error file.

15. Executing UNIX Commands

UNIX commands can be executed with the sh instruction, which has the form

sh *X any-UNIX-command X*

where *X* is any character not used in the UNIX command.

As an example, suppose that the data in the file rawdata is to be plotted and, at the same time, a straight line is to be fitted to this data by using the *least-squares* technique as shown in the following graph:

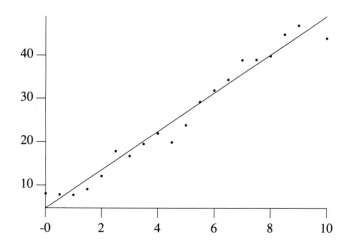

Straight line coefficients are computed using a user-supplied least squares program
lc. Using these coefficients, a line is drawn from (x_{min}, y^c_{min}) to (x_{max}, y^c_{max}); x_{min}
and x_{max} are the smallest and largest x-values in the data, and y^c_{min} and y^c_{max} are the
corresponding y-values computed using the least squares coefficients.

The graph shown above was specified as

```
.G1
first = 1
frame top invis right invis
copy "rawdata" thru {
    if first then
    {
        min_x = $1; max_x = $1
        first = 0
    } else {
        min_x = min($1, min_x)
        max_x = max($1, max_x)
    }
    bullet at $1, $2
}
sh X lc <rawdata >/usr/nhg/TEMP/coeff X
copy "/usr/nhg/TEMP/coeff" thru {
    line from min_x, $1+$2*min_x to\
                    max_x, $1+$2*max_x
}
sh X rm /usr/nhg/TEMP/coeff X
.G2
```

The smallest and largest x-values, determined from the data in the file `rawdata`, are stored in the variables `min_x` and `max_x` (line 7). These variables are both initialized to the first data value and then adjusted after examining subsequent data values. Variable `first` controls the initialization step.

The output of the program `lc` is stored in file `/usr/nhg/TEMP/coeff` (line 15).

16. Examples

We will now illustrate the use of `grap` with a variety of examples. In this section, we will focus on drawing graphs for which `grap` does not provide explicit facilities. Specifically, the examples illustrate how to specify a graph with its axes in the middle of the frame, a pie chart, a pictogram, a range-column chart, a thermometer and a graph with a thick line. Because of the absence of explicit facilities in `grap` for drawing the examples shown, many trial-and-error attempts were required to fine tune each graph.

16.1 Graphs with X- and Y-Axes Intersecting at Their Middle Points

Consider the following graph of a sine curve whose X and Y axes intersect:

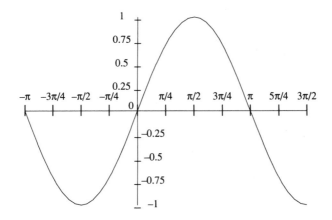

The sine function

The axes and the ticks in the above graph were explicitly constructed. The `line` instruction was used to draw the axes and the symbols `vtick` and `htick` were placed at appropriate points on the axes to print the tick marks. The symbol π was printed using its `troff` name \ (*p.

Here is the specification of the above graph:

```
    .G1
    pi = 3.14159265
    frame invis; ticks off; draw solid
    label bot "\fBThe sine function\fP"
 5  for i = -180 to 270 by 10 do
    {
        next at i, sin(i/180*pi)
    }
    line from (-180, 0) to (270, 0)
10  for i = -180 to 270 by 45 do
    {
        vtick at (i, 0.0)
    }
    line from (0, -1) to (0, 1)
15  for i = .25 to 1 by 0.25 do
    {
        htick at (0, i-0.035)
        htick at (0, -i-0.035)
    .ps -2
20      plot i at (-25, i)
        plot -i at (25, -i)
    .ps
    }
    plot "\s-20\s0" at -10, 0.05
25
    "\s-2\-\(*p\s0" at (-180, .15)
    "\s-2\-3\(*p/4\s0" at (-135, .15)
    "\s-2\-\(*p/2\s0" at (-90, .15)
    "\s-2\-\(*p/4\s0" at (-45, .15)
30  "\s-2\(*p/4\s0" at (45, .15)
    "\s-2\(*p/2\s0" at (90, .15)
    "\s-23\(*p/4\s0" at (135, .15)
    "\s-2\(*p\s0" at (180, .15)
    "\s-25\(*p/4\s0" at (225, .15)
35  "\s-23\(*p/2\s0" at (270, .15)
    .G2
```

16.2 Pie Charts

Consider the following pie chart that shows the marital status of female heads of household in the United States in 1975 [Freund 1981]:

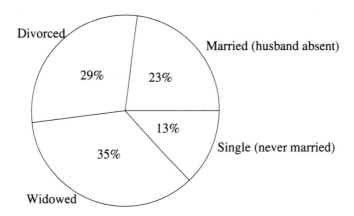

Pie charts must be hand crafted because grap does not provide facilities for directly specifying pie charts.

This pie chart shown above was specified as

```
   .G1
   frame invis ht 3.0 wid 3.0; ticks off
   coord x -1.5, 1.5 y -1.5, 1.5
   pi = 3.14159265; pi2 = pi * 2
5  r = 1.0
   m1 = 0.23*pi2
      #angle in radians: married but husband absent
   m12 = 0.23/2*pi2   #half the angle for % label
   d1 = (0.23+0.29)*pi2   #divorced angle
10 d12 = (0.23+0.29/2)*pi2
   w1 = (.52+.35)*pi2   #widowed angle
   w12 = (.52+.35/2)*pi2
   s12 = (.87+.13/2)*pi2

15 circle at 0,0 radius r
   line from 0,0 to r,0
   line from 0,0 to r*cos(m1),r*sin(m1)
   "23%" at r/2*cos(m12),r/2*sin(m12)
   line from 0,0 to r*cos(d1),r*sin(d1)
20 "29%" at r/2*cos(d12),r/2*sin(d12)
   line from 0,0 to r*cos(w1),r*sin(w1)
   "35%" at r/2*cos(w12),r/2*sin(w12)
   "13%" at r/2*cos(s12),r/2*sin(s12)

25 "   Married (husband absent)" ljust\
      at r*cos(.115*pi2),r*sin(.115*pi2)
   "Divorced            " above\
      at r*cos(.375*pi2),r*sin(.375*pi2)
   "Widowed      " rjust\
30    at r*cos(.695*pi2),r*sin(.695*pi2)
   "  Single (never married)" ljust\
      at r*cos(.935*pi2),r*sin(.935*pi2)
   .G2
```

16.3 Pictograms [Freund 1981]

The following pictogram shows the increase in the United States population:

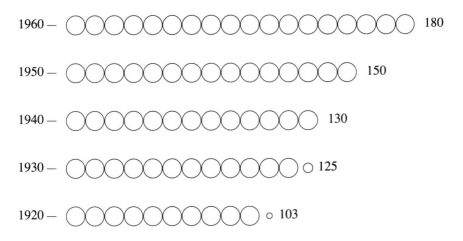

Population of USA
(in millions)

The data for the above pictogram is taken from the file pop, which contains lines of the form

year$_1$ *population-in-thousands*$_1$
year$_2$ *population-in-thousands*$_2$
...

Here is the specification of the preceding pictogram:

```
    .G1
    frame wid 4.75 ht 2.0 invis
    coord x 0, 23 y 1920, 1960
    ticks bot off
5   ticks left from 1960 to 1920 by -10
    label "Population of USA" "(in millions)" left 0.5i
    r = 0.1
    copy "pop" thru {
        for i = 1 to $2/10 by 1 do
10      {
            circle at i, $1 radius r
        }
        f = $2/10 - (i-1) #fractional part
        if f > 0 && f < 1.0 then
15      {
            circle at i, $1 radius f*r
            plot "$2" at i+1, $1
        } else {
            plot "$2" at i+0.5, $1
20      }
    }
    .G2
```

Here is another pictogram showing the rise in electricity production in USA:

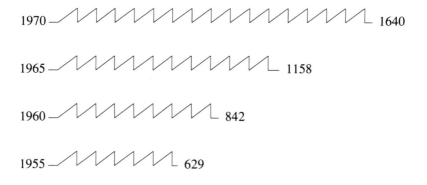

Electricity Production in USA
(Billions of Kilowatt Hours)

The data for this pictogram is taken from the file `elect`, which contains lines of the form

year$_1$ *electricity-production-in-billions-of-KWH*$_1$
year$_2$ *electricity-production-in-billions-of-KWH*$_2$
...

Here is the specification of the preceding pictogram:

```
   .G1
   frame wid 4.5 ht 2.0 invis
   coord x 0, 22 y 1950, 1970
   ticks off
5  ticks left from 1955 to 1970 by 5
   label bot "Electricity Production in USA"\
        "(Billions of Kilowatt Hours)" up 0.4 left 0.5
   copy "elect" thru {
        p = $2/100
10       for i = 1 to p do
        {
             line from i-1, $1 to i, $1+1.5
             line from i, $1+1.5 to i, $1
        }
15      f =  p - (i-1)
        if f > 0 && f < 1 then
        {
             line from i-1, $1 to p, $1
        }
20      "  $2" ljust at p, $1
   }
   .G2
```

16.4 Range-Column Charts [Selby 1979]

The following range-column chart is used to show the average trading range of a group of selected stocks that are traded on the New York Stock Exchange (NYSE); this average is called the Dow Jones Industrial Average (DJIA):

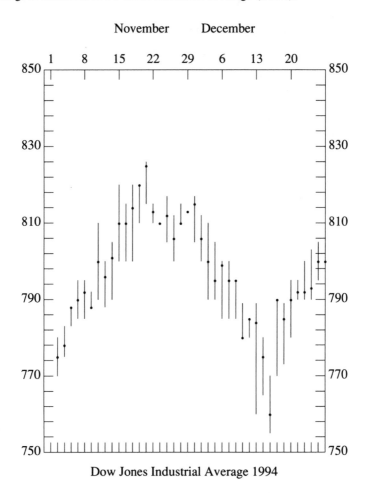

Dow Jones Industrial Average 1994

The top and bottom of each vertical line indicates the highest and lowest values for the DJIA on the day in question. The bullet mark on each vertical line indicates the price at the NYSE closing time.

The above range-column chart was specified as

```
     .G1
     frame ht 4.0 wid 3.0
     coord x 0, 41 y 750, 850

5    ticks bot in from 1 to 40 ""
     label bot "Dow Jones Industrial Average 1994"\
                                          up 0.2
     ticks top in at 1 "1", 6 "8", 11 "15",\
        16 "22", 21 "29", 26 "6", 31 "13", 36 "20"
10   label top "November         December"

     ticks left in from 750 to 850 by 4 ""
     ticks left in from 750 to 850 by 20

15   ticks right in from 750 to 850 by 4 ""
     ticks right in from 750 to 850 by 20

     i = 1
     copy "dj" thru {
20       i = i + 1
         line from i, $1 to i, $2
         bullet at i, $3
     }
     .G2
```

16.5 Thermometer

Consider the following figure of a thermometer:

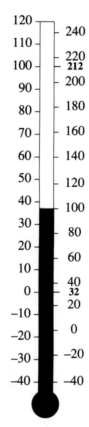

The thermometer shown above was specified as

```
   .G1
   frame ht 4.0 wid 0.15
   coord x 0, 1 y -50, 120
   ticks bot off
5  ticks left out 0.05 from -40 to 120 by 10
   for f = -40 to 240 by 20 do
   {
       c =  int((f-32)*5/9)
       ticks right out 0.05 at c ""
10     plot f at 2.5, c
   }

   "\s-2\fB32\fP\s0" at 2.5,  0
   htick ljust at 1, 0
15 "\s-2\fB212\fP\s0" at 2.5, 100
   htick ljust at 1, 100

   #draw the solid stem
   temp = 37
20 .ps +12
   for i = 0.05 to 1.00 by 0.05 do
       { line from i, -50 to i, temp }
   .ps

25 #the bulb
   "\s+(48\(bu\s0" below at 0.50, -55
   .G2
```

The line for drawing the solid stem was made thicker by increasing the point size
(line 20) by 12 points to 22 points. The point size that is actually used for drawing
this line on our typesetting system is 7 points. This is because the postprocessor for
our typesetter, when drawing lines, uses a dot whose size is one third of the current
point size.

16.6 Using `troff` Point-Size Instructions to Print a Thick Line

As an example of a graph with a thick graph line, consider the following graph that shows the amount of individual savings [Meyers 1970]:

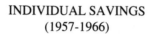

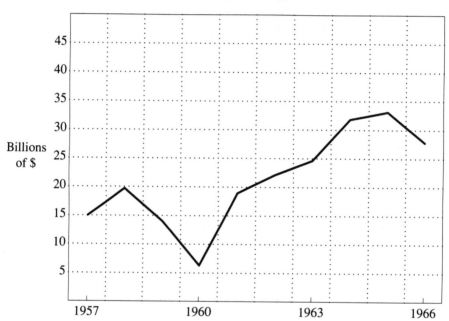

This graph was specified as

```
     .G1
     frame ht 3.0 wid 4.0
     coord x 1956.5, 1966.5 y 0, 50
     ticks bot in 0.05 from 1957 to 1966 by 3
  5  grid bot dotted from 1957.5 to 1965.5 ""
     grid left dotted from 5 to 45 by 5
     label left "Billions" "of $"
     label top "INDIVIDUAL SAVINGS"\
           "(1957-1966)" down 0.2
 10  .ps 48
     draw solid
     copy "savings"
     .ps
     .G2
```

The graph line was made thicker by increasing the point size (line 10) to 48. However, as mentioned earlier, the point size actually used for drawing this line is 16 (one third of 48).

17. Final Comments

The discussion in this chapter has been mainly about how to use grap. We have not really addressed the issues involved in drawing good and effective graphs. Readers interested in these issues should read *The Visual Display of Quantitative Information* by Tufte [1983].

18. Exercises

1. Explain the difference between the new and draw instructions.

2. What are the pros and cons of including data directly in a graph specification vis-a-vis reading it from a file.

3. Write a specification to draw the following graph that illustrates the Law of Large Numbers [Freund 1981]. Applied to coin tossing, this law states that the distribution of heads and tails approaches 0.5 as the number of tosses increases:

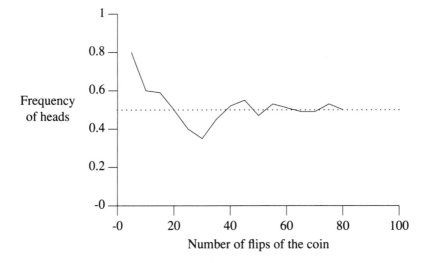

    The data values to be used for this graph are

Tosses	Heads	Tosses	Heads
5	0.8	45	0.55
10	0.6	50	0.47
15	0.59	55	0.53
20	0.5	60	0.51
25	0.4	65	0.49
30	0.35	70	0.49
35	0.45	75	0.53
40	0.52	80	0.5

4. In the histogram example given in Section 9.1, the starting and end points of
    the arrow pointing to the mode column and the position of the label "mode"
    could have been computed from the data. Instead, values of these items, which
    are all based on the value and frequency of the mode, were pre-computed
    outside the graph specification and used directly for specifying the arrow and
    label coordinates (lines 35-36). This makes the graph data dependent, i.e., a
    change in the data is likely to require a change in these values. Modify the
    histogram specification so that these values are computed in the specification
    itself.

5. Write a specification for the following Business Week style graph that shows
    the changes in the leading and production indexes:

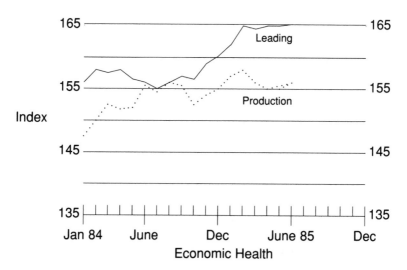

The data values to be used for the graph are

	Leading Index			Production Index	
Year	Month	Index	Year	Month	Index
1984	1	156	1984	1	147.5
1984	2	158	1984	2	150
1984	3	157.5	1984	3	152.5
1984	4	158	1984	4	151.75
1984	5	156.5	1984	5	152
1984	6	156	1984	6	155.5
1984	7	155	1984	7	154.5
1984	8	156	1984	8	156
1984	9	157	1984	9	155.5
1984	10	156.5	1984	10	152.5
1984	11	159	1984	11	154
1984	12	160.25	1984	12	155
1985	1	162	1985	1	157
1985	2	165	1985	2	158
1985	3	164.5	1985	3	156
1985	4	165	1985	4	155
1985	5	165	1985	6	156
1985	6	165.25	1985	5	155

6. Write a grap specification for the following horizontal bar graph:

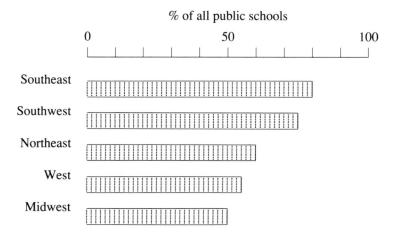

Percent of Public Schools Having
National School Lunch Program

Chapter 2

Specifying Viewgraphs and Slides

The mv macro package [DWB 1986a] provides facilities for specifying viewgraphs and slides, collectively called *foils* or *transparencies*, for display on overhead and 35mm projectors. Viewgraphs of several sizes, 35mm slides and 2" × 2" super slides can be made with mv. It has facilities for specifying titles, lists, fonts, point sizes, and so on. mv can be used in conjunction with preprocessors such as grap, pic, tbl and eqn.

Making foils is a two-stage process. In the first stage, the information to be displayed on the foil is printed on a typesetter or on a laser printer in the exact format in which it is to appear on the foil. This formatted output is then used to make the viewgraph or slide. A viewgraph is made by transferring the printed page image to a transparency using a device such as the Thermofax® machine. The document used to make the viewgraph is rendered unreadable by the heat and the pressure used to transfer the printed material from the page to the viewgraph. Consequently, in case of expensive or hard to make originals, copies, not originals, should be used to make transparencies.

Slides are made by professional photographers from the original formatted output. Two kinds of slides can be made: slides with opaque letters on clear or colored background (*positive* slides) or transparent letters on opaque background (*negative* slides).

1. Examples of Foils

To give you a flavor of how foils are specified, we will look at two viewgraphs that were used by Transcendental Transportation at their 1988 annual meeting. Here is the first viewgraph:[1]

---

1. Because of page size constraints, the foils shown in this chapter are approximations, not exact replicas, of the foils that are actually produced.

Transcendental Transportation Products

TIRES

- circular (conventional)
- square (revolutionary, fuel-efficient)
- elliptic (revolutionary, fuel-efficient)
- semi-circular (revolutionary, super fuel-efficient)

MISCELLANEOUS

- Automobile Repair Kits
- Levitation Training

This viewgraph was specified as

```
  .VS 1 "TTI Annual Meeting" "2/30/88"
  .T "Transcendental Transportation Products"
  .sp
  .ce
5 TIRES
  .B
  circular (conventional)
  .B
  square (revolutionary, fuel-efficient)
10 .B
  elliptic (revolutionary, fuel-efficient)
  .B
  semi-circular (revolutionary,
  super fuel-efficient)
15 .sp 2
  .ce
  MISCELLANEOUS
  .B
  Automobile Repair Kits
20 .B
  Levitation Training
```

The first line in the above specification is the foil-start instruction .VS which specifies a 7" × 7" viewgraph. Each foil *must* begin with a foil-start instruction. The .VS instruction takes three arguments that identify the foil. Identification information is printed on the top right hand side of the foil, just above the projection area. In this case, the three arguments specify

1. the viewgraph number,
2. the occasion and
3. the date of the occasion.

By default, mv uses the Helvetica font. This sans serif font is less dense and easier to read at a distance than the Times Roman font that is used by other tools such as mm and ms. The .VS instruction specifies an 18 point font for the viewgraph. With this font up to 21 lines can fit on a page.

The second line is the title instruction .T, which prints its argument in the center of the line using a 22-point font (current point size plus 4). The next two lines (lines 3 and 4) are troff instructions: .sp outputs a blank line and .ce centers the next input line (line 5). The .T instruction was not used to center the text on line 5 because it prints its argument in a larger font. Note that troff instructions are routinely used with mv (for troff details, see Chapter 4).

Line 6 is the second-level-indentation instruction .B, which specifies that the text following it is to be indented and that the first text line is to be tagged with a bullet.

The indented text is terminated by the next mv instruction. The remaining instructions are similar to the ones we have just discussed.

The second viewgraph is interesting because it contains a graph that demonstrates the integration of grap and mv:

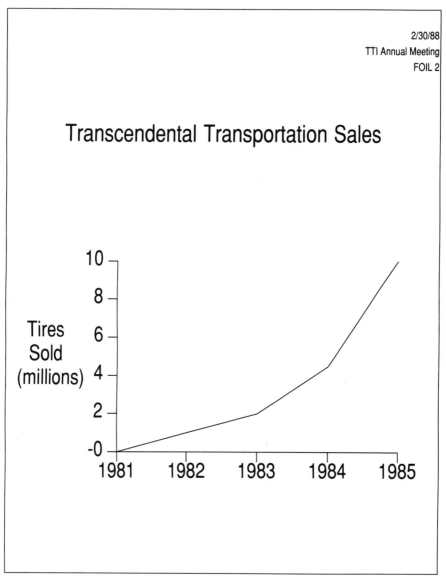

This viewgraph was specified as

```
     .VS 2 "TTI Annual Meeting" "2/30/88"
     .T "Transcendental Transportation Sales"
     .sp 4
     .in +0.5i
 5   .G1
     frame invis left solid bot solid
     coord x 1981,1985 y 0,10
     label left "Tires" "Sold" "(millions)" left 0.4i
     draw solid
10   1981, 0
     1982, 1
     1983, 2
     1984, 4.5
     1985, 10.0
15   .G2
     .in
```

Like the first viewgraph specification, this specification also begins with the .VS and
.T instructions. These are followed by two troff instructions, .sp and .in. The
.sp instruction (line 3) outputs four blank lines and the .in instruction (line 4)
increases the indentation by 0.5". Line indentation is increased to center the graph.
It was necessary to change the indentation to center the graph because mv, unlike mm
and ms, does not provide a facility for centering item blocks. The amount of
indentation required was determined by trial and error.

Lines 5-15 contain the specification of the graph. (Graphs are specified using grap
instructions; cee Chapter 1 for details about grap.)

The last line of the viewgraph specification restores the original indentation.

2. Foil Specification Format

Each foil specification has the form:

> *foil-start instruction*
> *instructions, and text*

Each foil specification can be kept in a separate file or, alternatively, several
specifications can be kept in one file.

3. Foil-Start Instructions

mv provides several foil-start instructions for specifying foils of different sizes.
Foil-start instructions have the form

.xy [*n* [*id* [*date*]]]

All the three arguments of the foil-start instructions are strings: *n* is the foil number, *id* contains additional identifying information such as the presentation title, and *date* is the date to be printed on the foil. These arguments are printed on the top right-hand corner of the foil:

If the foil-start instruction arguments are omitted, then default values are used: the current foil number for *n*, the company name for *id* and the current date for *date*:

```
                                                   current-date
                                                   company-name
                                        FOIL current-number
```

The names of the foil-start instructions have been constructed systematically. The first character of the instruction name can be V (for viewgraphs) or S (for 35mm slides). The second character indicates the foil shape:

- S (square),
- w (small wide),
- h (small high),
- W (big wide) or
- H (big high).

The following is a list of the different foil sizes that are supported by mv:

instruction	explanation
.VS	7" × 7" viewgraph or 2" × 2" super-slide
.Vw	7" × 5" viewgraph
.Vh	5" × 7" viewgraph
.VW	9" × 7" viewgraph
.VH	7" × 9" viewgraph
.Sw	7" × 5" 35mm slide
.Sh	5" × 7" 35mm slide
.SW	9" × 7" 35mm slide
.SH	7" × 9" 35mm slide

Each foil-start instruction terminates the previous foil, if any, and begins a new one. The .VW and the .SW foil-start instructions, which specify foil dimensions to be 9" × 7", produce formatted output whose dimensions are actually 7" × 5.4". This is because the width of the commonly used typesetter paper is less than 9.0 inches [DWB 1986a]. Consequently, the formatted output must be enlarged by a factor of 9/7 before making viewgraphs or slides.

The following figures (0.2 × original size) illustrate the relative sizes of the different foils:

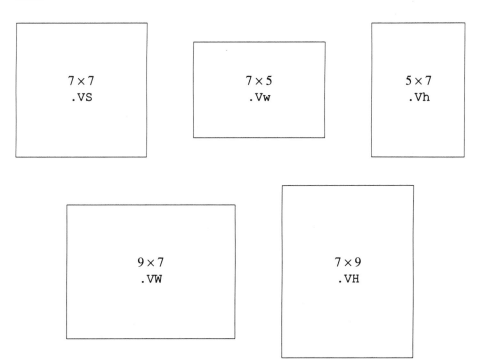

4. Default Parameters: Point Size, Dimensions, Etc.

Foil-start instructions use default values for foil parameters such as the point size, the foil dimensions and the aspect ratio (width/height). These values determine the amount of text that can fit on a foil. The parameter values used are listed in the following table:

inst-ruction	point size	max. lines	nominal				actual text			
			W	H	AR	1/AR	W	H	AR	1/AR
.VS	18	21	7	7	1	1	6	6.8	1.13	0.88
.Vw	14	19	7	5	0.71	1.4	6	4.8	0.8	1.25
.Vh	14	27	5	7	1.4	0.71	4.2	6.8	1.6	0.62
.VW	14	21	7	5.4	0.77	1.3	6	5.2	0.87	1.15
.VH	18	28	7	9	1.3	0.77	6	8.8	1.5	0.68
.Sw	14	18	7	4.6	0.67	1.5	6	4.4	0.73	1.4
.Sh	14	27	4.6	7	1.5	0.67	3.8	6.8	1.8	0.56
.SW	14	18	7	4.6	0.67	1.5	6	4.4	0.73	1.4
.SH	18	28	6	9	1.5	0.67	5	8.8	1.76	0.57

W, H and AR denote the width (in inches), the height (in inches) and the aspect ratio of the foil, respectively. Nominal dimensions refer to physical foil dimensions; actual text dimensions specify dimensions used for placing the text.

The vertical spacing used is 1.25 times the current point size.

5. Titles and Centered Lines

Viewgraph titles are printed with the title instruction .T, which has the form

.T "*title*"

The title is centered and printed using a point size equal to the current point size plus 4 points. Title centering is not affected by any changes to the indentation (specified with the .I or the .in instructions).

The troff center instruction .ce should be used to center lines in the current point size:

```
.ce [ n ]
line₁
line₂
...
lineₙ
```

n is the number of lines to be centered. If n is not specified, then it is assumed to be 1.

6. Specifying Lists

Typically, foils consist of lists itemizing the main points of the presentation. mv provides special facilities, called indentation-level instructions, for specifying such lists. There are four (progressively increasing) indentation levels: A (unindented), B,

C and D. The amount of indentation depends upon the foil type.

The following table shows how items with different indentation levels are specified:

List Level	Item Mark	Item Specification	Comments
A		.A [no] *item-text*	Output lines corresponding to the item text are printed starting at the left margin. Unless argument no is given, the .A instruction inserts a half blank line before the item text. The .A instruction is automatically invoked by the foil-start instructions.
B	●	.B [*mark* [*size*]] *item-text*	Level-B items are automatically indented with respect to level-A items. A half blank line is inserted before the item text.
C	—	.C [*mark* [*size*]] *item-text*	Level-C items are automatically indented with respect to level-B items. A half blank line is inserted before the item text.
D	●	.D [*mark* [*size*]] *item-text*	Level-D items are automatically indented with respect to level-C items. The bullet used for the level-D is smaller than the one used for level-B.

Argument *mark* specifies the alternative item mark that is to be printed in place of the default item mark. *mark* can be any sequence of characters, but if it contains blanks, then it must be enclosed within double quotes. Argument *size* specifies the point size to be used for the alternative *mark*. If *size* is negative, then the point size is decreased by *size*; otherwise it is increased by *size*.

The text associated with an item is terminated by the next mv instruction.

6.1 A List Example

As an example of lists, consider the following viewgraph:

There are several kinds of high-level languages:

- *Sequential*

  — Pascal

  — Fortran

  — C

- *Concurrent*

  — Concurrent Pascal

  — Concurrent C

This viewgraph was specified as

```
   .VS   15 AT&T 8/2/87
   There are several kinds
   of high-level languages:
   .B
5  \f(HISequential\fP
   .C
   Pascal
   .C
   Fortran
10 .C
   C
   .B
   \f(HIConcurrent\fP
   .C
15 Concurrent Pascal
   .C
   Concurrent C
```

Notice the use of the Helvetica Italic font (HI), which is specified with the troff instruction \f (lines 5 and 13).

We will now show you an alternative version of the above viewgraph in which the symbols ☞ and □ are used as item marks. These symbols, which are denoted as \(rh and \(sq, are given as arguments to the .B and .C instructions. Here is the viewgraph:

There are several kinds of high-level languages:

☞ *Sequential*

   ☐ Pascal

   ☐ Fortran

   ☐ C

☞ *Concurrent*

   ☐ Concurrent Pascal

   ☐ Concurrent C

6.2 Changing the Indentation Levels

The indentation used for the item lists can be changed using the indentation instruction .I. This instruction has the form

.I [*indent* [a [*x*]]]

Argument *indent* specifies the new indentation. If *indent* is unsigned, then the new indentation is the initial indentation plus *indent*; otherwise, it is the current indentation ± *indent*. If *indent* is null or omitted, then the initial indentation is restored. If the second argument a is specified, then the .I instruction invokes the .A instruction before completing. The third argument, if present, is used as the argument for the .A instruction.

The change in indentation specified with the .I instruction takes effect after the next .A, .B, .C or .D instruction (including a .A instruction invoked by the .I instruction).

The indentation cannot be made negative; if the specified decrement results in a negative value, then the indentation is assumed to be zero.

6.3 Vertical Spacing and the Indentation-Level Instructions

By default, indentation-level instructions .A, .B and .C output half a vertical space (0.5v) before the item text. Instruction .D does not output any vertical space. The amount of space output by these instructions can be changed by using the .DV instruction:

.DV [*av* [*bv* [*cv* [*dv*]]]]

Arguments *av*, *bv*, *cv* and *dv* specify the vertical space to be output by the instructions .A, .B, .C and .D, respectively. A null argument " " specifies that the space output is *not* to be changed.

Initially, the vertical space output by the indentation-level instructions corresponds to the settings specified by the instruction

.DV 0.5v 0.5v 0.5v 0.0v

7. Point Size and Line Length

The .S instruction is used for changing both the point size and the line length. This instruction has the form

.S [*ps* [*ll*]]

Argument *ps* specifies the new point size. If *ps* is signed, then it specifies a relative change in the current point size. If *ps* is null or omitted, then the previous point size is restored. If *ps* is greater than 99, then the original (default) point size is restored.

Argument *ll* specifies the line length. If this argument is not scaled, i.e., *ll* is just a number that is not followed by units such as i (inches) or m (ems), then the scale used will depend upon the value of *ll*. If *ll* is less than 10, then it is assumed to be in inches; otherwise, it is assumed to be a value scaled in troff's internal units.

The point size can also be changed with the following troff instructions, which can be embedded in the text:

instruction	effect
\s*d* \s (*dd*	Switch to point size *d* or *dd* (*d* is a single digit).
\s±*d* \s± (*dd*	Change point size by ±*d* or ±*dd* (*d* is a single digit).
\s0	Restore the previous point size.

8. Font Changes

By default, mv uses the Helvetica font. Other fonts can be specified with the `troff` switch-font instruction .ft:

.ft [*f*]

f is the new font name; if *f* is omitted or if it is the letter P, then the .ft instruction restores the previous font.

Alternative fonts can also be specified with `troff` font instructions that can be embedded in the text:

instruction	effect
\f*x* \f (*xx*	Change to font *x* or *xx*.
\fP	Restore the previous font.

9. Miscellaneous

- Text can be underlined with the .U instruction, which has the form

  .U *string₁* [*string₂*]

  string₁ will be underlined and *string₂*, if present, will be concatenated to *string₁* without underlining.

- String * (Tm generates the trademark symbol as in Apple™.

- Instructions .S, .DV and .U do not cause a line break. The .I instruction causes a break only if invoked with more than one argument.

10. Useful `troff` Instructions

For a finer control over the viewgraph format, `troff` instructions can be used with mv instructions. The following `troff` instructions can be used safely:

`troff` instruction	explanation
`.ad`	adjust output
`.br`	break
`.ce`	center output lines
`.fi`	switch to fill mode
`.ft`	switch font
`.hy`	hyphenate
`.na`	do not adjust output
`.nf`	switch to no-fill mode
`.nh`	do not hyphenate
`.nx`	switch to next file
`.so`	include contents of file
`.sp`	space vertically
`.ta`	set tabs
`.ti`	temporary indentation (for one output line)

mv recognizes the .AD, .BR, .CE, .FI, .HY, .NA, .NF, .NH, .NX, .SO, .SP, .TA and .TI instructions as synonyms for the corresponding `troff` instructions with lower-case letter names.

11. Hints for Making and Managing Foils

Here are some suggestions for making foils and for managing a large number of foils.

11.1 Making Foils

- Commonly used viewgraph sizes are 7" × 7" and 7" × 5".

- Commonly used slides are the 2" × 2" super slide and the 7" × 5" 35mm slide.

- Do not "crowd" the foils with too much information. Put only the important points on the foils.

- Avoid reducing the default point size. The default point sizes have been selected so that the foils can easily be read by an audience of a dozen or more people.

- The Helvetica sans serif font, the default font used by mv, is easier to read than the Times Roman serif font, which is the default font used by `troff`, mm and ms. The Times Roman font allows you to pack in more characters in a viewgraph than the Helvetica font. With the Helvetica font, remember to use Helvetica Italic (HI) and Helvetica Bold (HB) fonts and not the Times Italic (I) and Times Bold (B) fonts.

- Use fonts and point sizes consistently.

- Do not use too many fonts in one foil; otherwise, you will confuse the viewer about the significance of the different fonts.

- About 20-25 foils are appropriate for a one-hour technical presentation. This includes the time spent fielding some questions from the audience.

11.2 Managing a Large Number of Foils

1. Keep each foil specification in a separate file because this facilitates manipulation and alteration of individual foil specifications.

2. Specify at least the foil number (the first argument) in the foil-start instruction. This will allow you to print the individual foils separately with the correct foil number.

3. Use a file naming convention for files containing foil specifications that will allow you to conveniently access foil specifications, both individually and collectively. For example, we use the following naming convention for a foil with a two-digit number *dd*

   > *namedd*

   where the prefix *name* is the mnemonic name identifying the foil set. Each foil *dd* can now be typeset individually by using the command

   mvt *namedd*

   (mvt is the UNIX system command that invokes troff with the mv macros).

   Alternatively, all the foils can be typeset collectively with the command

   mvt *name*[0-9[0-9]

   The foils will be printed in the right order because the UNIX shell expands the above command to

   mvt *name*01 *name*02 *name*03 *name*03 *name*04 ...

   Note that a leading zero is used for the first 9 foils.

12. Interaction with Other Document Preparation Facilities

The preprocessors grap, pic, tbl and eqn for specifying graphs, figures, tables and equations can be used harmoniously with mv.

mv, unlike mm and ms, does not provide a facility for centering chunks (blocks) of the document. Specifically, this means that there is no facility for centering figures or graphs. Centering equations and tables is not a problem because they can be centered using eqn and tbl facilities. But to center figures, graphs and other blocks of text, it is necessary to improvise. For example, a graph or figure can be centered by increasing the line indentation before its specification and then restoring the original indentation after the specification. Centering items using this technique is a trial-and-error process.

13. Using mv

The `mv` macro package is invoked with the `mvt` command or by specifying the option `−mv` in the `troff` command:

`mvt` *options input-files*
`troff −mv` *input-files* >*output-file*

The `mvt` command can send the output directly to the printing device. In case of the `troff` command, the *output-file* must be sent explicitly to the printing device after processing it with a program called a *postprocessor*.

If the document also contains graphs, figures, tables and equations, then the appropriate preprocessors can be invoked by using the following versions of the `mvt` and `troff` commands:

`mvt −e −p −g −t` *options input-files*
`grap` *input-files* `| pic | tbl | eqn | troff −mv` >*output-file*

14. Notes

1. Some printers produce output in a continuous sheet. `mv` automatically prints cut marks indicating where the formatted output is to be cut for each foil. The actual projection area is marked by plus signs. These signs are used to position viewgraphs on the viewgraph mounts. On all foils, except the square ones, horizontal or vertical crop marks are printed to indicate how much of the foil will be projected if it is made into a slide instead of a viewgraph.

2. As in `eqn`, the tilde character ˜ denotes an unpaddable space[2] (in `troff` it is denoted by a backslash followed by a blank).

3. Do not use names beginning with either) or] for `troff` variable or macro names because such names are used internally by `mv`.

---

2. Spaces are of two kinds: *paddable* and *unpaddable*. Paddable spaces are spaces that can be padded with other spaces when right justifying a line. Normal spaces are paddable spaces. Padding may sometimes destroy the desired alignment or placement of text. In such cases unpaddable spaces should be used because spaces cannot be appended to unpaddable spaces. The spacing between two words separated only by unpaddable spaces will not be changed nor will these words be placed on different lines.

15. Exercises

Write specifications for the following two viewgraphs:

1.

Concurrent C Program Characteristics

- Every program must contain function `main`, the initial process.

- Process creation steps:

    — Declare process types.

    — Declare process variables.

    — Instantiate processes by using the `create` operator.

2.

6/27/87
AT&T
FOIL 02

Utilization of Multiple CPUs

Multiprocessor

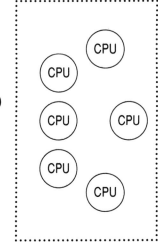

Monolithic
Sequential
Program

?

How do we Distribute the Program?

Chapter 3

Specifying the Document Format with ms

The ms macro package [Lesk 1978a, UNIX 1985], like the more varied mm macro package, is a collection of troff macros for specifying document formats. ms has been used for producing a wide variety of documents such as papers, books, letters and programming manuals. ms provides higher-level facilities than those provided by troff. It allows the user to specify items such as

- the document type (format),
- paragraphs,
- section headings,
- footnotes,
- a block of text which is to be kept together and
- two-column format.

ms does not attempt to hide troff. Instead, it attempts to facilitate the use of troff. Typically, troff instructions are used for the facilities not provided by ms. For instance, troff instructions are used for skipping to a new line or skipping to a new page because ms does not provide a new-line and a new-page instructions.

1. An Example of Document Formatting

To give you a flavor of ms, we will show you the specification of a two-page letter from the president of Transcendental Transportation Incorporated to a potential investor. For ease of presentation, we will discuss each page of the letter separately. Here is the first page:

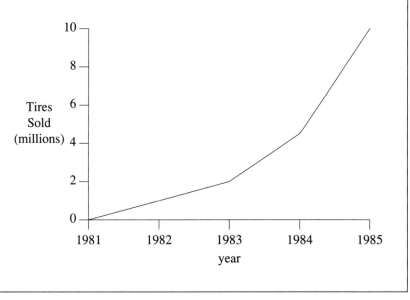

**Transcendental Transportation Inc.
Three Wheel Drive, Busted Axle, Wyoming**

April 1, 1986

Mr. A. L. Psmith
113 Niagara Falls Boulevard
Wheeling, West Virginia

Dear Mr. Psmith:

We are in receipt of your letter dated February 29 inquiring about
investment opportunities in our company. Enclosed is a copy of our
last year's annual report. Ever since our inception, our sales and
revenues have grown astronomically as illustrated by the following
graph:

The letter format and text were specified using ms and troff instructions. The
graph was specified using grap, a pic preprocessor. Preprocessors such as grap,
pic, tbl and eqn for specifying graphs, figures, tables and equations, respectively,
can be used with ms. The raw (input) document corresponding to the initial part of
the first page (up to the graph) is

```
    .LP
    .rs
    .sp |2.25i
    .po 1.0i
5   .tl '''April 1, 1986'
    .DS L
    Mr. A. L. Psmith
    113 Niagara Falls Boulevard
    Wheeling, West Virginia
10  .sp 3
    Dear Mr. Psmith:
    .DE
    .sp
    .LP
15  We are in receipt of
    your letter dated February 29 inquiring
    about investment opportunities
    in our company.
    Enclosed is a copy of our last
20  year's annual report.
    Ever since our inception, our
    sales and revenues have
    grown astronomically as illustrated by
    the following graph:
```

An ms instruction *must* precede the text in the raw (input) document so that ms parameters and variables are initialized properly. This instruction (usually the first instruction in a document) is used by ms to determine the document type. ms knows about some document types such as technical papers and memorandums; for other document types, the user must specify the document format explicitly by suitably positioning the document items.

The first instruction in the above letter is the left-adjusted paragraph instruction .LP, which is given so that the ms variables and parameters are initialized properly. (From the .LP instruction, ms determines that the document is not of a predefined type.) Lines 2 and 3 are troff instructions; they specify that 2.25 inches of blank space is to be output at the top of the page. (Note that lower-case letters are used for the names of troff instructions while upper-case letters, and occasionally digits, are used for names of ms instructions.)

Line 4 is a troff instruction that sets the page offset to one inch. Line 5 is the troff title instruction .tl that is used to print the date on the right-hand side of the page. The .tl instruction has the form

.tl *' left' center' right'*

left, *center* and *right* are character strings that may include blanks. .tl left adjusts, centers and right adjusts its arguments.

Next, enclosed within a display (lines 7-11) is the recipient's address and the line addressing the receiver:

.DS L
address of recipient
and the salutation
.DE

Instruction .DS signals the beginning of a left-justified (indicated by the argument L) display and instruction .DE signals its end. Material within a display is processed in no-fill mode and is not split across pages. If it is not possible to print the displayed material on the current page, then the rest of the current page is left blank and the displayed material is printed on the next page. Within the display is the vertical-space instruction .sp 3 (line 10), which instructs troff to output three blank lines; these lines separate the receiver's address from the salutation.

Following the display is the .sp instruction (line 13), which outputs one blank line. After this comes the left-adjusted paragraph instruction .LP (line 14), which indicates the beginning of a new paragraph. The remaining lines specify the text before the graph.

Now let us take a look at the graph specification:

```
     .DS  L
     .G1
     frame invis left solid bot solid
     coord x 1981,1985 y 0,10
 5   label left "Tires" "Sold" "(millions)"
     label bottom "year"
     draw solid
     1981,  0
     1982,  1
10   1983,  2
     1984,  4.5
     1985,  10.0
     .G2
     .DE
```

The graph specification is enclosed in a display (lines 1-14) to prevent the graph from being split across pages. (For details of graph specifications, see Chapter 1.)

The second page of the letter is

-2-

Our sales will be boosted further by our new super efficient semi-circular tire that we will soon market along with our circular, square and elliptic tires:

The following table compares the efficiency, on a typical automobile, of the standard circular tire and our revolutionary tires:

tire	miles/gallon
circular	30.0
square	36.0
elliptic	40.0
semi-circular	42.0

We appreciate your interest in our company.

Sincerely,

M. M. Yogi
President

Encs.
Transcendental Trans. Annual Report

The page number at the top of the page is automatically printed by ms. The figure was specified using pic and the table was specified using tbl. Here is the raw document for the initial part of the second page (up to the table):

```
    .LP
    Our sales will be boosted further
    by our new super efficient semi-circular
    tire that we will soon market
 5  along with our circular, square
    and elliptic tires:
    .DS B
    .PS
    r = 0.5
10  L: line right 2*r
    arc from L.start to L.end\
        with .c at L + (r, 0)
    .PE
    .DE
15  .LP
    The following table compares
    the efficiency,
    on a typical automobile,
    of the standard
20  circular tire and our
    revolutionary tires:
```

The first line is the left-adjusted paragraph instruction; this is followed by text lines
(lines 2-6) and a display (lines 7-14) containing pic instructions specifying the
semi-circular tire. Argument B of the display-start instruction .DS centers the semi-
circular tire. The display containing the figure is followed by the left-adjusted
paragraph instruction .LP (line 15). Then come several lines of text.

Here is the remainder of the letter specification:

```
     .DS
     .TS
     center;
     cb   cb
5    a n.
     tire☛miles/gallon

     circular☛30.0
     square☛36.0
10   elliptic☛40.0
     semi-circular☛42.0
     .TE
     .DE
     .LP
15   We appreciate your interest in our company.
     .sp 2
     .nf
     .in 3.0i
     Sincerely,
20   .sp 2
     M. M. Yogi
     President
     .in
     .sp 3
25   Encs.
     \fITranscendental Trans.\fP Annual Report
```

First, there is a display (lines 1-13) that contains a table specification. Table entries are separated by the tab character (denoted by the visible symbol ☛). The table is enclosed within the display to ensure that it is not split across pages.

After the display is the left-adjusted paragraph instruction .LP (line 14), which left justifies the text (one line in this case) following it. Next comes the troff instruction .sp 2, which outputs 2 blank lines. This is followed by the troff instruction .nf (line 17), which causes a switch to the no-fill mode. Then the indentation is increased to 3.0 inches by troff instruction .in so that the formal closing "Sincerely", and the writer's name and title are appropriately indented. Then come instructions (lines 23-24) that restore the original indentation and output 3 blank lines. Finally, there is text specifying the document enclosures.

2. Basics

ms knows about the format of some document types such as papers prepared for publication or general distribution, intra-company technical memorandums and intra-company letters. For other documents, such as books, the document format must be explicitly specified by the user by placing document items in appropriate places.

2.1 Form of the Formatting Instructions

The document format is specified by inserting ms instructions, along with troff and preprocessor instructions, in the text. ms instructions have the general form

.*XY* [*parameters*]

where *X* and *Y* are upper-case letters. There are some exceptions: two instructions begin with a digit instead of a letter, and three instructions have a one-letter name.

troff instructions are used when appropriate facilities are not available in ms. Line-oriented or stand-alone troff instructions are similar to ms instructions except that they use lower-case letters. In-line troff instructions (also called escape sequences), which can be embedded in the text, begin with the backslash character \. Finally, preprocessor instructions are used to specify graphs, figures, tables and equations.

2.2 New Sentences

An input text line ending with a period, question mark or an exclamation mark is recognized by troff as the end of a sentence. An extra space is automatically inserted between sentences.

2.3 Page Dimensions

The default page and line lengths used by ms are 11 and 6 inches, respectively. The *page length* refers to the physical length of a page, and it includes space for the upper and lower margins. The *page width* is the sum of the line length plus the left margin (called the *page offset*) whose default value is 26/27 inches. The page width (as understood by troff) must be less than or equal to the physical page width. The line length is divided into two parts:

1. the *indentation*: text is right indented by this amount from the page offset, and

2. the *centering (actual line) length*: items are centered with respect to this length.

2.4 Spaces

There are two kinds of spaces: *paddable* and *unpaddable*. Paddable spaces are spaces to which other spaces can be added (by troff) to right justify a line. Normally spaces are paddable. An unpaddable space is specified by prefixing a normal space with the escape character \.

Padding may sometimes destroy the desired alignment or the placement of text. In such cases, unpaddable spaces should be used because spaces cannot be appended to unpaddable spaces. Spacing between two words separated only by unpaddable spaces is not changed. Also, such words are always placed on the same line.

As an example illustrating the use of unpaddable spaces, consider the following four lines of a raw document:

```
In the above time-series program,
the second assignment statement ''X = 1''
causes variable X to be assigned
the value one.
```

Right justification of the formatted output may cause extra spaces to be inserted between words as in

In the above time-series program, the second assignment statement "X = 1" causes variable X to be assigned the value one.

Suppose the phrase ''X = 1'' is to be kept intact, that is, it is not to be split across output lines (and no extra spaces are to be inserted within it); then the two spaces in this phrase must be made unpaddable by prefixing them with backslashes, for example, ''X\ =\ 1''. After this change, the above text will be printed as

In the above time-series program, the second assignment statement "X = 1" causes variable X to be assigned the value one.

Multiple spaces between words are not discarded; however, trailing spaces on an input line are discarded. An input line beginning with a space causes a break (i.e., the current output line is printed without right justification and a new output line is started). A blank input line causes a blank line to be printed.

3. Variables

Numeric variables are used for storing document parameters, and as flags and counters. String variables are often used as convenient abbreviations for long strings. Because ms does not provide numeric or string variables, troff numeric variables (registers) and string variables (strings) are used.

3.1 Numeric Variables

Numeric variables can be defined and their values changed with the troff instruction .nr, which has the form

.nr *r v*

where *r* is a one- or two-character numeric variable name to which the value *v* is assigned. Values of variables with one- and two-character names *x* and *xx* are obtained by referencing them as \n*x* and \n (*xx*, respectively.

The following predefined variables specify default values for some document format and style parameters:

variable	defines	change takes effect	default value
CW	column width	next multi-column instruction	$7/15 \times$ LL
FL	footnote length	next footnote	$11/12 \times$ VS
FM	bottom margin	next page	1 inch
GW	inter-column gap	next multi-column instruction	$1/15 \times$ LL
HM	top margin	next page	1 inch
LL	line length	next paragraph	6 inches
LT	title length	next paragraph	6 inches
PD	paragraph spacing	next paragraph	0.3 VS
PI	paragraph indent	next paragraph	5 ens
PO	page offset	next page	26/27 inches
PN	page number for output; register format determines page number format	immediate	arabic
PS	point size	next paragraph	10 points
VS	vertical spacing	next paragraph	12 points

The document format and style can be changed by changing values of these variables. However, the change may not take effect immediately; to make the change immediate, the corresponding troff instruction should also be given (see Chapter 4). Suppose the line length is to be changed to 4.5 inches. If the new length is specified by just changing the value of the line-length variable LL, then the new line length will take effect starting with the next paragraph. To make this change take place with the next line, the line change must also be specified with the troff instruction .ll, for example,

```
.nr LL 4.5i
.ll 4.5i
```

Note that alternative page lengths and page numbers are specified with the troff instructions .pl and .pn. The page number is printed using the format of the page number variable PN (its default format is arabic; alternative formats such as Roman and alphabetic can be specified; see Chapter 4 for details about variable formats).

3.2 String Variables

String variables are defined by using the troff define-string instruction .ds, which has the form

.ds *s* *str*

s is a one- or two-character variable name that is associated with the string *str*. Long strings can be continued on the next line by ending the current line with a backslash. Values of string variables with one- and two-character names *x* and *xx* are obtained by referencing them as *x and * (*xx*, respectively.

Examples of string definitions are

```
.ds uN UNIX System
.ds tR \f(CWtroff\fP
```

A reference to uN, i.e., * (uN, is replaced by the string "UNIX System"; similarly, * (tR is replaced by the string "\f(CWtroff\fP"

3.3 Accent Marks (Diacritics)

To facilitate specification of foreign words, ms provides predefined string variables for some commonly used accent marks (diacritics):

symbol/string	denotation	example
acute accent	*'	*'e prints as é
grave accent	*`	*`e prints as è
umlaut	*:	*:u prints as ü
circumflex	*^	*^e prints as ê
tilde	*~	*~a prints as ã
breve	*C	*Ce prints as ĕ
cedilla	*,	c*, prints as ç

The cedilla string immediately follows the letter below which the cedilla mark is to be printed. All other strings immediately precede the letter over which the corresponding mark is to be printed.

3.4 Special Characters Defined by troff

troff extends the keyboard character set by defining a large number of special characters that have names made up of characters available on most keyboards. Names of these characters have the form "\ (*xy*" where *x* and *y* are ASCII characters. Examples of a few of these special characters and their denotations are

character	denotation	name	character	denotation	name
•	\(bu	bullet	°	\(de	degree
□	\(sq	square	†	\(dg	dagger
~	\(ap	approximates	○	\(ci	circle
σ	\(*s	sigma	Σ	\(*S	Sigma

For a complete list of the special characters, see Chapter 4.

3.5 Dashes, Hyphens and Minus Signs

The character – is interpreted as the hyphen character. Special notation is provided for printing minus signs and dashes:

character	printed as	denotation
hyphen	-	–
minus sign	–	\-
dash	—	\(em

4. Fonts

ms provides facilities only for specifying italic, bold and Roman fonts. To specify other fonts, troff instructions must be used.

4.1 ms **Font Instructions**

instruction	explanation
.I	Change to italic font.
.I *string*	Print *string* in italic.
.B	Change to bold font.
.B *string*	Print *string* in bold.
.R	Change to Roman (default) font.

4.2 troff **Font Instructions**

The following in-line troff font instructions can be embedded in the text to change fonts:

instruction	effect
\fx	Change to font x, where x is a one-character font name.
\f (xy	Change to font xy, where xy is a two-character font name.
\fP	Change back to the previous font, that is, the font in use prior to the last font change request.

Here is some sample text that uses troff instructions to change fonts:

```
The UNIX system document
macro packages, such as \f(CWmm\fP and
\f(CWms\fP, preprocessors ...
In addition to the
\fIdocument formatting tools\fP ...
```

This text is printed as

> The UNIX system document macro packages, such as mm and ms, preprocessors ... In addition to the *document formatting tools* ...

There is a minor problem with troff that becomes obvious when changing to a font whose space character has a noticeably different width than the space character of the previous font. troff prints the space preceding an in-line font change instruction using the new font instead of the old font. If the two fonts have markedly dissimilar character widths, then the resulting output may look ugly because troff will leave a little more or a little less space than expected. For example, notice the extra space before the words mm and ms in the above example. Fortunately, when changing between most of the commonly used fonts, this troff problem either does not occur or it is inconsequential. If different fonts use the same space character (as can be the case with most text fonts for a specific printing device), then there is simply no problem. Alternatively, if the space characters belonging to different fonts have approximately the same width then this troff problem is not noticeable.

One way of bypassing this problem is to use the escape sequence \&\f(CW; the zero-width non-printing character \& forces troff to output the space before the font change takes effect. Using the escape sequence with the zero-width character, the above example will be printed as

> The UNIX system document macro packages, such as mm and ms, preprocessors ... In addition to the *document formatting tools* ...

In formatting this book, we used the escape sequence *(cW to change to constant-width font. This escape sequence refers to the string cW, which we defined as

```
.ds cW \&\f(CW
```

The line-oriented `troff` instruction `.ft` can also be used to change fonts. This instruction has the form

`.ft [f]`

where *f* is the name of the new font. If the font name is omitted or if the font name P is used, then the `.ft` instruction restores the previous font.

4.3 Changing Fonts—Our Preference

In general, we prefer to use in-line `troff` instructions for changing fonts because they can be

- embedded in the text,

- used to change to any font,

- used to specify the fonts of ms instructions arguments and

- used in conjunction with other formatting tools such as `tbl` and `pic` (eqn provides its own facility for changing fonts).

ms instructions can be used only to change to default Roman, bold or italic fonts.

Occasionally, we use the `troff` instruction `.ft` to change fonts. A line containing just an in-line `troff` instruction implies an empty input line and produces a blank output line. In such cases, we use the `.ft` instruction to change the font because it does not produce a blank output line.

5. Point Size

The *point size* of a font is the size of the characters in the font. Character sizes are usually measured in *points*, which is a printer's unit of measurement; one point is equal to 0.01384 inches (approximately 1/72 of an inch). Point sizes can be changed using ms and `troff` instructions.

5.1 ms **Point Size Instructions**

ms provides limited facilities for changing the point size:

instruction	explanation
.LG	Increase point size by 2 points.
.SM	Decrease point size by 2 points.
.NL	Change to normal (default) point size, which is 10 points (value of variable PS).

5.2 `troff` Point Size Instructions

The following `troff` instructions can be embedded in the text to change the point size:

instruction	effect
`\sd` `\s(dd`	Switch to point size *d* or *dd* (*d* is a single digit); if this is not a valid point size, then switch to the closest available point size. For historical reasons, a two-digit point size *dd* can also be specified as `\sdd`, but *dd* cannot be greater than 36.
`\s±d` `\s±(dd`	Change point size by ±*d* or ±*dd*, if possible; otherwise switch to the closest valid point size.
`\s0`	Switch back to the previous point size.

Here is some sample text with in-line `troff` instructions to change the point size:

```
The point size can be \s-3decreased\s0
or \s+3increased\s0 in-line just as
the fonts can be \fBchanged\fP in-line.
```

This text is printed as

The point size can be decreased or increased in-line just as the fonts can be **changed** in-line.

The line-oriented `troff` instruction `.ps` can also be used to change the point size. This instruction has the form

`.ps [[±]n]`

which changes the point size to *n* or, if the argument is preceded by a plus or minus sign, changes the current point size by ±*n* points. If the argument is omitted, then the `.ps` instruction restores the previous point size. In case the requested point size is not available, then the closest available point size is used.

5.3 Changing Point Size—Our Preference

As in the case of the font instructions (see Section 4.3), we generally prefer to use the in-line `troff` point-size instructions.

6. Vertical Spacing

The *vertical spacing* (or *leading*) is the distance between the base lines of two consecutive lines in the finished document. When the point size is increased, it is a good idea to increase the vertical spacing also; otherwise, consecutive lines will be too close to each other and characters may even overlap. The default point size is 10 points and the default vertical spacing is 12 points. According to one rule of thumb, vertical spacing should be equal to the point size plus two points.

Vertical spacing is changed by assigning an appropriate value to the vertical spacing variable VS. However, the change takes effect only in the next paragraph. To make the change immediate, the new vertical spacing should also be specified by using the troff vertical spacing instruction .vs, which has the form

.vs [[±] *n*]

This instruction changes the vertical spacing to *n* points (or, if a leading sign is present, to the current vertical spacing ±*n* points). If *n* is not given, then the .vs instruction restores the previous vertical spacing.

7. Document Structure

A raw (input) document consists of the following four logical components:

Definitions, Style and Appearance Parameters:
> Macro, string and eqn definitions used in the document are given here along with parameters that specify the style and appearance of the document; examples of parameters specified here are page length, page width and page offset.

Prelude:
> Items that occur only at the beginning of a document, e.g., document type, date, document title, author name and abstract.

Body:
> The document text along with formatting instructions, graphs, figures, tables and equations.

Postlude:
> Items that occur only at the end of a document, e.g., signature lines in letters.

Document Organization

The formatted document consists of two components: an optional cover sheet and the body.

8. Document Definitions, Style and Appearance Parameters

The first component of a raw document contains definitions that will be used in the document and instructions specifying the style and appearance of the document:

- eqn definitions (delimiters and shorthand notation for frequently used mathematical symbols and expressions),
- macro and string definitions,
- global parameter definitions (i.e., instructions changing the values of the predefined numeric variables),

- specification of right justification,
- specification of double spacing and
- a request to perform hyphenation.

For a discussion of eqn, see the companion book by Gehani [1987]. Numeric and string variable definitions were discussed earlier in Section 3, and macro definitions are discussed later in this chapter. See Chapter 4 for a discussion of the other items.

9. Document Prelude

Instructions given in the initial part of a document, the *document prelude*, specify the document type and information such as the document title, the name of the author and the institution, and the abstract. These instructions must appear in the following order:

```
     document type instruction (.RP, .IM, .TM, .LP)
     date instruction (new-date instruction .ND or date instruction .DA)
     .TL (title instruction)
     lines specifying the document title
 5   .AU (author)
     author information, such as name
     .AI (author institution)
     author institution
     .AB (abstract-begin instruction)
10   lines specifying the abstract
     .AE (abstract-end instruction)
     .CS (cover-sheet instruction)
     text ...
```

The document type instruction must be given; other instructions can be omitted.

9.1 Document Type

ms determines the document type by examining the first ms instruction in the raw document; this instruction must precede the raw document text for the proper initialization of ms. The following instructions are used to specify the document type explicitly:

instruction	document type
.RP	Released paper (paper prepared for publication or general distribution); a cover sheet is automatically generated.
.TM *t# c# f#*	Technical memorandum (paper prepared for distribution within the company); arguments *t#*, *c#* and *f#* specify the technical memorandum number, case number and file number, respectively.
.IM	Internal memorandum (intra-company letter).
.LP	No special format; you must give some ms instruction before the input text to initialize ms properly; the .LP instruction, which is the left-justified paragraph instruction, does the job; you can also use the .PP, .TL, .SH or .NH instructions.
.MR	Memorandum for record.
.MF	Memorandum for file.
.EG	Engineer's notes.
.LT	Letter; this instruction has been recently added (see Section 15.1).

Only one version of an ms document needs to be stored. To print the document in an alternative format, just the first instruction in the document is changed. ms ignores instructions that are inappropriate for the specified document type.

9.2 Document Date

There are two instructions for controlling the printing of the date: .DA and .ND. The .DA instruction is used for specifying the date printed at the bottom of a page and the .ND instruction is used for specifying the date printed in the ''date'' fields associated with a document.

By default, the current date is printed on the cover pages of a released paper and a technical memorandum as well as in the date fields of the first page of technical and internal memorandums. The date is printed in the format illustrated by the example date

May 1, 1986

nroff prints the date at the bottom of each page; to make troff do the same, use the date instruction .DA without arguments.

Instead of the current date, a user-supplied date can also be printed at the bottom of each page; the user-supplied date is specified using the .DA instruction:

`.DA` *date*

An alternative date can also be specified with the new-date instruction `.ND`; however, this instruction suppresses printing of the date at the bottom of each page. The `.ND` instruction has the form

`.ND` [*date*]

If the date is omitted, then no date will be printed.

If both the `.ND` and the `.DA` instructions are given, only the last one applies.

9.3 Title

The title is specified by using the title instruction `.TL` followed by the title text:

```
.TL
one or more lines
of text specifying the title
```

The title will be printed on one or more lines as determined by ms. To specify each output line of a multi-line title explicitly, the troff break instruction `.br` is used:

```
.TL
title line_1
.br
title line_2
.br
. . .
title line_n
```

The first ms instruction following the title text indicates the end of the title.

9.4 Authors and Author Information

Author names and other items of information are specified with the author and author-institution instructions `.AU` and `.AI` instructions, respectively:

```
.AU [ room-no [ extension ] ]
author₁ name
.AI
author₁ institution
.AU [ room-no [ extension ] ]
author₂ name
.AI
author₂ institution
...
.AU [ room-no [ extension ] ]
authorₙ name
.AI
authorₙ institution
```

Lines containing the author name and the author institution are printed as separate centered lines. Arguments *room-no* and (telephone) *extension* of the .AU instruction are printed in appropriate places on the cover sheet and the first page of a technical or an internal memorandum.

If all the authors (or a subset of successive authors) belong to the same institution, then only one .AU and one .AI instruction need be given for them:

```
.AU
author₁ name
author₂ name
...
.AI
authors' institution
```

If a single .AU instruction is used for multiple authors, then individual room numbers and extensions cannot be specified.

As an example, consider the following raw document segment specifying the document title, and the name and the institution of the two authors:

```
.TL
Specifying Customized Microprocessors
.AU
Doug Comer
.AI
Purdue University
West Lafayette, Indiana 47907
.AU
Narain Gehani
.AI
.MH
```

Note that the .MH instruction is a special implementation-dependent instruction available at AT&T Bell Laboratories (in Murray Hill, NJ) for conveniently specifying the local address.

The information specified above will be printed on the cover sheet and on the first page of a released paper as shown below:

Specifying Customized Microprocessors

Doug Comer

Purdue University
West Lafayette, Indiana 47907

Narain Gehani

AT&T Bell Laboratories
Murray Hill, New Jersey 07974

9.5 Abstract

Document abstracts are specified using the abstract-begin instruction .AB and the abstract-end instruction .AE. An abstract specification has the form

```
.AB [ no ]
lines of text plus formatting instructions
specifying the abstract
.AE
```

Normally a line with the word "*ABSTRACT*" is printed before the abstract. Giving the argument no to the .AB instruction suppresses printing of this line.

The abstract line length is equal to five sixths of the document line length. An alternative abstract line length can be specified with the `troff` instruction `.ll`; this instruction must be given after the abstract-begin instruction, but before the abstract text.

9.6 Cover Sheet

The cover sheet of a document contains information such as the document title, the author's name and affiliation, and the document abstract. An example of a released paper cover sheet is shown at the end of this chapter. Released paper cover sheets are printed automatically. Technical memorandum cover sheets are printed with the cover-sheet instruction `.CS`. This instruction has the form

`.CS` *text-pages other-pages total-pages #figures #tables #references*

The format of technical memorandum cover sheets is implementation dependent. The `.CS` instruction is ignored for all document types other than a technical memorandum.

10. Document Body

The portion of a raw document corresponding to the document body consists of text intermixed with instructions specifying items such as headings, paragraphs, displays, lists, footnotes, preprocessor instructions (specifying graphs, tables, equations and figures) and `troff` instructions.

In this section we will discuss the ms instructions used in specifying the document body. Wherever appropriate or necessary, we will also discuss some `troff` instructions.

10.1 Paragraphs

There are three instructions for specifying paragraphs:

paragraph instruction	explanation
`.LP`	Left-justified ordinary paragraph.
`.PP`	Ordinary paragraph with first line indented.
`.IP [[`*l*`]` *i*`]`	Indented paragraph (all lines are indented). The paragraph label *l* is not indented. Argument *i* specifies the text indentation; if this argument is not given, then the paragraph is indented by a standard amount.

A paragraph is terminated by the next ms instruction that is encountered.

Here is an example illustrating different types of paragraphs:

Computer document preparation consists of editing, formatting and viewing:

1. *Editing*: the document is entered into the computer, or an existing document is modified.

2. *Formatting*: the document is processed as specified.

3. *Viewing*: the processed document is viewed or printed.

Document preparation tools have revolutionized the way people write and prepare documents.

There are five paragraphs in the above example: an ordinary paragraph with the first line indented, three indented paragraphs with labels and one left-justified paragraph. Note the use of indented paragraphs to specify lists. This example was specified as

```
   .PP
   Computer document preparation consists of
   editing, formatting and viewing:
   .IP 1.
 5 \fIEditing\fP: the document
   is entered into the computer, or an existing
   document is modified.
   .IP 2.
   \fIFormatting\fP: the document is processed
10 as specified.
   .IP 3.
   \fIViewing\fP: the processed document is viewed
   or printed.
   .LP
15 Document preparation tools have
   revolutionized the way
   people write and prepare documents.
```

10.1.1 Quoted Paragraphs: Quoted paragraph text is both left and right indented. Individual quoted paragraphs are specified with the quoted-paragraph instruction .QP:

```
.QP
```
quoted paragraph text

A quoted paragraph specified with the .QP instruction is terminated by the next ms instruction.

Multiple quoted paragraphs are specified with the instructions .QS and .QE, which specify the start and end of quoted text, respectively:

```
.QS
quoted paragraph₁ text
.LP
quoted paragraph₂ text
. . .
.LP
quoted paragraphₙ text
.QE
```

Here is an example of quoted paragraphs:

Now let me tell you what Charles Goren has to say about the game backgammon [1974]:

> Backgammon is so ancient that none can say exactly when it was originated; traces of similar games go back as far as five thousand years.

> It is an enthralling game because a single cast of the dice can turn imminent disaster into sure victory.

These paragraphs were specified as

```
   .LP
   Now let me tell you what Charles Goren has
   to say about the game backgammon [1974]:
   .QS
5  Backgammon is so ancient that none can say
   exactly when it was originated;
   traces of similar games go back as far
   as five thousand years.
   .LP
10 It is an enthralling game because a single
   cast of the dice can turn imminent disaster
   into sure victory.
   .QE
```

10.2 Headings

A *heading* is text printed at the head of a document section to introduce the section contents. The heading is normally made to stand out from the rest of the text by printing it in a bold font.

ms provides instructions for specifying two kinds of headings: numbered and unnumbered. Numbered headings are specified using the .NH instruction.

Numbered heading specifications have the form

.NH [*heading-level*]
heading text

If the argument *heading-level* is omitted, then it is assumed to be 1. If *heading-level* is equal to zero, then it is like specifying a level-one heading except that the heading numbers are reset to start from one. The heading text can span several lines and is terminated by the next ms instruction. To separate the heading text from the section text, a paragraph instruction, e.g., .PP or .LP, is often used.

As an example, consider the following numbered headings:

---

8. Poetry
8.1 Medieval Poetry
8.1.1 Old English Period
8.1.2 Middle English Period

These headings were specified as follows:

```
.NH 1
Poetry
.NH 2
Medieval Poetry
.NH 3
Old English Period
.NH 3
Middle English Period
```

Note that the appropriate section and subsection numbers are printed automatically.

10.2.1 Unnumbered Headings: Unnumbered headings are specified using the .SH instruction. Unnumbered heading specifications have the form

.SH
heading text

As in case of numbered headings, the heading text can span several lines and it is terminated by the next ms instruction.

As an example, consider the following unnumbered headings:

Humor
Sarcasm

These headings were specified as follows:

```
.SH
Humor
.SH
Sarcasm
```

10.3 Keeps

A *keep* is used to keep a portion of the document, such as a table, together on the same page. There are two kinds of keeps: static and floating.

A *static* keep ensures that the kept material has the same relative position in the finished document as it has in the raw document. If the kept material cannot fit on the current page, then the rest of the current page is left blank and the kept material is printed starting at the top of the next page. Ordinary keep specifications have the form

```
.KS
part of document that is not to be split across pages
.KE
```

A *floating* keep is similar to a static keep, but it does not guarantee that the kept material will have the same relative position in the finished document vis-a-vis its position in the raw document. If the kept material cannot fit on the current page then, as in case of static keeps, it is printed starting at the top of the next page. However, unlike static keeps, the remainder of the current page is not left blank; it is filled with items that follow the floating keep in the raw document. Note that the relative ordering of floating keeps is always preserved.

Floating keep specifications have the form

```
.KF
part of document that is not to be split across pages
.KE
```

10.4 Displays

Displays are used to specify blocks of text and other items that are to be kept together without any rearrangement. Displayed material, unlike kept material, is processed in no-fill mode. A display specification has the form

```
.DS [ style [ indent ] ]
material to be displayed
.DE
```

The different values allowed for argument *style* and their effects are discussed in the following table:

style	**comments**
I or *omitted*	*Indented display*: the displayed material is indented 0.5 inches (8 spaces in nroff) by default. Argument *indent* can be used to specify an alternative indentation.
L	*Left-justified display.*
C	*Line-by-line-centered display*: each line of the display is centered individually.
B	*Block-centered display*: the display is first left justified and then centered as a block.

We will use the following limerick [Lear 1964] to illustrate the different display styles:

```
There was a young person in pink,
Who called out for something to drink;
But they said, 'O my daughter,
There's nothing but water!'
Which vexed that young person in pink.
```

If it is not enclosed in a display, then the above text will be printed as

> There was a young person in pink, Who called out for something to drink; But they said, 'O my daughter, There's nothing but water!' Which vexed that young person in pink.

Lines of the above limerick are rearranged because the limerick is processed in fill-mode. Displayed material, on the other hand, is processed in no-fill mode. For example, if the limerick is enclosed in an indented display (using the instruction .DS), then it will be printed as

> There was a young person in pink,
> Who called out for something to drink;
> But they said, 'O my daughter,
> There's nothing but water!'
> Which vexed that young person in pink.

If the limerick is enclosed in a left-justified display (using the instruction .DS L), then it will be printed as

> There was a young person in pink,
> Who called out for something to drink;
> But they said, 'O my daughter,
> There's nothing but water!'
> Which vexed that young person in pink.

If the limerick is enclosed in a line-by-line centered display (using the instruction .DS C), then it will be printed as

> There was a young person in pink,
> Who called out for something to drink;
> But they said, 'O my daughter,
> There's nothing but water!'
> Which vexed that young person in pink.

If the limerick is enclosed in a block-centered display (using the instruction .DS B) then it will be printed as

> There was a young person in pink,
> Who called out for something to drink;
> But they said, 'O my daughter,
> There's nothing but water!'
> Which vexed that young person in pink.

As in the case of kept material, displayed material is not split across pages. For long displays, the instructions .CD, .LD and .ID should be used, because they allow the displayed material to be split across page boundaries:

long display	instruction to be used
line-by-line-centered	.CD (instead of .DS C)
left-justified	.LD (instead of .DS L)
indented	.ID (instead of .DS I)

10.5 Lists

ms does not provide a special facility for constructing lists. Fortunately, they can easily be constructed using the indented paragraph instruction .IP as follows:

```
.IP  label₁
text for list item 1
.IP  label₂
text for list item 2
. . .
.IP  label
            n
text for list item n
```

The list is terminated by the end of the document or by the first ms instruction after the last list item, whichever comes first.

The item labels are not indented. If the labels are to be indented, then they must be preceded by spaces, for example,

```
.IP  "   1."
```

Here is an example list (from a driving manual):

> There is no simple way to tell you *exactly* how long it will take you to stop at a certain speed. Your stopping distance depends on:
>
> 1. Your own reaction time.
>
> 2. Weather and road conditions.
>
> 3. The weight of the vehicle.
>
> 4. The condition of the brakes.
>
> 5. The condition and type of tires.
>
> One thing is sure. The faster you are going, the longer it will take you to stop.

This list was specified as

```
     .LP
     There is no simple way to tell you
     \fIexactly\fP how long it will take you to
     stop at a certain speed.
  5  Your stopping distance depends on:
     .IP "  1."
     Your own reaction time.
     .IP "  2."
     Weather and road
 10  conditions.
     .IP "  3."
     The weight of the vehicle.
     .IP "  4."
     The condition of the brakes.
 15  .IP "  5."
     The condition and type of tires.
     .LP
     One thing is sure.
     The faster you are going, the longer it
     will take you to stop.
```

10.5.1 Nested Lists: Lists can be nested within other lists. Before the nested list, the right-shift instruction .RS must be used to increase the indentation for the nested list. The original indentation is restored at the end of the nested list with the instruction .RE. A nested list specification has the form

```
     .RS
     specification of the list
     .RE
```

Here is an example that illustrates nested lists:

There are several kinds of high-level languages:

1. *Sequential*

    - Pascal

    - Fortran

    - C

2. *Concurrent*

    - Concurrent Pascal

    - Concurrent C

The above lists were specified as

```
    .LP
    There are several kinds of high-level
    languages:
    .IP "  1."
 5  \fISequential\fP
    .RS
    .IP "  \s-1\(bu\s0"
    Pascal
    .IP "  \s-1\(bu\s0"
10  Fortran
    .IP "  \s-1\(bu\s0"
    C
    .RE
    .IP "  2."
15  \fIConcurrent\fP
    .RS
    .IP "  \s-1\(bu\s0"
    Concurrent Pascal
    .IP "  \s-1\(bu\s0"
20  Concurrent C
    .RE
```

10.6 Footnotes

Footnotes are specified as

```
. . . label
.FS
label  footnote text
.FE
. . .
```

Here is some example text illustrating footnotes:

> Concurrent C is a superset of C for parallel programming.* In this paper, I
> will briefly discuss suitability of Concurrent C for programming robots.†
>
> _____
>
> * Its facilities are based on the *rendezvous* model.
>
> † For more details, please see *Concurrent C and Robotics* by Narain Gehani

This text was specified as

```
    Concurrent C is a superset of C for
    parallel programming.*
    .FS
    * Its facilities are based on
5   the \fIrendezvous\fP model.
    .FE
    In this paper, I will briefly discuss
    suitability of Concurrent C for
    programming robots.\(dg
10  .FS
    \(dg For more details, please
    see \fIConcurrent C and Robotics\fP
    by Narain Gehani
    .FE
```

10.6.1 Footnote Label Position and Point Size: Footnote labels are not automatically printed as superscripts nor are they automatically printed in a smaller point size. (The footnote label asterisk * looks like a superscript because of the way an asterisk is printed.) To print a footnote label in the text as a superscript and in a smaller point size, the following paradigm can be used:

```
...\u\s-2label\s+2\d
.FS
label  footnote text
.FE
...
```

`troff` in-line instructions `\u` and `\d` raise and lower the printing position by half an em; instruction `\s` is used to change the point size.

11. Document Postlude

The final part of the document, the *document postlude*, contains items that occur at the end of the document.

11.1 Signature

Memorandums are signed by their authors at the end of the document. The signature is usually placed just above the author's name, which is printed at the end of the document. Authors' names, indented and with sufficient space for signatures, are printed by the signature instruction `.SG`. The name of each author specified with the `.AU` instruction is printed.

The signature instruction has the form

`.SG` [*reference-data*]

String *reference-data* contains identification information such as the typist's initials; if given, *reference-data* is printed, left adjusted, on the same line as the name of the last author. For example, if two authors are specified, then the `.SG` instruction will print

	author$_1$
reference-data	*author$_2$*

The signature instruction is ignored for released papers.

12. Page Headers and Footers

A page header consists of three parts: left-, center- and right-adjusted headers. Current values of the string variables `LH`, `CH` and `RH` are printed as the left, center and right headers. By default, ms sets the center header to print the page number in the format

- n -

on all pages except the first page. Left and right headers are set to null.

Page headers can be changed by redefining the string variables mentioned above with the define-string instruction .ds. For example, the definitions

```
.ds LH \\\\n%
.ds RH \fB\s-1Introduction\s0\fP
```

set the left header to the current page number (the value of the predefined variable %), and the right header to the string ''\fB\s-1Introduction\s0\fP'', which is printed as ''**Introduction**''. (To find out why four backslashes are needed to specify the current page number, see Section 27 of Chapter 4.)

Similarly, a page footer consists of three parts: left-, center- and right-adjusted footers. Current values of the string variables LF, CF and RF are printed as the left, center and right footers. Footers can be changed by redefining the string variables LF, CF and RF. By default, ms, when used with nroff, sets the center footer to print the date; when used with troff, it sets the center footer to the null string. Left and right footers are, by default, always set to the null string.

13. Multi-Column Format

Text can be printed in multi-column format:

instruction	explanation
.2C	Change to two-column format.
.MC [*cw* [*gw*]]	Change to multi-column format; *cw* specifies the column width and *gw* specifies the *gutter width* (space between the columns). Depending upon the values of *cw* and *gw*, ms fits as many columns as possible on a page. If *cw* and *gw* are not specified, then the .MC instruction is equivalent to the .2C instruction.
.1C	Change to one-column format.

Changing the number of columns, except when switching from one-column format to multi-column format, causes a skip to a new page.

Here is a two-column format example [Marx 1983] produced by using the .2C instruction:

I believe the emphasis on popcorn and other noise-making foods has helped drive many people away from the movies and I think the commercial pounding that the television listeners are subjected to will eventually drive many of them away from their sets.

Where they will go I don't know. Perhaps they will take up fox hunting or glass blowing, or maybe they will just roam the streets at night searching for peace and quiet.

My comments are necessarily brief and quiet, for in my profession, it is extremely hazardous for a comedian to outrage the sponsor, for without the commercial he hasn't got a job and without a job he is hardly a comedian.

Here is the same text in three-column format produced by using the .MC instruction:

I believe the emphasis on popcorn and other noise-making foods has helped drive many people away from the movies and I think the commercial pounding that the television listeners are subjected to will eventually drive many of them away from their sets.

Where they will go I don't know. Perhaps they will take up fox hunting or glass blowing, or maybe they will just roam the streets at night searching for peace and quiet.

My comments are necessarily brief and quiet, for in my profession, it is extremely hazardous for a comedian to outrage the sponsor, for without the commercial he hasn't got a job and without a job he is hardly a comedian.

14. Miscellaneous Instructions

14.1 Boxes

Strings and blocks of text can be enclosed in boxes. The box instruction .BX, which has the form

.BX *string*

encloses its argument in a box $\boxed{string}$. If *string* contains embedded blanks, then it must be enclosed within double quotes.

The box-begin and box-end instructions .B1 and .B2 are used for enclosing a block of text within a box. These instructions are used as

```
.B1
text
.B2
```

For example, the following box and text [Lear 1964]

> There was an Old Man with an owl,
> Who continued to bother and howl;
> He sat on a rail, and imbibed bitter ale,
> Which refreshed the Old Man and his owl.

were specified as

```
.DS
.B1
.sp
There was an Old Man with an owl,
Who continued to bother and howl;
He sat on a rail, and imbibed bitter ale,
Which refreshed the Old Man and his owl.
.sp
.B2
.DE
```

The box instructions and text are enclosed within a display so that the text is processed in no-fill mode and is not split across pages.

14.2 Underlining

The .UL instruction is used for underlining strings. This instruction has the form

.UL *string*

If *string* contains embedded blanks, then it must be surrounded by double quotes; embedded blanks are also underlined.

Here is an example illustrating the use of the underline instruction:

> We make three kinds of tires: the conventional circular tire and the revolutionary fuel-efficient square and elliptic tires.

The preceding text was specified as

```
We make three kinds of tires: the
conventional circular tire and the
.UL revolutionary
fuel-efficient square and elliptic tires.
```

14.3 Tabs

Tab positions are specified with the .TA instruction, which has the form

.TA t_1 t_2 ... t_n

Tab positions are specified in ens. The default tab positions are 5 ens, 10 ens, etc.

14.4 UNIX System Trademark Instruction

The UNIX system trademark instruction

.UX

prints "UNIX" (in current point size minus one) along with the footnote

UNIX is a registered trademark of UNIX System Laboratories, Inc.

The footnote, which is printed only by the first use of the .UX instruction, is labeled by a dagger † (asterisk * in nroff).

14.5 Local Addresses

An implementation may provide instructions for conveniently specifying local addresses. For example, at AT&T Bell Laboratories the instruction

.MH

is provided as an abbreviation for the company address at Murray Hill, NJ. The .MH instruction is typically used after the .AI instruction.

15. ms Extensions

Some implementations of the ms macro package provide instructions for specifying a letter format, letter attachments and persons receiving copies.

15.1 Specifying Letter Document Type

The letter format is specified with the letter-type instruction .LT:

.LT
address of receiver

The .LT instruction prints the current date, and switches to the no-fill mode for the recipient's address. It also defines a new version of the signature instruction .SG that automatically prints the formal closing line with the word "Sincerely". After printing its argument (the sender's name), the .SG instruction skips to the next page.

As an example, consider the following letter printed on company letterhead:

Transcendental Transportation Inc.
Three Wheel Drive, Busted Axle, Wyoming

July 1, 1987

Mr. A. L. Psmith
113 Niagara Falls Boulevard
Wheeling, West Virginia

Dear Mr. Psmith:

We are in receipt of your letter dated June 28 inquiring about getting
a dealership for our tires.

We would like to meet with you to discuss this. Please let us know
when would it be possible for you to visit us.

Sincerely,

M. M. Yogi

This letter was specified as

```
      .LT
      Mr. A. L. Psmith
      113 Niagara Falls Boulevard
      Wheeling, West Virginia
   5  .sp 3
      Dear Mr. Psmith:
      .sp
      .LP
      We are in receipt of
  10  your letter dated June 28 inquiring
      about getting a dealership for our tires.
      .LP
      We would like to meet with you
      to discuss this.
  15  Please let us know when would
      it be possible for you to visit us.
      .SG "M. M. Yogi"
```

The `.LP` instruction restores the fill mode that was turned off by the `.LT` instruction.

15.2 Specifying Attachments

Attachments can be specified using the instruction `.AT`, which prints the word "Attached" and then switches to the no-fill mode. This instruction is used as

```
      .AT
      attachment₁
      attachment₂
      . . .
      attachmentₙ
```

The input shown above will be printed as

```
      Attached:
      attachment₁
      attachment₂
      ...
      attachmentₙ
```

The attachment instruction is normally given after the signature instruction `.SG`. The fill mode turned off by the attachment instruction can be restored after the attachments with the `.LP` instruction or the `troff` fill-mode instruction `.fi`.

15.3 Specifying Persons Receiving Copies

Name of persons receiving copies of a document can be specified on the document by using the .CT instruction, which prints the words "Copies to" and then switches to the no-fill mode:

```
.CT
person 1
person 2
. . .
person n
```

The above .CT instruction will produce the following output:

```
Copies to:
person 1
person 2
...
person n
```

The fill mode can be restored after the "copy to" list by using the .LP instruction or the troff fill-mode instruction .fi.

16. troff **Instructions and Macros**

We will now briefly discuss some of the troff facilities that are often used with ms. For a detailed discussion of troff instructions, see Chapter 4.

16.1 troff **Instructions**

The following troff instructions are commonly used with ms because ms does not provide the corresponding facilities:

instruction	comments
.bp	break page (skip to next page)
.br	line break (skip to next line)
.de	define macro
.ds	define string variable
.in	indent
.ll	line length
.na	no adjustment
.nr	define/initialize numeric variable
.po	page offset
.sp	vertical space

16.2 Macros

A *macro* facility allows a group of instructions and/or text to be given a symbolic name, called the *macro name*; the group of instructions and/or text is called the *macro body*. A macro invocation (call) is replaced by the body of the macro.

Macros are a convenient mechanism for symbolically referencing frequently used groups of instructions and blocks of text. Macros can be used to reduce the input document size. They make document modifications easier because, in changes involving macros, usually only the macro definitions will need to be changed instead of all the places where the macros are called.

ms does not have facilities for defining macros. Consequently, troff macro facilities are used. troff macro definitions have the form

```
.de  x
instructions and/or text, that is, macro body
..
```

where *x* is a one- or two-character name of the macro being defined or redefined. The body of the macro begins on the next line and is terminated by a line with two dots:

```
..
```

Macros can be parameterized with up to 9 parameters; these parameters are referenced in the macro body as \\$i ($1 \leq i \leq 9$). Parameters are replaced by the corresponding arguments, which are values supplied in the macro call. The ith argument is used as the value of the ith parameter.

Macro calls have the form

```
.xx  arguments
```

where *xx* is a one- or two-character macro name. Arguments must be separated by spaces; moreover, arguments with embedded blanks must be enclosed within double quotes. If all the arguments do not fit on one line, then they can be continued on the next line by ending the line to be continued with a backslash.

As examples of macros, consider the two macros named (P and) P which begin and end constant-width font displays. These macros were defined as

```
.de (P
.DS
.ft CW
..
.de )P
.ft P
.DE
..
```

A call to the macro (P, i.e., . (P, is replaced by the two instructions

```
.DS
.ft CW
```

which start a display and change the current font to the constant-width font. Similarly, a call to the macro) P is replaced by the two instructions

```
.ft P
.DE
```

which restore the previous font and end the display.

16.2.1 Automatically-Numbered Lists: ms does not provide facilities for automatically-numbered lists. However, facilities for specifying automatically-numbered lists can easily be provided by defining a set of macros. As an example, here are two user-defined macros for implementing automatically-numbered lists:

macro	definition/explanation
.AL	Begin a new automatically-numbered list; first item text follows.
.LI	Text for a list item follows.

The list is terminated by the end of the document or the first ms instruction after the last list item, whichever comes first. Note that list items cannot contain ms instructions.

The format of automatically-numbered lists specified using these macros is

```
.AL
item₁ text
.LI
item₂ text
.
.
.LI
itemₙ text
```

Instructions .AL and .LI are calls to the macros AL and LI, respectively, which were defined as

```
.de AL
.nr j 0 1
.IP "   \\n+j."
..
.de LI
.IP "   \\n+j."
..
```

Every occurrence of the .AL instruction is replaced by the two instructions

```
.nr j 0 1
.IP "   \n+j."
```

The .nr instruction initializes the number variable j to 0 and sets its auto-increment value to 1. Instruction .IP begins an indented paragraph that is labeled with the item number. This item number is the new value of j, which is equal to the old value plus the auto-increment value.

Each occurrence of the .LI instruction is replaced by the instruction

```
.IP "   \n+j."
```

For instance, consider the following list:

The following list summarizes the basic sailing maneuvers:

1. Whenever you change course, you must retrim sail either out or in to find the luff.

2. Changing tacks when sailing to windward is called *coming about* or *tacking*.

3. Changing tacks when sailing to leeward is called *jibing*.

This list was specified as

```
    The following list summarizes the
    basic sailing maneuvers:
    .AL
    Whenever you change course, you must
5   retrim sail either out or in to find
    the luff.
    .LI
    Changing tacks when sailing to windward is
    called \fIcoming about\fP or \fItacking\fP.
10  .LI
    Changing tacks when sailing to leeward is
    called \fIjibing\fP.
```

The above macros cannot be used to construct nested lists; this is because each list must have its own item counting variable, but these macros use the same counting variable j for all the lists. Note that the item text alignment fails after nine items.

16.2.2 Automatically-Numbered Footnotes: Some versions of the ms macros, but not all, provide a mechanism for specifying automatically-numbered footnotes. If your ms does not support automatically-numbered footnotes, then you can easily implement them as follows. Use a variable, say f, to store the last footnote number; increase f by one for every new footnote. In addition, define a string variable F and a macro AF as follows:

1. The next footnote number is printed by referencing F; the value of variable f is automatically increased by 1.

2. Beginning of the footnote text is indicated by the macro call .AF. End of the footnote text, as before, is indicated by the instruction .FE.

Automatically-numbered footnote specifications will have the form:

```
...\*F
.AF
footnote text
.FE
...
```

where variable f, string F and macro .AF were defined as

```
.nr f 0 1
.ds F \u\s-2\\n+f\s0\d
.de AF
.FS
.IP \\nf.
..
```

Note that the footnote text will be indented.

Here are examples of automatically-numbered footnotes specified using the above macros:

Concurrent C is a superset of C for parallel programming.[1] In this paper, I will briefly discuss suitability of Concurrent C for programming robots.[2]

---

1. Its facilities are based on the *rendezvous* model.
2. For more details, please see *Concurrent C and Robotics* written by Narain Gehani

---

These footnotes were specified as

```
     Concurrent C is a superset of C for
     parallel programming.\*F
     .AF
     Its facilities are based on
5    the \fIrendezvous\fP model.
     .FE
     In this paper, I will briefly discuss
     suitability of Concurrent C for
     programming robots.\*F
10   .AF
     For more details, please
     see \fIConcurrent C and Robotics\fP written
     by Narain Gehani
     .FE
```

17. ms and Other Document Preparation Tools

Graph, figure, table and equation specifications can be included within a document specified using ms; these items are specified using the tools grap, pic, tbl and eqn, respectively. Graphs, figures, tables and equations should be kept within displays or keeps to prevent them from being split across pages. Displays are also used for centering figures and graphs.

17.1 Preprocessor Interface Instructions

1. grap graph specifications have the form

   ```
   .G1
   graph specification
   .G2
   ```

2. pic figure specifications have the form

   ```
   .PS  (or  .PF)
   figure specification
   .PE
   ```

3. tbl table specifications have the form

   ```
   .TS  option
   table specification
   .TE
   ```

4. eqn equation specifications have the form

   ```
   .EQ  [x  [y]]
   definitions and equation specifications
   .EN
   ```

   Argument x can be I, L or C specifying that the equation is to be indented, left-justified or centered; if x is omitted, then it is assumed to be C. Argument y specifies the equation number.

   Equations can be embedded (given in-line) in the text; in-line equations are delimited by characters specified as eqn delimiters.

18. Using ms

The ms macro package is invoked with the −ms option of troff or nroff.[1] For example, if the document contains only ms and troff instructions, then the following command may be used:

---

1. nroff documents containing multi-column output or tbl tables should be processed with the UNIX system program col before printing them on terminals that do not support reverse line feeds, and forward and reverse half-line feeds. col performs the line overlays implied by such line feeds.

troff −ms *input-files* >*output-file*

If the document also contains graphs, figures, tables and equations, then the following command may be used:

grap *input-files* | pic | tbl | eqn | troff −ms >*output-file*

The output of troff, *output-file*, is printed after processing it with a program, called a *postprocessor*, associated with the printing device.

19. A Final Example

In this example, we will show you the complete specification of an article (paper) that was produced using ms. The paper, which is shown below along with its specification, is a radically shortened version of a paper titled *Concurrent C* by N. H. Gehani and W. D. Roome [1984]. (The page and line lengths used for the paper are 6 and 3.5 inches, respectively.)

For ease of presentation, we will discuss the paper one page at a time. First, we will show you a page of the paper in its finished form, commenting when necessary. Then we will show you how this page was specified, that is, the corresponding portion of the raw input text.

A paper consists of two parts: a cover sheet and the body of the paper. The cover sheet, which comes before the paper body, consists of the title of the paper, the names of the authors and their affiliations, and the abstract of the paper. The cover sheet of our example paper is

Concurrent C

N. H. Gehani
W. D. Roome

AT&T Bell Laboratories
Murray Hill, New Jersey 07974

ABSTRACT

Concurrent C is a superset of C that provides concurrent
programming facilities.

May 31, 1985

Cover Sheet of a Released Paper

The raw document corresponding to the cover sheet is

```
     .RP
     .pl 6.0i
     .nr LL 3.5i
     .ND "May 31, 1985"
 5   .TL
     Concurrent C
     .AU
     N. H. Gehani
     .AU
10   W. D. Roome
     .AI
     .MH
     .AB
     .LP
15   Concurrent C is a superset of C that
     provides concurrent programming facilities.
     .AE
```

Notice that troff instructions were used to specify the page and line lengths.

Now let us take a look at the first page of the body of the paper:

Concurrent C

N. H. Gehani
W. D. Roome

AT&T Bell Laboratories
Murray Hill, New Jersey 07974

1. Introduction

Concurrent programming is becoming increasingly important because multicomputers are becoming attractive alternatives to maxicomputers.

Concurrent programming has many advantages:

1. Concurrent programming facilities can lead to notational convenience and conceptual elegance.

2. Concurrent programming can reduce program execution time.

Page 1 of Released Paper

The raw document corresponding to the first page of the paper is

```
      .NH
      Introduction
      .LP
      Concurrent programming is becoming
  5   increasingly important because
      multicomputers are becoming attractive
      alternatives to maxicomputers.
      .LP
      Concurrent programming has many
 10   advantages:
      .IP 1.
      Concurrent programming facilities can lead to
      notational convenience and conceptual elegance.
      .IP 2.
 15   Concurrent programming can reduce program
      execution time.
```

Notice that the author name, affiliation and location information are not specified again for page one even though this information is printed on page one. As in the case of the cover sheet, this information is printed using the information supplied in the .AU, .AI and .MH instructions given earlier.

Now let us take a look at the second page of the paper:

-2-

2. Concurrent Programming

Few major programming languages offer concurrent programming facilities:

language	concurrent programming
Fortran	No
PL/I	Yes (low-level)
Pascal	No
C	No
Ada	Yes

3. Concurrent C

The concurrency model in Concurrent C is based on the
rendezvous concept. A Concurrent C program consists of
one or more processes cooperating to accomplish a common objective.

A *process* is an instantiation of a process type. A process
has its own flow-of-control; it executes in parallel with
other processes.

Page 2 of Released Paper

The portion of the raw document corresponding to page two is

```
   .NH
   Concurrent Programming
   .LP
   Few major programming languages
5  offer concurrent programming facilities:
   .DS
   .TS
   box, center;
   c | c
10 a | a.
   language☞concurrent programming
   =
   Fortran☞No
   PL/I☞Yes (low-level)
15 Pascal☞No
   C☞No
   Ada☞Yes
   .TE
   .DE
20 .NH
   Concurrent C
   .LP
   The concurrency model in Concurrent C is
   based on the \fIrendezvous\fP concept.
25 A Concurrent C program consists of one or more
   processes cooperating to
   accomplish a common objective.
   .LP
   A \fIprocess\fP is an instantiation of a
30 process type.
   A process has its own flow-of-control; it
   executes in parallel with other processes.
```

The table specification (to be processed by tbl) is enclosed within a display (lines 6-19) to ensure that the table is not split across pages. The first line in the table specification (line 8) indicates that the table is to be enclosed within a box and it is to be horizontally centered. Lines 9 and 10 respectively specify that the table will have two columns and the format of the table entries. Following these lines are the data lines (lines 11-17) that specify the table entries. As before, symbol ☞ denotes the tab character. The data line containing just the character = specifies that a double horizontal line is to be drawn. See *Document Formatting and Typesetting on the UNIX System* [Gehani 1987] for details about table specifications.

Let us now move on to the final page of the paper:

-3-

4. Conclusions

Concurrent C is a versatile language that can be used for
a variety of applications.

Page 3 of Released Paper

The last portion of the raw document is

```
.NH
Conclusions
.LP
Concurrent C is a versatile language that
can be used for a variety of applications.
```

20. Exercises

1. What are the pros and cons of undoing the font changes with the in-line instruction \fP, which restores the previous font and the in-line instruction \fR, which specifies a switch to the Roman font?

2. Define two macros dS and dE to begin and end centered italic font displays. The effect of calling .dS and .dE is similar to the effect produced by .DS C and .DE instructions, respectively, except that the text enclosed by them will be printed in italic font (I). State your assumptions about the use of these macros.

3. Give the text and formatting instructions to print the text

    procedure SWAP(X, Y: **in out** FLOAT) **is**
       T: FLOAT;   —temporary variable
    begin
      T := X;
      X := Y;
      Y := T;
    end SWAP;

4. Describe specifically, with an example showing what happens, why the paradigm for implementing automatically-numbered lists discussed in Section 16.2.1 cannot be used for implementing nested lists. Describe a strategy for implementing automatically-numbered lists that can be nested.

Chapter 4

Typesetting Documents with `troff`

`troff` (pronounced TEE-roff) is a text formatter used to produce high-quality documents. `troff`'s beginnings are roughly contemporary with those of the UNIX system. It descends from a group of formatters that grew from J. E. Saltzer's RUNOFF, developed at MIT in the 1960s. The acronym *roff* was coined by Brian Kernighan for a primitive formatter he wrote for his own use as a graduate student. `troff` (*typesetter roff*) was originally written in PDP assembly language (c. 1973) by Joseph F. Ossanna. During the same period, Ossanna also developed `nroff` (pronounced EN-roff), which is essentially a subset of `troff` and used with typewriter-like printers. Ossanna rewrote both formatters in the C language completing the project in 1976.

`troff` formats documents to be printed on typesetters, laser printers and ink jet printers producing, for example, an output such as this:

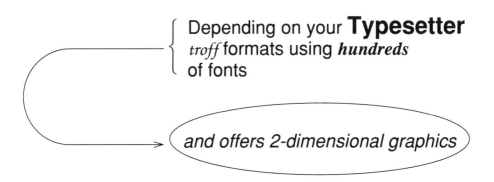

`nroff` formats output for typewriter-like devices such as dot matrix printers, daisy wheel printers and other impact type printers that do not offer sophisticated printing capabilities. Devices capable of digital typography can, of course, be used (or under-used) to produce `nroff` output as well. `nroff` output looks like this:

```
Name_____

Address_____

Phone_____

   1. Make and model of car:


   2. Type of insurance requested:


                    Signed_____
```

Brian Kernighan rewrote `troff` to make it device-independent [Kernighan 1982b]. Kernighan again revised `troff` in 1984, which was presented by AT&T as part of DOCUMENTER´S WORKBENCH Software (DWB) Release 2.0. [DWB 1984b]. This chapter describes the version of `troff` released in DWB 2.0.

`troff` is the heart of UNIX system text formatting [DWB 1986a]. It is the language in which macro packages such as mm, ms and mv are written. It is also the language into which eqn, `pic` and `tbl` instructions are translated (`grap` instructions are translated into `pic`). The following figure describes how `troff` interacts with these facilities:

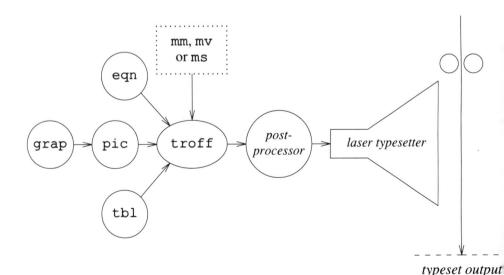

typeset output

`nroff` is similar to `troff` though it cannot format figures or graphs. For equations an `nroff`-specific `eqn` (called `neqn`) must be used:

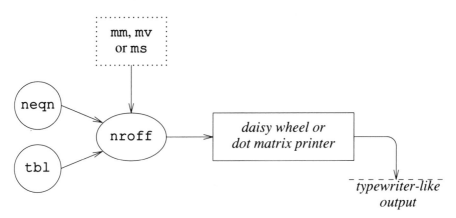

`nroff` and `troff` have been traditionally referred to with the single, generic name "`troff`." We adopt that convention in this book.

Generally speaking, `nroff` will successfully interpret a `troff` input file ignoring instructions that specify the size and typeface of characters. `nroff` and `troff` are highly compatible with one another, and it is almost always possible to prepare documents acceptable to both formatters.

`troff` is a simple typesetting language that can be quickly learned by the user. A relatively small set of specifications such as those for font, point size, margin control and so forth will accomplish most general typesetting tasks. `troff` is also a powerful text processing language with facilities such as arithmetic and logical expressions; control instructions; macro definitions; variables; line-drawing functions; and, perhaps most important, the ability to position text and figures dynamically based on their formatted size.

1. An Example of a `troff` Specification

To illustrate the use of `troff`, we will discuss the specification of the following letter:

A. L. Psmith, Ph.D., C.P.A., D.Sc., etc.
Freelance Financial Consultant

April 7, 1991

Transcendental Transportation Inc.
Three Wheel Drive
Busted Axle, Wyoming

Sir:

We thank you for your letter of 1 April and for the graphs and figures demonstrating your sales, approaching 10 million dollars. This is all the more impressive when one considers the savings represented by your semi-circular tire, which we imagine requires precisely half of the materials required for the manufacture of conventional tires.

By our calculations the additional funds supplied by my clients could significantly boost your profits. The following represents our estimates for sales growth at the investment levels to which we anticipate committing:

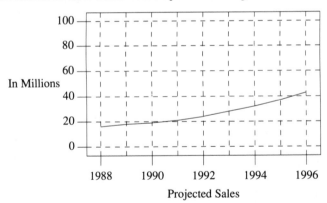

Projected Sales

Please send additional information you deem relevant to our possible investment in your concern.

Your humble servant,

A. L. Psmith
Freelance Financial Consultant

We will discuss the input specification of this letter in logical chunks. If you do not understand them at first, read on; they will be explained later in the chapter. The input given below is for 6" × 9" stationery. (Note that the preceding example has been altered to fit on the page.)

The first chunk specifies the general characteristics of the letter:

```
     .po 1i
     .ll 4i
     .ps 9p
     .vs 11p
5    .\"              Print letter head
     .rs
     .sp 0.25i
     .ft HB
     .vs +4p
10   .ce 3
     \s+4A. L. Psmith, Ph.D., C.P.A., D.Sc., etc.
     Freelance Financial Consultant\s-4
     \D'l 3.5i 0'
     .vs
```

The page-offset instruction `.po` (line 1) sets a 1 inch left margin. The right margin is specified (line 2) with the line length instruction `.ll`. (Using 6" × 9" stationery, Dr. Psmith would have a one inch right margin.) Lines 3-4 specify the character point size and vertical spacing (the vertical distance between lines) to be ''9 on 11,'' (9 point characters set on 11 point lines).

A comment (line 5) identifies instructions that specify the letterhead. `troff` ignores all characters that follow the comment instruction `.\"` and precede a new line. Spaces (not tabs) are used to indent the comment itself.

The restore-spacing instruction `.rs` (line 6) turns on spacing at the top of a new page, and the space instruction (line 7) specifies a top margin of a quarter inch. The font instruction `.ft` (line 8) specifies that characters should be printed in the Helvetica Black (HB) font, and the in-line point size instruction (escape sequence) `\s+4` (line 11) specifies the character size to be 13 points, 4 points higher than the current point size. The 9 point character size is restored before the text of the letter is printed using the complementary instruction `\s-4` (line 12). The larger characters are given additional vertical spacing (line 9), and the previous vertical spacing is restored (line 14). The first three input text lines (lines 11-13) are specified to be centered (line 10). The line-drawing instruction (line 13) draws a horizontal line 3.5 inches long.

Input for the letter's inside address and salutation is as follows:

```
15  .ft R
    .sp 0.5v
    .ti 2.5i
    April 7, 1991
    .sp 0.5v
20  Transcendental Transportation Inc.
    .br
    Three Wheel Drive
    .br
    Busted Axle, Wyoming
25  .sp 0.5v
    Sir:
    .sp 0.5v
```

Letter text is set in the Times Roman font (line 15). A half vertical space is generated before and after the date (lines 16 and 19). The temporary-line-indentation instruction (line 17) indents the date 2.5 inches from the page offset. The letter's inside address contains line breaks (lines 21 and 23) to force input lines 20 and 22 each to begin on a new output line. The next chunk specifies the letter body:

```
    .ti 2m
    We thank you for your letter of 1 April and for
30  the graphs and figures demonstrating your sales,
    approaching 10 million dollars.
    This is all the more impressive when one
    considers the savings represented by your
    semi-circular tire, which we imagine requires
35  precisely half of the materials required for the
    manufacture of conventional tires.
    .sp 0.5v
    .ti 2m
    By our calculations the additional funds supplied
40  by my clients could significantly boost your
    profits.
    The following represents our estimates for sales
    growth at the investment levels to which we
    anticipate committing:
45  .G1
    copy "Lgrap_input"
    .G2
    Please send additional information you deem
    relevant to our possible investment in your
50  concern.
```

Each temporary line indentation in this section is specified to be 2 ems (lines 28 and

38) to indent the first line of each new paragraph. The graph in the letter is specified at lines 45-47 using `grap` instructions (see "Chapter 1: Specifying Graphs").

The final chunk specifies the letter closing:

```
     .sp 1v
     .na
     .ti 2.5i
     Your humble servant,
55   .sp 3v
     .in +2.5i
     A. L. Psmith
     .br
     Freelance Financial Consultant
```

2. Simple Typesetting Instructions

The straightforward tasks of typesetting — alterations of font, character size and page size — are easy to specify in `troff` and can be mastered quickly.

Most `troff` instructions have the general form

.xy arguments

where *xy* is a two-character (usually lower-case alphabetic) instruction name. Arguments are numeric specifications, character strings or both. Each instruction stands alone in a line preceded by a control character — a dot (`.`) or a forward quote (`'`) — appearing in the first column. Note that tabs or spaces following the control character and preceding the instruction name are not significant and, as we will show, are used to enhance readability:

```
.if  condition  \{\
.       sp 1
.       in 0.5i
.       ll 5i \}
```

Numeric arguments are usually followed by a *scale indicator* specifying the unit of distance or size to be used (centimeters, inches, picas, points, vertical spaces and so forth). Unscaled numeric arguments are usually interpreted according to a default scale that applies to the instruction. For example, the

```
.sp 3
```

instruction specifies a positive (downward) motion of 3 `v`s, or vertical spaces. By default, each vertical space is 12 points.

Numeric arguments can be fractional (in decimal notation) though `troff` will truncate minute fractional specifications (more than three places after the decimal point) to thousandths.

In addition to these line-oriented (or *stand-alone*) instructions, `troff` provides in-line instructions for a finer level of typographical control. (These are known as *escape sequences* because they begin with the escape character \.) In-line instructions occur in a variety of forms including the simple general forms

\c or \ (cc

where *c* is a single character. Instructions such as these either perform simple functions or are the names of special characters (e.g., \ (dg is the name of the dagger symbol †).

Another group of in-line instructions accepts arguments. Those accepting one-character arguments usually have the form

\ca

where *c* is a one-character instruction name and *a* is a one-character argument. As an example, \fB specifies the Times Bold font, and \s8 specifies 8-point characters.

In-line instructions accepting two-character arguments generally precede those arguments with a left parenthesis such as

\c (aa

where *c* is a one-character instruction name and *aa* is a two-character argument. For instance, \f (PB specifies the Palatino Bold font, and \s (12 specifies 12-point characters.

In-line instructions can also accept strings as arguments having the general form

\c ´string´

where *string* is a signed or unsigned number, an expression, or a string of characters enclosed in delimiters (normally single forward quotes).

In-line instructions frequently appear in places where stand-alone instructions would be awkward to use such as between characters. For example, the following output, alternating Times Roman and Times Italic characters,

S*tr*in*g*

was specified by preceding each character with an in-line instruction:

```
.ps 16
\fBS\fIt\fBr\fIi\fBn\fIg\fR
.ps
```

3. Comments

All comments in `troff` are preceded by the stand-alone instruction

`.\"`

and are terminated with the next new line. Each new line on which a comment appears must begin with the comment instruction. Unlike some "free format" languages, `troff` understands blank lines to be significant (in fill-mode they are interpreted as horizontal spaces on output; in no-fill mode they are interpreted as blank lines on output).

The only valid comment instruction in `troff` is `.\"`. While it is possible to derive the effect of a comment by preceding it with an undefined instruction (e.g., `'\"` or `'''`), such a practice relies on side effect is consequently undesirable.

4. Specifying Sizes and Distances

`troff` provides a set of scale indicators for specifying size and distance. They are appended to numeric (integer or real) arguments and must not be preceded by white space. The scale indicators include both typesetting measures as well as everyday units of scale:

scale indicator	meaning
P	pica = 1/6 inch
c	centimeter
i	inch
m	em = S points (where S is the current point size)
n	en = em/2
p	point = 1/72 inch
u	internal unit (device-dependent)
v	vertical line space
none	default (see below)

In the absence of an explicit scale indicator, a default scale is selected according to the instruction. A list of default scale values appears below:

function	scale by default	instruction
horizontal motion	em (m)	`.in, .ll, .lt, .mc,` `.po, .ta, .ti, \h, \l`

vertical motion	vertical line space (v)	`.ch, .dt, .ne, .pl,`
		`.rt, .sp, .sv, .wh, \L,`
		`\v, \x`

internal dimensions	internal unit (u)	`.ie, .if, .ne`
characters and vertical spaces	point (p)	`.ps, .vs, \H, \s`

4.1 Relative and Absolute Values

Distances can be specified relative to the current position or in absolute terms. Many instructions accept signed numbers indicating that the argument is to be added or subtracted from a current value. To place a character or string of characters 1 inch to the right of and 2 inches down from the current position, for example, you would give the indentation instruction `.in +1i` and the space instruction `.sp +2i`. Of course, that resulting location would then become your new current position, and all succeeding specifications would be calculated relative to it. Instructions such as `.in` can be specified in absolute terms simply by using an unsigned argument.

`troff` also provides an operator for specifying absolute values: the vertical bar (|). The `.sp |2i` instruction, for instance, indicates a vertical spacing 2 inches down from the established top page margin.

5. Specifying Fonts

Fonts are specified with the font instruction `.ft`, which has the general form

`.ft [c]`

where *c* is a one- or two-character (usually upper-case alphabetic) argument naming a font. If no argument is specified, then the previous font is restored. The output

| **Bold plods.** Roman ambles. *Italic runs.* |

was specified as

```
.ft B
Bold plods.
.ft R
Roman ambles.
.ft I
Italic runs.
.ft R
```

5

Fonts can also be specified using in-line instructions. The general form for the in-line font instruction is

\f*x*

where *x* is a one-character font name or

\f (*xx*

where *xx* is a two-character font name. The example shown above could also have been specified as

\fBBold plods. \fRRoman ambles. \fIItalic runs.\fR

The in-line instruction \fP restores the previous font.

As we discussed in "Chapter 3," the horizontal space preceding an in-line font specification is set in the new font. This can produce a disturbing effect if the old font and new font have markedly dissimilar character widths. As an example, consider the use of the wide Constant Width (CW) font adjacent to the narrow Helvetica (H) font:

```
A mixture of  wide  and narrow spaces  produces   an    uneven
spacing between words.
```

Notice that the horizontal spaces between words set in Constant Width are much wider than spaces separating words set in Helvetica. The preceding example was specified as

```
\f(CWA \fHmixture of \f(CWwide and \fHnarrow
spaces \f(CWproduces an uneven \fHspacing
between \f(CWwords\fR.
```

To eliminate this ugly effect, each in-line font specification is preceded with the zero-width character: \&. Here is the modified output:

```
A mixture of  wide  and narrow spaces  produces   an    uneven
spacing between words.
```

The zero-width character forces `troff` to print the space preceding the \& in the old font.

5.1 Font Positions

`troff` looks for current fonts at physical locations called *font positions*. Fonts may be specified either by name or by font position. Specifically, Times Roman is usually mounted at font position 1, Times Italic at font position 2 and Times Bold at font position 3. Our earlier example of alternating fonts could have been specified as

`\f3Bold plods. \f1Roman ambles. \f2Italic runs.\f1`

That is, where before we had said, in effect, "print using the Times Roman font," we now are saying "print using the font at position 1," which by default is Times Roman.

The font-position instruction `.fp` is used to mount fonts explicitly at the various font positions. The `.fp` instruction has the general form

`.fp` *n f*

where *n* is the numerical position corresponding to the mounted font and *f* is the font name.

Specifying fonts by number instead of name can be confusing, but in some cases it can be used to advantage. For example, if all fonts are specified numerically, global changes can be accomplished quickly by mounting the new font in the position where the old font had been. Suppose that Times Roman, Times Italic and Times Bold are mounted on positions 1, 2 and 3, respectively. The following example changes all instances of Times Roman to Palatino, all instances of Times Italic to Palatino Italic and all instances of Times Bold to Palatino Bold:

```
.fp 1 PA
.fp 2 PI
.fp 3 PB
```

On most implementations, the Times Roman, the Times Italic and the Times Bold fonts are mounted on font positions 1, 2 and 3, respectively. Suppose that the Helvetica Italic font were mounted on position 2 using the `.fp` instruction. Font calls of the form `\fI` would no longer refer to font position 2, now occupied by the Helvetica Italic font. Instead it would refer to position 0, where `troff` dynamically mounts fonts that are called but not currently mounted. Note that instruction `\f(HI` refers to the Helvetica Italic font.

To find out which fonts are mounted by default, look at `troff`'s output before it is sent to the printer. A section near the top of the file lists the fonts in the following manner:

```
x font 1 R
x font 2 I
x font 3 B
x font 4 H
x font 5 CW
x font 6 S
x font 7 S1
x font 8 GR
```

This excerpt reveals the following information:

position	font
1	Times Roman
2	Times Italic
3	Times Bold
4	Helvetica
5	Constant Width
6	Special font
7	Special font prime (1)
8	Greek

It is important that new fonts not be mounted on the positions occupied by the special fonts. No matter which fonts are currently in use, icons in the special fonts such as ‡ (\ (dd), ® (\ (rg) or ¢ (\ (ct) will continue to be needed.

Access to unmounted fonts through dynamic mounting at position 0 is convenient, but it should not be viewed as an alternative to explicitly mounting fonts. For example, if two unmounted fonts are called within a single output line, that line will not be adjusted properly because `troff` will not calculate the width of all characters correctly. In addition, only one unmounted font can be specified during the course of a single diversion (discussed later).

Here are some sample fonts:

name	font
R	Roman
I	*Italic*
B	**Bold**
S	Special (☛ ∫ ○)
BI	***Bold Italics***
CB	`Constant Width Bold`
CI	*`Century Bold Italic`*
CW	`Constant Width`
CX	***`Constant Width Bold Oblique`***
GR	Greek (α β γ)
H	Helvetica
HB	**Helvetica Black**
HI	*Helvetica Italics*
PX	***Palatino Bold Oblique***
ZI	*ZEE III*

5.2 Emboldening Fonts

`troff` offers facilities for printing bold characters in any font. The embolden instruction `.bd` specifies that characters in a named font be replotted at a specified offset. Instruction `.bd` effectively supplements the number of available fonts by allowing light fonts to made bold and bold fonts to be made bolder. The embolden instruction has the general form

`.bd` f [w]

where f is the font name (or font position) and w specifies the emboldening width in internal units. Omitting the second argument turns off emboldening. As an example, consider the following plain versus emboldened Times Italics characters:

These characters are printed in plain italics.
These characters are printed in emboldened italics.

The above text was specified as follows:

```
      .ft I
      These characters are printed in
      plain italics.
      .ft
5     .bd I 3
      .ft I
      These characters are printed in
      emboldened italics.
      .bd I
```

The argument 3 (line 5) specifies the width of emboldening to be 3 internal units (device dependent).

6. Specifying Point Size

The size of a character, known as its *point size*, is specified with the `.ps` instruction. The point size instruction has the general form

`.ps [[±]n]`

where *n* is a number of points (one point is 1/72"). Omitting an argument restores the previous point size.

Consider the following example [Milton 1667]:

Into a limbo large and broad.

This was specified as

```
Into a
.ps 12
limbo
.ps 16
large
.ps 20
and
.ps 24
broad.
.ps 10
```

Point size can also be specified using the in-line instruction `\s`. The in-line point size instruction has the general form

`\s[±]n`

for single-digit size specifications and

`\s([±]nn`

for two-digit size specifications. The `\s0` instruction restores the previous point size.

The following in-line point size instructions could have been used to specify the previous display:

`Into a \s(12limbo \s(16large \s(20and \s(24broad.\s(10`

Note that the line returns to ten points, the default size for most text. Relative specifications are also possible. Consider the following alternative:

```
Into a \s+2limbo \s+4large \s+4and \s+4broad.\s-(14
```

7. Specifying Vertical Spacing

When point size changes, the vertical distance between lines, called *vertical spacing*, should be changed proportionately. (Compositors refer to this inter-line spacing as *leading*.) The vertical spacing normally used is 2 points greater than the current point size.

The vertical-spacing instruction `.vs` has the general form

`.vs [±]`*n*

where *n* is the distance between lines. (If *n* is unscaled, then it is assumed to be in points.)

If the vertical spacing is comparatively small, the text will appear cramped. Consider the following claustrophobic case [Poe 1975]:

> It was now midnight, and my task was drawing to a close. I had completed the eighth, the ninth, and the tenth tier. I had finished a portion of the last and the eleventh; there remained but a single stone to be fitted and plastered in.

The point size and vertical spacing here was specified as "12 on 10" [Poe 1975]:

```
.ps 12
.vs 10
```

Increasing the vertical spacing will give your text room to breathe. The following output, for example, was specified to have a point size and vertical spacing of 12 on 14:

> "Let us go nevertheless. The cold is merely nothing. Amontillado! You have been imposed upon. And as for Luchesi—he cannot distinguish Sherry from Amontillado."

Using a `.vs` instruction without an argument restores the previous vertical spacing.

Because the `.sp` instruction with an unscaled argument specifies the generation of some number of vertical spaces, its behavior is closely linked to `.vs`. That is, `.sp` will generate spaces whose size is determined by the most recent vertical spacing specification.

7.1 Extra Space

Extra vertical spacing can be allocated on a per-line basis by using the `\x` instruction, which has the general form

\x[±]*n*

A positive value increases vertical spacing of the following line; a negative value increases vertical spacing of the preceding line. For example, the following text

> The how-it-is is the plush pleasure of the pleased. The long lines of lengthy and learned disquisitions that unfailingly foretell
>
> # The Coming of the Goths cannot compare
>
> with the gaudy Gothic histories that vindicate the vanquishers. Dead languages comprise the tales of dead men.

was specified as

```
    .ps 12
    .vs 14
    The how-it-is is the plush pleasure of the pleased.
    The long lines of lengthy and learned disquisitions
 5  that unfailingly foretell \x'-1v'\f(HB\s+8The
    Coming of the Goths\s0\fP\x'+1v' cannot compare
    with the gaudy Gothic histories that vindicate
    the vanquishers.
    Dead languages comprise the tales of dead men.
10  .ps 10
    .vs 12
```

The vertical spacing preceding and following "The Coming of the Goths" was specified to be 1 vertical space higher (lines 5-6) than the prevailing vertical spacing, which is 14 points (line 2).

7.2 Line Spacing

Closely related to the vertical spacing is the notion of line spacing. While `.vs` specifies the *size* of vertical spaces, the line-spacing `.ls` instruction specifies the *number* of spaces that must be generated after each line of text. The line-spacing instruction has the general form

`.ls [[±]n]`

where *n*−1 is the number of blank lines appended to each line of text. Instruction

`.ls 1`

specifies that zero blank lines be appended to each line of text, which is the default condition. By contrast "double-spaced" text is specified as

```
.ls 2
```

8. Filling and Adjustment of Text

`troff` both left- and right-adjusts its output by default. During processing, `troff` places lines of text in a *line buffer* where it decides the number of words that will fit on a line, the spacing between those words for right-adjustment and any necessary hyphenation of words appearing at the end of a line. This process, called *filling* and *adjustment*, continues until the end of the page. Printing is then suspended; the line of text at the bottom of the page (called a *footer*) and the text at the top of the next page (called a *header*) are printed (if they have been specified); then the cycle of buffering and printing begins again.

The instruction for specifying text adjustment has the general form

`.ad` [*style*]

where *style* specifies the adjustment styles:

style	explanation
l	adjust left margin only
r	adjust right margin only
c	center
b or n	adjust both margins
none	unchanged

The no-adjust instruction

`.na`

specifies that no adjustment be applied, causing a "ragged right" margin and equal spacing between words. Sentences are automatically followed by two spaces. (On input, new sentences should begin on a new line; `troff` recognizes a line ending with a period, question mark or exclamation mark as the end of a sentence).

The no-fill instruction

`.nf`

turns off filling. In no-fill mode input lines are copied to the output without any rearrangement though typesetting functions such as font and point size changes continue to be performed.

The fill instruction

`.fi`

turns on filling. Note that text adjustment continues to be controlled by the `.ad` and the `.na` instructions.

9. Line and Page Breaks

`troff` provides instructions for interrupting the page-filling process at the line and page levels.

9.1 Line Breaks

The line-break instruction

```
.br
```

is used to interrupt the filling process without turning off fill mode. When the `.br` instruction is encountered, `troff` prints the partial line it has collected in the line buffer (i.e., it flushes the line buffer). The text following the `.br` instruction is printed on a new line. For example, consider the following input:

```
To demonstrate the length of the filling
output line,
this first sentence will be on the long side.
The
.br
next sentence,
.br
however,
.br
will be short.
```

(5 in margin)

This is printed as

```
To demonstrate the length of the filling output line, this first sentence will be on
the long side.  The
next sentence,
however,
will be short.
```

9.2 Page Breaks

The break-page instruction is similar to the line-break instruction except that the text following it is printed on a new page. The `.bp` instruction has the general form

```
.bp [n]
```

where *n* is the number printed on the next page; omitting *n* causes the new page to have a page number that is one greater than the current page number. Transition to a new page is as usual: printing is suspended, footers and headers (if any) are printed and text printing is then resumed on the new page.

9.2.1 Page Transition: The transition from one page to the next is handled by a facility called *page traps*, which we will discuss later. For now it is important to know that `troff` does not provide page transition facilities automatically (or associated page headers and footers and the pagination they perform). Headers and footers must be specified explicitly, and traps must be set explicitly. Otherwise, pages will fill one after another governed only by the page length, which is specified with the page-length instruction `.pl` (page length is 11 inches by default).

The following specification is that of a general-purpose header and trap, designed to be used until you have learned to specify your own headers and traps. It is suitable for an 8.5" × 11" sheet and prints the name of the file and page numbers at the top of each page:

```
.de pH
.lt \\n(.lu
'bp
.rs
'sp 1i
.\"  if not page 1, header is filename and page number
.if !\\n%=1 .tl ''\s9\fB\\n(.F'%\fP\s0'
'sp 0.25i
.lt
..
.wh -1.5i pH
```

This block should appear near the top of your document file before text.

Note that page transition is a basic function provided by a macro package such as mm or ms.

9.3 Break and No-break Control Characters

Certain instructions cause a line break at the point they are encountered. The following table is a complete listing of these instructions:

instruction	name
`.bp`	break page
`.br`	line break
`.ce`	center
`.fi`	fill mode
`.fl`	flush line buffer
`.in`	line indentation
`.nf`	no-fill mode
`.sp`	space
`.ti`	temporary-line-indentation

To suppress the line break caused by these instructions, the no-break control character, by default the forward quote (′), is used instead of the break control character, by default the dot (.). As an example, consider the following output:

```
Normally the indentation of this line would increase 8 centimeters following the
                                             second word. The  ´
                                             character suppresses
                                             indentation until the
                                             next line.
```

This was specified as

```
Normally the
'in 8c
indentation of this line would increase 8
centimeters following the second word.
The \' character suppresses indentation until
the next line.
.in
```

Because the line buffer is not flushed when the ′in instruction is encountered, the indentation does not take effect until the next line of output.

The line-break in-line instruction \p is a variant of the .br instruction. Unlike the .br instruction, the \p instruction fills and adjusts the output line. Strings containing \p are treated as whole words on output and not split across lines.

Note that . is to stand-alone instructions as \ is to in-line instructions. Both the control character . and the escape character \ can be changed by the .cc and .ec instructions respectively.

10. Spaces, Tabs and Leaders

10.1 Proportional Font Spacing

Fonts may be mono-spaced (as on a typewriter) where all characters are allocated the same horizontal space regardless of the character's width, or they may be proportional. A tabular display manually aligned on input with spaces will not align on output unless a mono-space, or constant-width, font is used. Here is an input file containing columns arranged with by using the right number of spaces:

```
.ft CW
.nf
Here are  The        The
some      first      second
5 columns:  column     column
          is         is
          set        a
          only       continuation
          with a     of the
10          space      same row.
          bar.
.fi
.ft
```

Although the display is formatted in no-fill mode (line 1), `troff` formats characters proportionally causing misalignment of columns:

```
Here are The    The
some    first  second
columns: column  column
    is    is
    set    a
    only   continuation
    with a  of the
    space   same row.
    bar.
```

10.2 Paddable and Unpaddable Spaces

During filling, `troff` pads the distance between words in order to right-adjust the line. Such manipulated spaces are said to be *paddable*, meaning they can be widened or split across lines. `troff` provides escape sequences for specifying unpaddable spaces:

escape sequence	**function**
space	unpaddable ordinary space character
`\0`	digit-width space character
`|`	1/6 em narrow-space character (zero width in `nroff`)
`\^`	1/12 em half-narrow-space character (zero width in `nroff`)
`\&`	non-printing, zero-width character

Strings with embedded spaces that should not be split across lines can be specified using unpaddable spaces as follows:

```
Ms.\ Ramat\ S.\ Hennahead arrives on the
Deccan\ Princess on January\ 1,\ 1970
```

The narrow-space instructions are used for fine-tuning the position of characters on output. For instance, in the following output

```
UNIX® is a registered trademark of UNIX System Laboratories, Inc.
```

the space following the trademark is too small. It can be increased slightly by using the narrow-space character \ | :

```
UNIX\(rg\|\| is a registered trademark of
UNIX System Laboratories, Inc.
```

This will be formatted as

```
UNIX®  is a registered trademark of UNIX System Laboratories, Inc.
```

As we have mentioned, when the characters . and ' appear in the first column, `troff` interprets them as control characters. Interpretation of these characters can be suppressed by prepending them with the zero-width character \&. All examples of instructions and macros displayed in this book, for instance, are entered as

\&.*xy*

Because . is no longer the first character on the line, it is not interpreted as a control character.

10.3 Tabs

Text formatted in columns that are read from left to right is specified using the tab instruction. Tabs can be right-, center- or left-adjusted. Typical uses include building tables ranging from simple left-justified columns to displays having opposing left- and right-justified columns such as tables of contents. Elaborate tables should be formatted using the `tbl` preprocessor [Gehani 1987].

Tab positions are specified with the set-tab instruction .ta, which has the form

.ta [[±]]n_1 [[±]]n_2 ... [[±]]n_k

Tab position i is specified by [±]n_i. Signed numbers specify that the current value is to be incremented or decremented; unsigned numbers specify a new absolute value. (The default value for n is ems.)

The input tab character is entered with the keyboard tab key, which produces a control-I (^I). If your keyboard does not have a tab key, you can use ^I. The escape sequence \t, which is an alternative tab input character, is interpreted during copy mode as a horizontal tab.

The following tabular display of New England states and capitals

	New England	
	State	Capital
	Connecticut	Hartford
	Maine	Augusta
	Massachusetts	Boston
	New Hampshire	Concord
	Rhode Island	Providence
	Vermont	Montpelier

was entered as follows (the tab character is represented by ☞):

```
   .nf
   .ta 1.6i
   ☞New England
   .ta 1.3i 2.4i
5  ☞State☞Capital
   .sp 0.5v
   .ta 1i 2.3i
   ☞Connecticut☞Hartford
   ☞Maine☞Augusta
10 ☞Massachusetts☞Boston
   ☞New Hampshire☞Concord
   ☞Rhode Island☞Providence
   ☞Vermont☞Montpelier
   .fi
```

The previous table could also have been specified using relative tab values:

```
☞New England
.ta 1.3i +1.1i
☞State☞Capital
.sp 0.5v
.ta 1i +1.3i
```

10.4 Tab Adjustment

Tabs are left-adjusted by default. Right-adjusted and centered tabs are specified by using R and C as suffixes to the tab positions:

tab type	instruction
right	`.ta` n`R`
centered	`.ta` n`C`

Right-adjusted tabs are useful for aligning columns of integers as the following table of contents demonstrates:

Introduction	1
Accelerated Notions	55
An Advanced Course	122

This table of contents was specified as follows:

```
.nf
.ta 4.5iR
Introduction←1
Accelerated Notions←55
An Advanced Course←122
.fi
```

The preceding table of contents would have been easier to read if a row of dots had connected the topics with the corresponding page numbers:

Introduction 1
Accelerated Notions 55
An Advanced Course...122

This is done with the tab-character instruction, which has the general form

`.tc` *c*

where *c* is the character replacing the repeated spaces that the `.ta` instruction generates by default. The default value is restored with the instruction

`.tc`

The preceding version of the table of contents was specified as

```
.nf
.ta 4.5iR
.tc .
Introduction←1
Accelerated Notions←55
An Advanced Course←122
.tc
.fi
```

10.5 Leaders

The horizontal dots connecting fields in a tabular display are called *leaders*. The default leader character is the dot character. This can be changed by using the leader-character instruction `.lc`. For example, the instruction

```
.lc _
```

changes the leader character to an underscore.

troff interprets the input character ^A (control-A) as designating a sequence of leaders which are printed on output. Alternatively, the escape sequence \a can also be used to indicate a sequence of leader characters.

As an example of leaders printed using the leader-character designator ^A, consider the following example:

Introduction	1
Accelerated Notions	55
An Advanced Course	122

The above example was specified as

```
.lc _
.ta 4.5iR
.nf
Introduction^A1
Accelerated Notions^A55
An Advanced Course^A122
.fi
```

As illustrated previously, leaders can also be printed by using the .tc instruction to convert the spaces generated by the .ta instruction to dots or some other printable character. This effectively makes the tab sequence designator ^I into a leader sequence designator. However, maintaining the distinction between the tab sequence designator (^I) and the leader sequence designators (^A and \a) is necessary in cases where both ordinary tabs (resulting in spaces printed) and leaders are to be printed on the same line as shown below:

i	Introduction	1
ii	Accelerated Notions	55
iii	An Advanced Course	122

The preceding example, which also demonstrated center-, left- and right-adjusted tabs, was specified as follows:

```
.ta 1iC 1.75i 4.5iR
.lc .
.tc
.nf
☞i☞Introduction^A1
☞ii☞Accelerated Notions^A55
☞iii☞An Advanced Course^A122
.fi
```

5

11. Automatic Hyphenation

In fill mode `troff` can automatically hyphenate words appearing (but not quite fitting) at the end of each line. Hyphenation can be turned on with the hyphenate instruction `.hy`, which has the general form

`.hy [n]`

where *n* specifies hyphenation style:

n	function
0	turns off automatic hyphenation (same effect as `.nh`)
1	turns on automatic hyphenation (all arguments to `.hy` greater than 1 turn on hyphenation)
2	words appearing on the last line of the page are not hyphenated
4	the last two characters of a word are not used in hyphenation
8	the first two characters of a word are not used in hyphenation

Values of *n* may be additive. That is, some arguments to `.hy` can be decomposed into a combination of hyphenation style specifiers. The specification `.hy 14`, for instance, invokes all hyphenation rules (2 + 4 + 8).

Although the hyphenation choices `troff` makes are usually satisfactory, they sometimes can be arbitrary and ungrammatical. Hyphenation of words not in `troff`'s vocabulary can be specified with the hyphenate-word instruction `.hw`, which has the general form

`.hw` *hyphenated-word*

where *hyphenated-word* contains a word that has been manually hyphenated. For example, the

`.hw chthon\%ian`

instruction specifies all hyphenations of "chthonian" to be done between the n and the i.

Automatic hyphenation is turned off with the no-hyphenation instruction `.nh`. Words that contain hyphens, dashes and minus signs on input, however, will continue to be subject to splitting across lines. Thus, the phrases

```
man-at-arms
UNIX System V\(emconsider it standard
expression\(miexpression
```

will continue to be split across lines even though no hyphenation (`.nh`) has been specified.

To check `troff`'s choices for word hyphenation, process the document using the `-a troff` option, which will send an `nroff`-like version of the processed document to the standard output (your terminal screen by default). Although the output will not be typeset, the words per line and their automatic hyphenations will be identical to the typeset version.

11.1 Changing the Hyphenate-word Character

By default, `.hw` understands `\%` to be the sequence for indicating automatic hyphenation breaks. The second character of this sequence, i.e., `%`, called the hyphenation character, can be changed using the hyphenation-character instruction `.hc` which has the form

`.hc [c]`

For example, the character # can be specified to be the hyphenation character as follows:

`.hc #`

Following this `.hc` instruction, the `.hw` instruction will understand the pound symbol to be the hyphenation character:

`.hw chthon\#ian`

Note that the hyphenation character is always preceded by the escape character. The escape sequence is used only as a marker for legal hyphenation points and is not printed.

12. Summary of Basic Page Characteristic Instructions

By now we have discussed a few of the basic instructions for controlling page dimensions and patterns of filling and adjustment. The following table, summarizing basic instructions for specifying page characteristics, fills out the picture:

instruction	name	effect
`.ad [`*c*`]`	adjust	specifies line adjustment: *c*=l (left-adjusted), *c*=r (right-adjusted) or *c*=b (both left- and right-adjusted)
`.bp [`*n*`]`	break page	print contents of line buffer following an ejection of the current page, which is paginated to be *n* (optional)
`.br`	break line	prints contents of the line buffer on next output line
`.ce [`*n*`]`	center	centers the next *n* input lines following it on output (if the argument is omitted, it is assumed to be 1)
`.fi`	fill mode	adjusts lines according to specifications of `.ad`
`.in [[±]`*n*`]`	indentation	makes local changes in the left margin; indentation is relative to the page offset
`.ll [[±]`*n*`]`	line length	controls the right margin
`.na`	no-adjust	specifies no right adjustment (ragged right margin)
`.nf`	no-fill mode	copies input to output without line adjustment
`.ns`	no-space-mode	turns off the `.sp` and `.bp` instructions (provided `.bp` is not followed by a page number)
`.pl [[±]`*n*`]`	page length	controls the bottom margin
`.pn` *n*	page number	sets next page number to be *n*
`.po [[±]`*n*`]`	page offset	specifies the general left margin
`.sp [[±]`*n*`]`	space	sets blank lines between lines of text
`.rs`	restore spacing	turns on the `.sp` and `.bp` instructions
`.ti [[±]`*n*`]`	temporary-line-indent	makes local changes in the left margin that apply only to the next line

The page width is determined by the following formula:

$$page\ width = page\ offset + line\ length$$

Indentation, but not page offset, is understood to be part of the line length. In particular, a change of indentation does not affect the right margin; a change of page offset does.

13. Titles

`troff` provides an explicit facility, the title instruction `.tl`, for printing titles in particular and for printing left-, center- and right-adjusted strings in general. The general form of the title instruction `.tl` is

`.tl ´l´c´r´`

where the ´ delimiters enclose a left-adjusted field *l*, a centered field *c* and a right-adjusted field *r*. Any character can be used as a delimiter provided it does not appear in one of the fields. Note that the `.tl` instruction interprets the input character % as the current page number.

The title string is not affected by the `.in` and `.ll` instructions. The left margin of a title is controlled by the `.po` instruction while its right margin is controlled by the title-length instruction `.lt`. This instruction has the general form

`.lt [[±]n]`

If no scale indicator is given, *n* is assumed to be in ems. The title length is usually set to be equal to the current line length.

14. Local Motions

`troff` provides a facility for specifying vertical and horizontal motions with in-line instructions.

14.1 Vertical Motion

The following table shows the available instructions for vertical motion:

vertical motion		
vertical motion	**effect in** `troff`	**effect in** `nroff`
`\u`	½ em up	½ line up
`\d`	½ em down	½ line down
`\r`	1 em up	1 line up
`\v ´[±]n ´`	move distance *n* (default is *n* blank lines)	

Vertical motion is used to elevate and lower individual characters and words. The following text was printed by using explicitly specified vertical motions:

$$\text{Up }^{\text{the}}\,^{\text{Down}}\,{}^{\text{S}}{}_{\text{T}}{}^{\text{A}}{}_{\text{I}}{}^{\text{R}}{}_{\text{C}}{}^{\text{A}}{}_{\text{S}}{}_{\text{E}}$$

The above example was specified as follows:

```
.ce
\v'+1'Up\v'-0.5' the\v'-0.5' Down \
S\v'+0.2'T\v'+0.2'A\v'+0.2'I\v'+0.2'R\v'+0.2'\
C\v'+0.2'A\v'+0.2'S\v'+0.2'E\v'-1.6'
```

The main line (the line unchanged by vertical motion) is the line where "Down" is sitting.

You can raise or lower characters with one instruction, the \v. To move the word "Up" downward, precede it with the instruction together with directions for the distance you want "Up" to travel:

\v´+1´Up

To return to the initial vertical position, give the opposite instruction argument: \v´−1´. Note that the absence of an operator causes a positive motion by default.

Unlike the font and point size instructions, \v encloses its argument in forward quotes.

The \u (up) and \d (down) instructions are frequently used as alternatives to the \v instruction. These do not have the range of \v, but their simplicity is appropriate for some commonly encountered words or expressions. As an example, the following output

Footnotes[7] 14[10] Trademarks[TM]

was specified as

```
Footnotes\u7\d
14\u\s610\s0\d
Trademarks\u\s6TM\s0\d
```

Notice the symmetry of specification. Like \v, which requires a companion instruction to return to the baseline, \u and \d complement each other: for every *down* there must be an *up* and vice versa (unless, of course, you don't want to balance the line).

14.2 Horizontal Motion

`troff` also offers a set of instructions for moving characters horizontally to the left or right. The complete set of horizontal motion instructions includes the narrow-space character instructions already described:

horizontal motion		
horizontal motion	**effect in** `troff`	**effect in** `nroff`
|	1/6 em space	ignored
\^	1/12 em space	ignored
\&	zero-width	zero-width
\h´[±]n´	move distance n	
\0	digit-size space	
\(space)	unpaddable space-size space	

The \h instruction requires its argument to be enclosed in forward quotes. Negative values specify leftward motion, and positive values specify rightward motion. Consider the following examples:

The preceding examples were specified as

```
   .ce 2
   .ps 36
   .vs 28
   [\h´-.35m´][\h´-.35m´][\h´-.35m´][\h´-.35m´]\
 5 [\h´-.35m´][\h´-.35m´][\h´-.35m´][\h´-.35m´]
   .sp
   }\h´-1n´{\h´-8p´}\h´-1n´{\h´-8p´\
   }\h´-1n´{\h´-8p´}\h´-1n´{
   .vs
10 .ps
```

The first set of icons was specified by shortening the space between each left and right square bracket. After the left square bracket is printed, a default inter-character space is generated; then .35 ems of leftward horizontal motion is generated. This causes each right square bracket to overstrike its predecessor.

The second icon is similar. The space between each curly brace (right and left) is shortened 1 en (ens were used in the demonstration for the sake of variety). Note that ems and ens are relative to both the current font and point size and are, therefore, appropriate for these tasks. The shortened distance between curly brace pairs is specified in points.

15. Manipulating Files

A `troff` document can be partitioned into multiple files to facilitate editing and to allow for logical sections to be stored separately. Typically, these files are included in a "master" file, which together constitute a whole document.

15.1 Including Files with `.so`

`troff` provides a facility for including files in a document. This is done with the switch-source instruction `.so`, which has the general form

`.so` *file*

The availability of the `.so` instruction allows users to split documents, especially large documents, into smaller and more manageable files ranging from chapters to individual displays. The `.so` instruction is especially useful for including files (such as program text) that are likely to be modified or processed independent of the file including them.

Each file can be edited as a separate document, yet included files will paginate and format as a single document applying parameters established in the original source file. Here is an example of an included file:

```
troff input text
.so example1
continuation of troff input
```

When `troff` encounters a `.so` instruction, it accepts input from the specified file — in this case `example1` — and then continues to process the remainder of the original input file. If the file specified in the `.so` instruction cannot be opened, then `troff` terminates.

`eqn` and `tbl` cannot process associated files using `.so` instructions. Files included with `.so` that contain `eqn` or `tbl` instructions must be preprocessed separately or must be included using `pic`'s include-file instruction `.PS`.

15.2 Substituting Source Files with `.nx`

`troff` provides a next-file instruction `.nx` for substituting one input source file with another. The `.nx` instruction has the general form

`.nx` *file*

When `troff` encounters a `.nx` instruction, it reads input from the specified file and then exits.

Note that executions of the `.so` and `.nx` instructions differ in that in case of the `.so` instruction, control returns to the file containing the `.so` instruction. By contrast, in case of the `.nx` instruction, control transfers to the specified file.

15.2.1 Generating Form Letters with `.nx`: We will illustrate the use of the `.nx` instruction by showing you how to generate form letters from a template. Because the `.nx` instruction replaces the file in which it is encountered with the included file, it is well-suited for form letter generation: the beginning of the letter is variant, but the bulk of the letter is standard boiler plate and can simply be appended to the opening section. The template parameters are the inside address, salutation and opening remarks. Here is a sample form letter:

Mr. and Mrs. Gorfield Zorgle
Bungalow A6, Henry Hudson Estates
Northwest Territories, Canada

My dear Mr. and Mrs. Zorgle,

May I wish you a warm welcome to Henry Hudson estates? This historic region where Henry Hudson's ship, the Half Moon, may have sailed is splendid recreation for the entire family.

You may notice that the heating facilities are not yet completed. A. L. Psmith Associates is working hard to solve this problem even as you read our special, personal greeting.

We have made arrangements for your supply of whale oil for heating and lighting to be delivered by the tribespeople in your district.

Our warmest regards,

A. L. Psmith Associates

This letter was specified as follows:

```
Mr. and Mrs. Gorfield Zorgle
.br
Bungalow A6, Henry Hudson Estates
.br
Northwest Territories, Canada
.sp
My dear Mr. and Mrs. Zorgle,
.nx welcome_letter
```

All text and instructions following the salutation, ''My dear ...'' is the contents of the file `welcome_letter` — invariant boiler plate.

Further automating the form letter, we add the `.rd` instruction for reading from the standard input (keyboard). The general form of the read instruction `.rd` is

`.rd` [*prompt*]

where *prompt* is any string not containing spaces soliciting input from the user. `troff` appends a colon to *prompt* by default. Omitting *prompt* causes `troff` to solicit input by sounding a bell.

For example, consider the following alternative for generating the preceding form letter. The following input file, called `form1`, looks like this:

```
.rd Name
.br
.rd Street
.br
.rd State_and_Country
.sp
.rd Salutation
.sp
.nx welcome_letter
```

Processing this input, `troff` echos requests for information onto the terminal (bold type represents strings typed at the keyboard; the arcing arrow denotes a carriage return):

```
$ troff form1 | postprocessor↵
Name: Mr. and Mrs. Gorfield Zorgle↵ ↵
Street: Bungalow A6, Henry Hudson Estates↵ ↵
State_and_Country: Northwest Territories, Canada↵ ↵
Salutation: My dear Mr. and Mrs. Zorgle,↵ ↵
$
```

`troff` allows for multi-line input, accepting user input until *two* new lines are encountered. Both literal text and instructions can be accepted as input.

15.2.2 Generating Multiple Form Letters Sets of form letters can be generated by specifying the `.nx` instruction to recursively include the file containing it. `troff` then begins execution again at the top of the same file. This continuous loop of self-invocation is ended with the exit instruction `.ex`, which causes `troff` to end processing just as if it had reached the end of the file. The input for generating multiple form letters looks like this:

```
     .rd Name
     .br
     .rd Street
     .br
  5  .rd State_and_country
     .sp
     .rd Salutation
     .sp
     .so welcome_letter
 10  .rd Stop?_(type_.ex)
     .bp 1
     .nx \n(.F
```

The boiler plate section of the letter, `welcome_letter`, is now included with the `.so` instruction (line 9) returning control to the original file since we want to generate additional form letters. In line 10 the user is asked if he or she wants to exit. Entering a carriage return causes processing to continue: `.bp 1` resets pagination for the new letter (line 11), and `.nx` reinvokes the current file starting at the top. The predefined variable for the current file name `\n(.F` permits generalization of this form letter tool. That is, `.nx` will call the current file, whatever its name is.

A sample session at the terminal looks like this:

```
$ troff forml | postprocessor↵
Name: Mr. and Mrs. Louis Mortemens↵ ↵
Street: Bungalow M37, Henry Hudson Estates↵ ↵
State_and_Country: Northwest Territories, Canada↵ ↵
Salutation: My dear Mr. and Mrs. Mortemens,↵ ↵
Stop?_(type_.ex): ↵↵
Name: Mr. and Mrs. Zero K. Nullworth↵ ↵
Street: Bungalow M51, Henry Hudson Estates↵ ↵
State_and_Country: Northwest Territories, Canada↵ ↵
Salutation: My dear Mr. and Mrs. Nullworth,↵ ↵
Stop?_(type_.ex): .ex↵ ↵
$
```

This session will generate two form letters similar to the one we demonstrated above.

16. String Variables

Up until now we have demonstrated how to specify formatted documents with text and in-line instructions. `troff` also allows you to define string variables, giving symbolic names to strings of text and in-line instructions. This is done with the define-string instruction, which has the general form

`.ds` *s* *character_sequence_without_blanks*

or

`.ds` *s* *"any character sequence*

where *s* is a one- or two-character symbolic name. A definition can be continued on the next line by terminating the current line with a backslash (which is not printed). Note that definitions containing blanks must begin, but not end, with a double quote. The double quote character may be entered in a definition by specifying two double quote characters.

String variables are evaluated with the sequence

*s

or

\ (*ss

where *s* is a single character.

String variables allow you to generalize elements of your document. The following example personalizes the form letter we demonstrated earlier by allowing placeholders to be inserted in the text with the use of string variables. The formatted letter below

---

Dear Mr. Merkle Dumont and Ms. Tamar Newberger:

Congratulations! You, Tamar Newberger and Merkle Dumont, may already have won a bungalow on Hudson Bay's beautiful north shore. Tamar Newberger, are you intrigued by history? Merkle Dumont, do you love the outdoors? Both are combined at Henry Hudson Estates, and A. L. Psmith Associates has selected you as members of an elite group of families for this offering.

Our heartiest congratulations,

A. L. Psmith Associates

---

was produced with a template and a letter-generation tool. The contents of the template are as follows:

```
    Dear Mr. \*(Mr and Ms. \*(Ms:
    .sp
    Congratulations!  You, \*(Ms and \*(Mr, may
    already have won a bungalow on Hudson Bay's
 5  beautiful north shore.
    \*(Ms, are you intrigued by history?
    \*(Mr, do you love the outdoors?
    Both are combined at Henry Hudson Estates, and
    A.\ L.\ Psmith Associates has selected you as
10  members of an elite group of families for this
    offering.
    .sp
    .in 2i
    Our heartiest congratulations,
15  .sp 3
    A. L. Psmith Associates
```

The string variable references at lines 1, 3, 6 and 7 access values that were supplied by the user at the keyboard. The generator looks like this:

```
    .rd Define_Mr
    .rd Define_Ms
    .so template
    .rd Stop?_(type_.ex)
 5  .bp 1
    .nx \n(.F
```

A session of form letter generation is as follows:

```
$ troff form_offer | postprocessor⏎
define_Mr: .ds Mr "Merkle Dumont⏎ ⏎
define_Ms: .ds Ms "Tamar Newberger⏎ ⏎
Stop?_(type_.ex): .ex⏎ ⏎
$
```

String variables can also be defined in terms of other string variables. The input

```
    .ds U "UNIX system
    .ds UI "\*U interface
    \*(UI
```

produces

UNIX system interface

Unlike `troff` instructions, strings cannot be parameterized and do not accept arguments.

Note that `troff` predefines the string variable `.T` as the name of the current output device.

16.1 Appending to String Variables

Existing string variables can be extended using the append-to-string instruction `.as`, which has the general form

`.as` *s* `"`*appended definition*

where *s* is an existing string variable name. The previous string definition, for instance, could have been specified by extending string U as

`.as U " interface`

Note that the appended definition here begins with a blank.

17. Numeric Variables

`troff` provides a facility for storing integer and floating-point values: the *numeric variable* (also known as the *number register*). Numeric variables are commonly used for counters; for incrementing markers, such as those used in section headings or numbered lists; and for storing typesetting parameters that will be used later in a document. Numeric variables are defined using the `.nr` instruction, which has the general form

`.nr` *x n m*

where *x* is a one- or two-character numeric variable name, *n* is the value initially stored and *m* is the value of auto-incrementation (or -decrementation). By default *n* is 0 and *m* is 1.

Numeric variables are evaluated using the sequence \n as shown in the following table. Notice that numeric variables having a two-character name are evaluated with a left parenthesis:

reference notation	effect on numeric variable	interpreted value
\n$x$	none	n
\n (xx	none	n
\n+x	x incremented by m	$n+m$
\n–x	x decremented by m	$n-m$
\n+ (xx	xx incremented by m	$n+m$
\n– (xx	xx decremented by m	$n-m$

x is a single character. The following example shows a numeric variable A being defined and evaluated

```
.nr A 0 2
The first three even integers
are \n+A, \n+A and \n+A.
.br
The greatest number in the sequence is \nA.
```

producing

```
The first three even integers are 2, 4 and 6.
The greatest number in the sequence is 6.
```

Note that A's value is first incremented and then evaluated.

17.1 Predefined Variables

`troff` predefines a large set of variables to store the values of most typesetting parameters. As parameters change, the values of the predefined variables change accordingly.

Predefined variables are either read-only, whose values can only be evaluated, or read-and-write, whose values can be evaluated and changed and whose format can be altered. These are frequently used in `troff` specifications. A complete list of predefined variables is given toward the end of the chapter.

An example of predefined variables is the page number variable %. Thus, the input

```
The current page number is \n%.
```

results in the output containing the current page number:

The current page number is 185.

Note that when it appears as an argument to the `.tl` instruction, `%` evaluates to the current page number whether or not it is preceded by the sequence `\n`.

17.2 Use of Numbered Items

Numeric sequences are tedious to revise if they have been specified with constant values. Inserting a new chapter in a numbered sequence or inserting a new item in a numbered list forces a manual renumbering of all subsequent items. The use of variables can spare us this task. For example, the numbered list

1.	Reference the variable with \n.
2.	Increment and reference the variable with \n+.
3.	Variables increment first, then evaluate.

was specified as

```
.nr N 0 1
.ta 0.3i
\n+N.☞Reference the variable with \en.
.br
\n+N.☞Increment and reference the variable
with \en+.
.br
\n+N.☞Variables increment first, then evaluate.
```

Adding an item to the front of the list simply increments the others by 1. Deleting one of the list items will not require any change to the rest of the list. (Note that `troff` input for a backslash is `\e`.)

17.3 Numeric Variable Format

Although numeric variable values are Arabic by default, their format can be changed using the alter-variable-format instruction `.af`, which has the general form

`.af` x f

where x is a numeric variable name and f is a code specifying the format. The available formats are given in the following table:

code	format
1	$0, 1, 2, 3, 4, 5, ...$
01	$00, 01, 02, 03, 04, 05, ...$
001	$000, 001, 002, 003, 004, 005, ...$
0001	$0000, 0001, 0002, 0003, 0004, 0005, ...$
i	$0, i, ii, iii, iv, v, ...$
I	$0, I, II, III, IV, V, ...$
a	$0, a, b, c, ..., z, aa, ab, ..., zz, aaa, ...$
A	$0, A, B, C, ..., Z, AA, AB, ..., ZZ,$ $AAA, ...$

The list items appearing in the example just shown can be changed to an alphabetical format with the

```
.af N A
```

instruction. The list will now be printed as

A.	Reference the variable with \n.
B.	Increment and reference the variable with \n+.
C.	Variables increment first, then evaluate.

An Arabic format having *n* digits specifies a field width of *n* digits. `troff`'s predefined, read-only variables and the string-width instruction (discussed later) are always Arabic.

Instructions \g*x* and \g(*xx* yield the format of one-character and two-character variable names respectively. \g returns a value corresponding to a variable format. If the variable format in question has not been altered, \g*x* returns 0.

Testing for the current format can be critical when evaluating variables. For example, testing to see if the current page number is greater than 1 will not yield the expected result if the format of the page number variable % is lower-case Roman.

Note that it is possible to pass values from one numeric variable to another only when they both store their values in the Arabic format. Thus the input

```
.nr V1 0 1
.nr V2 \n+(V1
The value of V2 is \n(V2.
.af V2 i
.nr V3 \n+(V2
The value of V3 is \n(V3.
```

5

produces

The value of V2 is 1. The value of V3 is 0.

17.4 Incrementing String Variables

String variables cannot be auto-incremented or -decremented. They can, however, contain auto-incrementing or -decrementing values. For instance, the list

I.   Item one.
II.   Item two.
III.   Item three.

is specified as

```
.nr X 0 1
.af X I
.ds K \\n+X
.nf
.na
\*K.\h'|0.4i'Item one.
\*K.\h'|0.4i'Item two.
\*K.\h'|0.4i'Item three.
```

Each invocation of the string variable increments the variable's contents. This technique is useful where several formats are used in a single list. While each list tag is specified with the same string variable, format and incrementation can be specified in the numeric variables used to define that single string variable.

17.5 Storing Vertical Page Positions in Variables

The current vertical position is stored in an explicit variable by using the mark instruction .mk. This variable can then be referenced with the space instruction .sp to return to the stored position. The mark instruction has the general form

.mk [x]

where x is a one- or two-character variable name in which the current vertical position is stored. If no argument is given, the current vertical position is stored in an internal numeric variable (which cannot be explicitly referenced).

The .rt instruction is used to return to a marked position stored in an internal numeric variable. This instruction has the general form

.rt [[±]n]

where n is a scaled relative position preceding (−) or following (+) the internally stored vertical position. The .rt instruction can only refer to the marked position immediately preceding it. That is, all of its returns are upward only.

The .sp instruction can be used to return to he position marked with the .mk instruction:

```
.sp |\nxu
```

x is the numeric variable containing the vertical position marked with the `.mk`
instruction. For example, if the vertical position is stored in variable k,

```
.mk k
```

then a return to that position is specified as

```
.sp |\nku
```

Use of `.mk` and `.rt` instructions is illustrated by the following 3-column output:

> Like single-column text, multiple columns are specified with indentation and
> line length instructions.
>
> This is text for the first   The second column will   Satisfactory   columnar
> column and will be   return to the top and print   printing must take into
> brief for this simple   within the specified boun-   account   bottom-of-page
> demonstration.   daries.   handling and be easy to
>   use.

The formatted columns were specified as

```
    Like single-column text, multiple columns
    are specified with indentation and line
    length instructions.
    .sp
5   .mk
    .in 0.1i
    .ll 1.4i
    .hy 14
    This is text for the first column and will be
10  brief for this simple demonstration.
    .br
    .rt
    .in 1.5i
    .ll 3i
15  The second column will return to the top and
    print within the specified boundaries.
    .br
    .rt
    .in 3.1i
20  .ll 4.6i
    Satisfactory columnar printing must take into
    account bottom-of-page handling and be easy to use.
```

The current vertical place is marked in line 5. Subsequent returns to this position are specified in lines 12 and 18.

17.6 Storing Horizontal Page Positions in Variables

In addition to the stand-alone instruction for storing the current vertical position, `troff` also provides an in-line instruction for storing the current horizontal position. This instruction has the forms

\k*x*   and   \k (*xx*

where *x* and *xx* are one- and two-character numeric variable names in which the current horizontal position is to be stored.

Having stored the horizontal position in variables, say *x* and *xx*, the following instructions can then be used to return to the stored position:

\h' | \n*x*u'   and   \h' | \n (*xx*u'

This facility is particularly useful for marking places during a session of line drawing. The following points on a line are an example:

```
 _____•_____•_____•_____•_____•_____
```

The points are drawn with bullets after returning to horizontal places marked with \k:

```
.ce
\D'l 0.5i 0'\ka\D'l 0.5i 0'\kb\D'l 0.5i 0'\kc\
\D'l 0.5i 0'\kd\D'l 0.5i 0'\ke\D'l 0.5i 0'\
\h'|\nau'\(bu\h'|\nbu'\(bu\h'|\ncu'\(bu\
\h'|\ndu'\(bu\h'|\neu'\(bu
```

Note that the \D´l *n n*´ instruction is used for line-drawing and that it is discussed later.

17.7 Scaled Variable Values

Besides storing integer values, variables can also store scaled values specifying size or distance. This facility is especially valuable for parameterizing a document. For example, the following instructions

```
.nr P 1i
.nr I 0
.nr L 5.5i
.nr S 10p
.nr V 12p
.po \nPu
.in \nIu
.ll \nLu
.ps \nSu
.vs \nVu
```

set the page offset to an inch (lines 1 and 6), the indentation to zero (lines 2 and 7),
the line length to 5.5 inches (lines 3 and 8), the point size to 10 points (lines 4 and 9)
and the vertical spacing to 12 points (lines 5 and 10). Once these variables have been
initialized, they can be used throughout the document guaranteeing consistency. If
the basic characteristics of the document must be revised, only the variables at the
top of the file need be redefined; individual instructions need never change.

While variable values are defined in familiar terms — inches, centimeters, etc. —
their values are stored internally as *machine units* (integer values are not affected).
We thus evaluate them in terms of units. The number of units equal to an inch is
specific to the output device on which your document will be printed. For instance,
should a phototypesetter have a resolution, dots per inch (dpi), of 723, then the page
offset instruction specified above would have been stored internally as 723 units.
Because this point has historically been a source for confusion, it is worth further
explanation.

Variables defined in terms of an unscaled integer value will yield the same integer
value when evaluated. For instance, the example of input below:

```
.nr X 1234
\nX
```

yields the following output:

1234

By contrast scaled values are converted to an equivalent value in units. As an
example, the following initialization

```
.nr X 7.3i
\nX
```

evaluated as \nX will yield

5256

Scaled variable values should always be evaluated by explicitly specifying the scale.

For example, specifying a downward spacing as follows:

```
.nr S 1.5i
.sp \nS
```

might appear to result in an inch and a half of blank vertical space. The variable S in this case, however, will evaluate to 1084 units (on the current output device). Because the default scale of .sp is vertical spaces (v), we have specified a downward motion of 1084 vertical spaces — a considerable number of blank pages. The correct specification is

```
.sp \nSu
```

18. Arithmetic Expressions

As we have mentioned, parameterizing a document using numeric variables simplifies later revisions to the page design. `troff`'s ability to compute expressions enhances this technique. Text display indentations can be specified in terms of the line length, which in turn can be specified with respect to the page length. This technique can be extended to other page instructions making for a proportionally specified document. Book production for a variety of stock sizes can quickly be toggled by changing only a few variables.

No blanks are allowed in expressions. Floating-point multipliers or divisors are truncated to integer values. There is no precedence among operators, and evaluation of expressions is from left to right. The unary operators + and − are interpreted by some instructions as incrementation or decrementation operators. `troff`'s arithmetic operators are as follows:

operator	function
+	addition
−	subtraction
/	division
*	multiplication
%	modulus

Now for some examples using the arithmetic operators. The following example specifies vertical spacing as two points greater than the current point size (stored in the predefined variable .s):

```
.vs \n(.su+2p
```

The following set of instructions is typical of documents specified with proportional page parameters:

```
.nr V 11i
.pl \nVu
.ll \nVu/2u
.po \nVu/10u
.in 0
.rs
.sp \n(.iu
```

The four page margins are all specified in terms of one value: the 11 inch page
length. Shifting to a 6" × 9" page is done simply by specifying one value (line 1):

```
.nr V 9i
```

Because `troff` operators all have the same precedence, evaluation is controlled
with parentheses. The following example demonstrates the technique. The input
specification

```
.in 0
Here is the normal indentation.
.in (72p+1i/2u)
But this is 2 inches divided in half.
.in 72p+(1i/2u)
This is a different story:
1 inch plus half an inch.
.in 0
```

produces

```
Here is the normal indentation.
                But this is 2 inches divided in half.
                        This is a different story: 1 inch plus half an inch.
```

In the presence of default scaling, every number in an expression must be followed
by a scale indicator.

19. Input Interpretation

`troff` interprets input in two stages. The first stage is known as *copy mode* when
input is read but (with a few exceptions) not interpreted. String and number
variables are evaluated and *macros* (discussed in the following section) are defined
and expanded during copy mode. The following is a list of character sequences
interpreted during copy mode:

sequence	interpretation
\n	the contents of numeric variables preceded by \n are evaluated
*	string variables preceded by * are interpolated
\$*i*	macro argument *i* denoted as \$*i* is interpreted
newline	concealed new lines are eliminated
.\"	comments indicated by .\" are eliminated
\t	\t is interpreted as a horizontal tab
\a	\a is interpreted as a sequence of leaders
\\	\\ is interpreted as \
\.	\. is interpreted as .

During the second (and final) stage of processing, all text and instructions — including variable values and the (now expanded) contents of macros — are interpreted into a formatted document.

It is sometimes desirable to delay interpretation of macros or variables during copy mode. Variables, for example, might be assigned a value that is not yet available during copy mode. Because two backslashes are interpreted as one during copy mode, referencing of variables is delayed until the final stage of input interpretation using the sequence \\n or *.

In general `troff`'s interpretation of \. as . and \\ as \ produces the effect of backslashes being stripped from instructions during copy mode, suppressing interpretation of stand-alone and in-line instructions until later.

In addition `troff` also provides a facility for suppressing interpretation of instructions so that they can be passed transparently through `troff` to a postprocessor for interpretation. The stand-alone instruction for *transparent throughput* has the general form

\!*instructions to be passed through*

The in-line transparent throughput instruction has the general form

\X´*instructions to be passed through*´

20. Macros

Macros are used for associating a symbolic name with a group of instructions and text that are functionally related to each other. For example, instructions specifying a new paragraph can be named P, or instructions specifying a hierarchy of section headings can be named H accepting integer arguments (1−5). The macro is `troff`'s primary control abstraction mechanism (there are no procedures or functions) and should be regarded as the `troff`'s basic building block.

Macro definitions have the general form

```
.de xx
macro_body
..
```

where *xx* is a one- or two-character ASCII sequence, and *macro_body* contains
`troff` instructions, macro parameters, text and calls to other macros.

To avoid clashes with macro names used by packages such as mm or ms, we
recommend using two-character names made up of one lower-case and one upper-
case letter. Note that macros and string variables cannot have the same name.

A macro is invoked as

.*xx* [*args*]

Macro arguments must be separated by spaces. A macro can have up to nine
arguments. Arguments containing embedded spaces must be enclosed in double
quotes. `troff` replaces a macro invocation with the corresponding *macro_body*,
but only after replacing the parameters with the corresponding arguments.

Parameters are referenced in the macro body using the notation

\\$*i*

where *i* indicates the parameter number. The *i*th parameter corresponds to the *i*th
argument. The predefined numeric variable `.$` can be used to determine the number
of arguments at the current macro level.

Note that parameters require two backslashes to suppress interpretation during copy
mode when the macro argument has not yet become available. In all macro and
string variable definitions, it is important to delay evaluation of variables (among
other constructs) whose interpretation during copy mode is likely to differ from that
during final processing. For instance, font or point size specification in the macro
body does not require delayed interpretation. Evaluation of numeric variables in the
macro body, however, requires delay when the numeric variables are themselves
initialized in a macro.

Macros are useful for encapsulating frequently used instructions and related text.
Suppose the following set of instructions is used to begin a paragraph:

```
.sp 1.25i
.ne 4
.ti +0.2i
```

By encapsulating these instructions in a macro

```
.de Pp
.sp 1.25i
.ne 4
.ti +0.2i
..
```

they can now be invoked though a macro call:

`.Pp`

If in an `.if` or in an `.ie` instruction the test fails, the part of the instruction depending upon the test is neither interpreted nor read during copy mode.

As an example of parameter use, consider the following macro `Bd` defined for specifying bold strings. The input

```
.de Bd
\fB\\$1\fP
..
Roman words before
.Bd "bold words"
and after.
```
5

produces

Roman words before bold words and after.

The parameter `\\$1` is replaced by the single argument `"bold words"` in the macro body. As mentioned earlier, macro calls are replaced by the macro body after parameter substitution. Note that macro arguments containing spaces must be enclosed in double quotes. The double quote characters do not print on output.

Macro arguments allow for variability in an otherwise invariant template. As an illustration, we will encapsulate the instructions and text specifying A. L. Psmith's letter and letterhead (from the example give above). Macro `Lh` accepts up to four arguments corresponding to a maximum four-line inside address (which, of course, must change from letter to letter). Here is an example illustrating the use of this macro:

```
.Lh "Transcendental Transportation" \
"Three Wheel Drive" "Busted Axle, Wyoming"
Sir:
```

Parameters with no corresponding argument (e.g., `\\$4`) evaluate to null. Notice the use of `\` to continue the macro call onto a new line.

Here is the definition of the letterhead macro `Lh`:

```
     .de Lh
     .po 1i
     .ll 4i
     .ps 9
 5   .vs 11
     .rs
     .sp 0.5i
     .ce 3
     .ft HB
10   .vs +4
     \s+4A. L. Psmith, Ph.D., C.P.A., D.Sc., etc.
     Freelance Financial Consultant\s-4
     \D'l 3.5i 0'
     .vs
15   .ft R
     .sp 0.5
     .ti 2.5i
     \(mo/\(dy/\(yr
     .sp 0.5
20   \\$1
     .br
     \\$2
     .br
     \\$3
25   .br
     \\$4
     .sp 0.5
     ..
```

20.1 Appending to Macros

The append-to-macro instruction `.am` allows an existing macro definition to be
extended by adding to the end of the existing definition. The general form of the
`.am` instruction is

```
.am xx
lines to be appended
..
```

For example, a stock opening paragraph could be added to macro Lh:

```
     .am Lh
     Dear Sir or Madam:
     .sp 0.5
     A. L. Psmith Associates, founded in 1948,
  5  has established a distinguished record of
     investment counseling.
     Our specific field of expertise\(eminnovations
     in engineering\(emhas proven to be a
     profitable market.
 10  Your recent inquiry was of particular
     interest to us.
     ..
```

All Lh macro calls will now also include this salutation and paragraph.

20.2 Removing Macros

When a macro or string variable is no longer needed, the remove-macro instruction
`.rm` can be used to free the macro or string variable name. Macros are often
removed to free memory currently allocated to them. The `.rm` instruction has the
general form

`.rm` *xx*

Note that macros and string variables can be redefined without prior removal.

20.3 Renaming Macros

It is sometimes desirable to remove (hide) a macro temporarily so that calls to it are
treated as null instructions; the net effect is as if no instruction had been encountered.
This hiding can be done with the rename-macro instruction `.rn`, which has the
general form

`.rn` *xx yy*

Macro *xx* is renamed *yy*. All calls to the macro *xx* are treated as null instructions
until the original macro name *xx* is restored with another `.rn` instruction as follows:

`.rn` *yy xx*

As an example illustrating the use of macro renaming, consider the following
problem. A first-level section heading must always begin on a new page preceded by
a full-width hair-line rule. All other pages begin, by contrast, with a partial rule and
page number. In order to print a header that is different from the headers on other
pages, the first-level-heading macro (which we will name H1) must usurp the
functionality of the page header macro. So that both macros are never called to
perform the same task, H1 must temporarily ''turn off'' the page header macro pH.
The input looks like this:

```
     .de H1
     .rn pH @#
     'bp
     'sp 1i
5    \D'l \n(.lu 0'
     'sp 0.5i
     \fB\s+4\\$1\s0\fP
     'sp
     .rn @# pH
10   ..
```

The pH macro is temporarily given the unlikely name .@# (line 2), nullifying calls
to pH while the macro H1 is in effect. The last instruction of this definition (line 9)
restores the original definition to pH. Calls to this macro for new pages will now be
successful again (until the next H1 is encountered). Note that the hair-line rule (line
5) has been specified to be equal to the current line length using the predefined
numeric variable \n(.lu.

21. Conditional Statements

`troff` provides the `if` instruction and the `.ie`-`.el` instruction pair for conditional
execution. The following table illustrates the various allowable forms of these
instructions:

instruction	explanation
`.if` *c anything*	if condition *c* true, execute *anything*
`.if` *!c anything*	if condition *c* false, execute *anything*
`.if` *n anything*	if expression $n > 0$, execute *anything*
`.if` *!n anything*	if expression $n \leq 0$, execute *anything*
`.if` ´*string$_1$* ´*string$_2$* ´ *anything*	if *string$_1$* is identical to *string$_2$*, execute *anything*
`.if` ! ´*string$_1$* ´*string$_2$* ´ *anything*	if *string$_1$* is not identical to *string$_2$*, execute *anything*
`.ie` *c anything$_1$*	if portion of *if-else*; all above forms (like `.if`)
`.el` *anything$_2$*	else portion of *if-else*

anything represents any combination of text and instructions including nested levels
of more *if* instructions. *anything* can span multiple lines provided it is enclosed in
the delimiters \{ and \}. For consistent indentation *anything* usually begins on a
new line preceded by the delimiter \{ \:

```
.if \\n(^Z>0 \{\
.      sp |2i
.      po 1i
.      in 0.5i
.      ll 5i \}
```

Note that the `.if` instruction and the `.ie`-`.el` instruction pair can be nested.

If the test should fail in either an `.if` or `.ie` instruction, the part of the instruction depending upon the test is neither interpreted nor read during copy mode.

The built-in condition names are

condition name	true if
o	current page number is odd
e	current page number is even
t	formatter is `troff`
n	formatter is `nroff`

In addition, the conditional instructions use logical expressions to test for conditions. Here are the `troff` logical operators:

operator	function
>	greater than
<	less than
= (or ==)	equal to
>=	greater than or equal to
<=	less than or equal to
&	logical AND
:	logical OR

As an example of the `if` instruction, we will show you how to print the current date in the English format, e.g., August 14, 1990. Using predefined numeric variables for the current month, day and year, you are able to define the current date as follows:

```
     .if \n(mo=1 .ds Mo January
     .if \n(mo=2 .ds Mo February
     .if \n(mo=3 .ds Mo March
     .if \n(mo=4 .ds Mo April
  5  .if \n(mo=5 .ds Mo May
     .if \n(mo=6 .ds Mo June
     .if \n(mo=7 .ds Mo July
     .if \n(mo=8 .ds Mo August
     .if \n(mo=9 .ds Mo September
 10  .if \n(mo=10 .ds Mo October
     .if \n(mo=11 .ds Mo November
     .if \n(mo=12 .ds Mo December
     .ti \n(.lu/2u
     \*(Mo \n(dy, 19\n(yr
```

The `.ie`-`.el` instruction pair is used to decide between two logically opposed conditions. For example, consider the following fragment of the page header macro pH.

```
     .de pH
     more instructions and text
     .if \\n%>1 \{\
  .      ie t \{\
  5  .          ie o .tl '''\fB%\fP'
     .          el .tl '\fB%\fP''' \}
     .      el \{\
     .          ie o .tl '''-%-'
     .          el .tl '-%-''' \} \}
 10  more instructions and text
     ..
```

This macro fragment provides for emboldened pagination if the formatter is `troff` (lines 5-6); it provides for hyphens flanking a number in the default font if the formatter is `nroff` (lines 8-9). It places the page number to the right if the page is odd (lines 5 and 8); the page number is left-adjusted if the page is even (lines 6 and 9). Finally, pagination prints only if the page number is greater than one (line 3):

For readability and clear presentation of logic, it is good practice to indent nested conditional instructions.

22. Diversions

It is seldom desirable to split displays of text or graphics across page boundaries. Ensuring that displays stay together requires that the depth of the display block and the depth of available page space be known before printing. `troff` provides a *diversion* facility and predefined numeric variables for evaluating this information.

The diversion facility is an important feature of `troff` [Witten, et al. 1982]. Without it, typesetting would be a trial-and-error process.

Diversions are used to divert text together with instructions into a buffer, or *save area*, where it is formatted and stored for later printing. Diversion definitions have the form

```
.di xx
input to be diverted
.di
```

The `.di` instruction begins and ends the diversion definition. *xx* is a one- or two-character macro name associated with the save area. Note that diversion names should not clash with macro or string variable names.

The line buffer should be flushed preceding the opening of a diversion and following the end of diverted input. This ensures that only intended lines are diverted.

The contents of the diversion are "read back" by calling the diversion macro in the same manner one calls a conventional macro:

`.xx`

Diversions can be nested.

The predefined numeric variables dn and dl contain the depth and width of the last completed diversion. With each new diversion the contents of these predefined variables are overwritten.

Macros containing diversions are usually defined in pairs: one to initiate the diversion, the other to end it. All text entered between the two macros becomes part of the diversion. The lead macro definition is typically brief, leaving more detailed instructions to the second once the size of the diversion is known.

As an example, suppose you wanted to set text in boxed displays (similar to the displays appearing throughout this book), defining one macro (Bx) to begin the display and another (Be) to end it. The size of the displays would be variable, of course, depending upon the volume of the text entered between the macros. Determining the dimensions of the box and controlling printing of the display based on available page space is done using a diversion.

Consider the following output [Snyder 1982]:

> Once at Cold Mountain, troubles cease—
> No more tangled, hung-up mind.
> I idly scribble poems on the rock cliff,
> Taking whatever comes, like a drifting boat.

This was specified as follows:

```
    .Bx
    .ps 14
    .vs 16
    .ft PA
5   Once at Cold Mountain, troubles cease\(em
    No more tangled, hung-up mind.
    I idly scribble poems on the rock cliff,
    Taking whatever comes, like a drifting boat.
    .ft
10  .vs
    .ps
    .Be
```

Macro `Bx`, which begins the box definition, is defined as follows:

```
    .de Bx
    .sp 1v
    .nr fI \\n(.u
    .nr iN \\n(.iu
5   .di @X
    .nf
    .in +1m
    ..
```

The `.sp` instruction (line 2) offsets the display 1 vertical space from the preceding text and flushes the line buffer before beginning the diversion. Current filling mode and indentation information is then evaluated for later restoration (lines 3-4). The current filling mode is recorded by referencing the predefined variable `.u` and storing the data in `fI` (line 3); the current indentation is predefined in `.i` and stored in `iN` (line 4). User input entered between `.Bx` and `.Be` is formatted and stored in a save area associated with the macro `@X`.

Note that the value of the predefined variable `.u` in line 3 is not interpreted in terms of internal units. This is because it returns a Boolean value.

Macro `Be`, which ends the box, is defined as follows:

```
     .de Be
10   .in -1m
     .di
     .nr || \\n(dnu+1v
     .nr -- \\n(dlu+1m
     .in (\\n(.lu-\\n(--u)/2u
15   .ie \\n(||u>=\\n(.tu .bp
     .el .sp
     .@X
     .br
     \D'l \\n(--u 0'\D'l 0 -\\n(||u'\
20   \D'l -\\n(--u 0'\D'l 0 +\\n(||u'
     .if !\\n(fI=0 .fi
     .in \\n(iNu
     .sp 1.5
     ..
```

The diversion is cleanly ended by flushing the line buffer (line 10) before actually closing the diversion (line 11). The depth of the diversion plus one vertical space (line 12) and the width of the diversion plus one em (line 13) are stored in the variables || and -- respectively. The display itself is centered by specifying the indentation in terms of the width of the block (line 14).

The *if-else* instruction (lines 15-16) compares the depth of the diversion to the remaining vertical space on the page, calculated by determining the distance to the footer trap (stored in the predefined variable .t). If the diversion's depth exceeds or is equal to the distance to the footer trap, then the page is ejected (line 15). Otherwise, a single blank line is printed (line 16). The contents of the save area (diversion) are printed in line 17. After positioning and printing of the diversion, a box is drawn around it using line drawing instructions (discussed later) that are specified according to the depth and width of the display. Note that these values always reflect the current point size, vertical spacing and font of the diverted text as our example demonstrates.

Restoration of some original parameters is done toward the end of the definition. The variable containing fill mode information (fI) is tested (line 21). A value of 0 indicates that the text preceding the display was in no-fill mode. Next, indentation is restored (line 22).

The following instructions and predefined variables are local to the diversion in which they are used:

instructions	
the diversion trap instruction (and corresponding macro)	`.dt` *xy*
the no-space instruction	`.ns`
numeric variables	
the internally-saved vertical position	saved with `.mk` and evaluated with `.rt`
the current vertical place	`.d`
the current high-water text base-line	`.h`
the current diversion name	`.z`

23. Traps

Traps are a facility for interrupting normal processing to do some special processing when some condition becomes true. There are three kinds of traps: *page traps*, *diversion traps* and *input-line-count traps*.

23.1 Page Traps

`troff` page traps provide a facility for associating text and instructions with specific vertical positions on a page. For example, specifying the running header or running footer to appear in the same vertical position on every page is done with the page trap instruction `.wh`. The general form of the `.wh` instruction — the *when* instruction — is

`.wh` *n* *xx*

where *n* is a vertical page position and *xx* is the name of the macro to be invoked when the vertical position *n* is met or swept past. A positive *n* specifies a distance from the top of the page (which is position 0); a negative *n* specifies a distance from the bottom of the page (established with the `.pl` instruction and is eleven inches by default).

As an example, here is an instruction that causes the page header macro pH to be invoked at the top of every page:

`.wh 0 pH`

The following instruction causes the page footer macro pF to be invoked 1.5 inches from the bottom of every page:

`.wh -1.5i pF`

The pH header macro prints the page number while the pF footer macro simply ejects the page:

```
.de pH
.rs
'sp |1i
.ie e .tl'%'''
.el .tl'''%'
'sp 0.4i
..
.de pF
'bp
..
```

5

Note that in both `pH` and `pF` macro definitions, flushing of the line buffer is suppressed by using the forward quote control character ´. Otherwise text that had been buffered for page transition would be flushed in an unpredictable fashion.

The position of an existing page trap can be altered with the *change* instruction `.ch`, which has a general form nearly identical to that of the `.wh` instruction:

`.ch` *n xx*

23.2 Diversion Traps

Formatting a large display on a single page can lead to display overflow, which is not discovered until the document is printed. Diversion traps make it possible to suppress printing of such documents while communicating this overflow information to the user. Such traps are specified with the diversion trap instruction `.dt`, which has the general form

`.dt` *n xx*

where *n* is a vertical position representing the diversion depth and *xx* is the name of the macro that is invoked when the vertical position *n* is met or swept past. For instance, the specification

`.dt 2.5i Dt`

will cause the macro `Dt` to be invoked when the diversion has grown to a depth equal to or greater than 2.5 inches. Control then returns to the diversion just after the point where the macro was called.

Overflow — a diversion whose depth is greater than the length of a single page — can be managed by sending a terminal message to the user, then aborting the job:

```
**********WARNING**********
diversion bG greater than page depth
available page depth = 11 inches
******file junk aborted******
```

Here is the specification of macro Dt, which produced the preceding output:

```
     .de Dt
     .nr Rs 1i
     .nr p> \n(.p/\n(Rs
     .tm **********WARNING**********
  5  .tm diversion \\n(.z greater than page depth
     .tm available page depth = \\n(p> inches
     .tm *****file \n(.F aborted******
     .ex
     ..
 10  .di bG
     .dt \n(.pu Dt
     big diversion
     .di
```

The current resolution (number of internal units per inch) is stored in the numeric variable Rs (line 2). In order to report dimensions in inches, Rs is used as a divisor (line 3). Error messages are written with the .tm instruction. The trap itself is set at a vertical position equal to the depth of a page (predefined in the variable .p). Note the name of the current diversion and file are stored in the predefined variables .z and .F.

Exit instruction .ex (line 8) terminates the formatting. Note that the abort instruction .ab is similar to the exit instruction, except that it also prints its argument on the standard error output.

23.3 Input-line-count Traps

The *input-line-count trap* is used to defer some action until a specified amount of input has been encountered. This facility is particularly useful when used in conjunction with the rename-macro instruction .rn. As we have demonstrated, .rn is used to hide macro definitions temporarily. Sometimes, it is not possible for a macro to be turned back on by the same macro that turned it off. The input-line-count trap is used as a method of deferral in such cases. The input-line-count trap instruction has the general form

.it *n xx*

where *n* is the number of input lines read before the trap is sprung and *xx* a one- or two-character macro name that is invoked when the number of lines *n* is read.

As an example, suppose that two macros — H1 and P — are potentially in conflict with each other. The heading macro H1 prints a blank line after each new heading. Anticipating that the P macro will sometimes follow H1, equal spacing after each new heading is ensured by turning off the P macro. H1 cannot restore P because it will always complete its execution before reading the next input line (i.e., before finding out whether or not the next line is a call to the macro P). The solution is to set an input-line-count trap:

5
```
.de H1
.rn P @
more instructions and text
.it 1 Po
..
.de Po
.rn @ P
..
```

This excerpt shows the section heading macro setting an input-line-count trap associated with the "paragraph on" macro Po, whose only function is to restore the macro P. If the line after the H1 is a P, then the macro call will have no effect because P has been hidden. Just after the first line, however, the macro P is made visible once again.

24. Environments

The scope of all user-defined `troff` variables is global. Some predefined variables, however, are local to specific execution areas called *environments*. These environments behave as "mini-documents" each with its own distinct parameters such as the current font, point size and vertical spacing. `troff` supports three environments. By default, execution begins in environment 0 where the bulk of formatting is done.

A new environment is entered with the `.ev` instruction, which has the following form:

`.ev` [*n*]

where *n* represents the environment numbers 0, 1 or 2.

The sequence of environments entered and exited is tracked on a last-in-first-out (LIFO) basis. Environments are thus manipulated in a push-down fashion. The most recently entered environment is at the top of a stack and is "popped" with the `.ev` instruction followed by no argument.

The following instructions (and, in some cases, associated predefined variables) are local to the current environment:

instruction	predefined variable	name
`.ad`	`.j`	adjust
`.c2`		change no-break control character
`.cc`		change control character
`.ce`		center
`.fi`	`.u`	fill
`.ft`	`.f`	font
`.hc`		hyphenation character
`.hy`		hyphenation
`.in`	`.i`	indentation
`.it`		input-line-count trap
`.lc`		leader character
`.ls`	`.L`	lines spacing
`.ll`	`.l`	line length
`.mc`		margin character
`.na`	`.j`	no-adjust
`.nf`	`.u`	no-fill
`.nh`		no hyphenation
`.nm`		number lines
`.nn`		no line numbering
`.ps`	`.s`	point size
`.ss`		set space character
`.ta`		tabs
`.tc`		tab character
`.ti`		temporary indent
`.tl`		titles
`.vs`	`.v`	vertical spacing

To illustrate the use of environments, we will create an environment (numbered 1) to be used for displays specified with the macros Ds (display start) and De (display end). Text in the display environment will be printed using larger margins, 9 on 11 point size/leading and characters set in the Helvetica font. Consider the following:

> Environment switching is done in a push-down fashion. Restoration of previous environments must be done by popping the current environment.
>> Note: a previous environment cannot be explicitly reentered. It must be popped.
>
> There are three environments: 0, 1 and 2.

which was specified using the Ds and De macros:

```
     Environment switching is
     done in a push-down fashion.
     Restoration of previous environments
     must be done by popping the current
5    environment.
     .Ds
     Note: a previous environment cannot
     be explicitly reentered.
     It must be popped.
10   .De
     There are three environments:
     0, 1 and 2.
```

The Ds macro specifies values for the display environment (1) while the De macro restores the default environment (0):

```
     .de Ds
     .br
     .ev 1
     .ll 4i
5    .in 0.5i
     .ft H
     .ps 9
     .vs 11
     ..
10   .de De
     .br
     .ev
     .br
     ..
```

Note that the macro De does not respecify parameters. The display parameters continue to be current, but only in environment 1.

25. Character Manipulation Features

`troff` provides a variety of instructions for character manipulation. The following table gives a synopsis of the general form of each instruction and summarizes the function of each instruction:

instruction	function
\H´[±]n´	sets character height to *n* without affecting character width
\s´[±]n´	sets character at *n* degree slant
\o´abc...´	prints characters *a*, *b*, *c* on the same space, overstriking them (centers of *a*, *b*, *c* are aligned)
\z´c´	prints character *c* without generating space (*c* is left-aligned with the character after it; \z does not accept quoted arguments)
\l´[±]n c´	draws a horizontal string of *c*s of length *n*
\L´[±]n c´	draws a vertical string of *c*s of length *n*
\b´abc´	prints bracket piece characters *a*, *b*, *c* (dedicated instruction for building brackets)
\w´string´u	calculates the width of *string* in units

25.1 The Character-height Instruction \H

Characters can be made taller with the `.ps` instruction or the `\s` instruction, but they are also made proportionally wider. The height instruction `\H` allows character height to be increased without affecting character width. Here is an example of tall characters:

WHEN THE TALL SHIPS SAIL IN

These characters were specified as follows:

```
.ft HB
.ps 16
WHEN \H´+9´THE TALL SHIPS\H´0´ SAIL IN
.ps
.ft
```

The `\H´+9´` instruction increments the character height 9 points. An unsigned argument specifies an absolute value in points. `\H´0´` restores character height to that commensurate with the current point size.

25.2 The Character-slant Instruction \s

Characters (including those in the italic fonts) can be made to slant either forward or backward with the \s´[±]*n*´ instruction, where *n* is a number of degrees by which the slant is to be changed. For example, the display

THE NEW YORK *MARATHON*

is specified as

```
.ft  HB
.ps  16
THE  NEW  YORK  \S´14´MARATHON\S´0´
.ps
.ft
```

A 0 argument restores characters to their original slant. The number of degrees available for character slanting is device-dependent.

25.3 The Overstrike Instruction \o

The overstrike instruction \o is used to plot characters on top of one another. Each character specified to be overstruck is centered on top of its predecessor. The width of the resulting character is that of the widest overstruck character. For example, the symbols

are specified by overstriking an equal sign and slash as well as two opposing arrows:

```
.ps  36
.ce
\o´\(eq/´        \o´\(<-\(->´
.ps
```

25.4 The Zero-width Escape Sequence \z

The zero-width instruction \z closely resembles the overstrike instruction functionally. Instead of centering the overstruck characters, however, they are left-aligned. For example, the following cone is made by reducing the size of a series of circles, elevating them slightly and using \z:

The input specification is as follows:

```
.in 0.5i
.ps 28
\z\(ci\s-2\v\'-0.17\'\z\(ci\s-2\v\'-0.17\'\
\z\(ci\s-2\v\'-0.17\'\z\(ci\s-2\v\'-0.17\'\
\z\(ci\s-2\v\'-0.17\'\z\(ci\s-2\v\'-0.17\'\
\z\(ci\s-2\v\'-0.17\'\z\(ci\s-2\v\'-0.17\'\z\(ci
.ps 10
.in
```

25.5 The Character-repetition Instructions \l and \L

`troff` also provides a facility for drawing lines of arbitrary length by repeating any specified character. The instruction for horizontal repetition is

\l'[±]nc'

where n is a scaled distance and c is a repeated character. Similarly, the

\L'[±]nc'

instruction is used for vertical character repetition. The following example

```
            L
            L
            L
            L
            L
            L
            L
            L  LLLLLLLL
```

is specified as

```
.ce
\L'1.1iL'\l'0.75iL'
```

The default character argument to the \l instruction is the underscore-rule sequence \(ru (_). The default character argument to the \L instruction is the bold-vertical-pipe sequence \(bv (|). As a consequence, these instructions were used as general purpose line-drawing functions in early releases of `troff`. (Their names are an artifact of that usage.) Later releases of `troff` support a more general class of line-drawing functions, which we shall discuss at length below.

25.6 The Bracket-building Instruction \b

\b is the bracket-building instruction. The following example demonstrates the large brackets built with \b:

$$\left[\left\{ \text{Else a great prince in prison lies} \right\}\right]$$

Here is the specification of the preceding example:

```
.ce
\b'\(lc\(lf'\b'\(lt\(lk\(lb' \
Else a great prince in prison lies \
\b'\(rt\(rk\(rb'\b'\(rc\(rf'
```

As the input specification demonstrates, the square brackets are each made of two characters while the curly brackets are each made of three. The individual bracket pieces are described below in the ''Special Characters'' section below.

25.7 The String-width Instruction \w

The string-width instruction \w calculates the width (among other characteristics) of a string. After each execution of \w´*string*´u, three predefined variables record the characteristics of *string*. The variable ct contains four possible values (0-3) depending on properties of the characters in *string*. The following table shows the range of values returned by ct:

variable value	string characteristic
1	characters in *string* had no descenders (e.g., *y*)
2	characters in *string* had no ascenders (e.g., *k*)
3	characters in *string* had ascenders and descenders
0	characters in *string* had no ascenders or descenders (e.g., *x*)

The variables st and sb record the highest and lowest extent of *string* above and below the baseline, respectively.

The following example uses the string width in order to overstrike one string with another at a slight offset. The result is an emboldened string:

Blackest **black**

Here is the corresponding input:

```
.ps 16
Blackest black\h`-\w`black`u+0.01i`black
.ps
```

Two identical strings are laid one over another; the amount of negative horizontal
motion is 0.01 inches less than the width of the string. For the sake of readability,
back quotes rather than forward quotes are used for the delimiters of the \w
instruction.

The string-width instruction is often used to govern string placement where constant
values are inappropriate or unknown. Consider the following example that correctly
aligns the periods among numerical list tags:

> **99.** The right side of this item will always be 1
> en to the left. The string-width instruction
> provides consistent right-adjusted items.
> **100.** The width of the item might change, but the
> alignment of items will not be affected.

This was specified as follows:

```
    .in 1i
    .ll -1i
    .ti -(\w'\fB99.\fP'u+1n)
    \fB99.\fP
 5  .sp -1
    The right side of this item will always be 1 en
    to the left.
    The string-width instruction provides
    consistent right-adjusted items.
10  .ti -(\w'\fB100.\fP'u+1n)
    \fB100.\fP
    .sp -1
    The width of the item might change,
    but the alignment of items will not be affected.
15  .ll
    .in
```

The individual tags, which vary in width, are right-adjusted and uniformly offset
from the body of the list by 1 en.

26. Underlining Words

The underline-string instruction `.ul` is treated differently by `nroff` and `troff`, and this has been cause for confusion among `troff` users. The general form for this instruction is

`.ul` *n*

where *n* lines of input are underlined in `nroff` but italicized in `troff`.

In fact, `troff` provides no instruction for *underlining*. Using the string-width instruction \w and the horizontal-repetition instruction \l, however, we can devise a general purpose line-drawing macro. The general form for use is

`.Ul` *string*

where *string* is a sequence of characters to be underlined. If *string* contains white space, then the entire sequence must be enclosed in double quotes.

The following output, then,

> After scanning ''Fowles in the Frith,'' several times, I was on fire. I read <u>Pearl</u>, then <u>Sir Gawain and the Green Knight</u>, and now I have put aside a year to come to terms with <u>The Canterbury Tales</u>.

was specified as

```
     After scanning ``Fowles in the Frith,''
     several times, I was on fire.
     I read
     .Ul Pearl ,
  5  then
     .Ul "Sir Gawain and the Green Knight" ,
     and
     now I have put aside a year to
     come to terms with
 10  .Ul "The Canterbury Tales" .
```

Macro Ul is defined as follows:

```
   .de U1
   .nr sL \w´\\$1´u
   .if \\n(.lu-\\n(.ku<=\\n(sLu .br
   \\$1\
5  \h´-\\n(sLu´\
   \v´2p´\
   \l´\\n(sLu´\
   \v´-2p´\
   \\$2
10 ..
```

The width of the string argument is calculated and stored in the numeric variable `sL` (line 2). Since, we cannot underline across new lines, the length of the string is compared to horizontal space remaining on the current line (line 3). (The predefined variable `.k` stores the length the partially collected current line, and the predefined variable `.l` stores the current line length.) If the passed string is longer than the space remaining, the line buffer is flushed (`.br`), forcing the string to be printed on the next line. After the string is printed (line 4), a negative horizontal motion is generated equal to the length of the string (the test on line 3 ensures we have sufficient space). Finally, a horizontal line is drawn equal to the length of the string (line 7). Note that 2 points of "breathing room" is generated on line 6 (then compensated for in line 8) for readability. The second argument to `U1` is expected to be punctuation, so it is printed last and not included in underlined text.

String arguments containing white space are quoted to associate the entire string with the single formal parameter `\\$1`.

27. Two-dimensional Graphics

`troff` provides instructions for drawing lines, circles, ellipses, arcs and splines. The picture-drawing language, `pic`, is specially designed for providing high-level instructions for two-dimensional graphics. `troff` line-drawing instructions are low-level but are more versatile in some cases. For instance, unlike figures made with `pic`, `troff` figures may be placed in-line with text. The ability to fill a line with figures as well as characters makes it possible to encapsulate new sets of characters in macros or string variables.

27.1 Line

The instruction for drawing lines has the general form

`\D´l` *x y*´

which specifies that a line is drawn from the current position to the relative position *x, y*. As an example, consider the box

A box: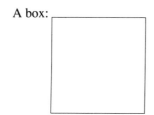

which was specified as

```
.ti (\n(.lu/2u)-0.5i
A box:
\D´l 1i 0´\D´l 0 1i´\D´l 1 -1i 0´\D´l 0 -1i´
```

Readability can be improved by splitting the line drawing instruction on to several lines (one per side):

```
.ti (\n(.lu/2u)-0.5i
A box:
\D'l 1i 0'\
\D'l 0 1i'\
\D'l -1i 0'\
\D'l 0 -1i'
```

If new lines were not escaped (terminated with a backslash) on input lines 3-5, a horizontal space would have been generated on output for each new line on input. (Recall that carriage returns are interpreted as spaces on output.)

27.2 Circle

The circle instruction has the general form

`\D´c d´`

where *d* is the diameter of the circle. The west side is treated as the current position:

Next, a circle: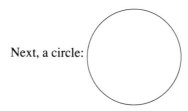

This figure was specified as

```
.ti 1.5i
Next, a circle:
\D´c 1i´
```

27.3 Ellipse

The ellipse instruction has the general form

`\D'e` *hd vd'*

where *hd* and *vd* are horizontal and vertical diameters of the ellipse. The west side is treated as the current position:

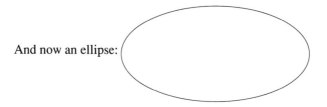

This ellipse was specified as

```
.ti 0.7i
And now an ellipse:
\D'e 2i 1i'
```

27.4 Arc

The arc instruction has the general form

`\D'a` x_1 y_1 x_2 y_2`'`

It draws an arc from the current position counterclockwise to the point x_1+x_2, y_1+y_2. The point x_1, y_1 represents the center of the partial or closed arc. The following arc

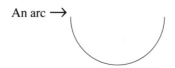

was specified as

```
.ce
An arc \s+4\(->\s-4 \D´a 0.5i 0 0.5i 0´
```

It is not possible to draw arcs in a clockwise direction.

27.5 Spline

The spline instruction has the general form

$$\backslash D\,'\,\tilde{}\ \ x_1\ y_1\ x_2\ y_2\ \cdots\,'$$

which draws a spline from the current position by x_1, y_1, then by x_2, y_2, and so on.
The following spline

A spline . . .

was specified as

```
.ti 1.25i
A spline . . .
\D'~ 0.4i 0.4i 0.4i -0.4i 0.4i 0.4i 0.4i -0.4i'
```

Note that each value pair is an incrementation of its predecessor and is not a pair of
absolute Cartesian coordinates. Specifically, x_{i+1}, y_{i+1} is relative to x_i, y_i.

27.6 Line Drawing and String Variables

The line-drawing functions are not display oriented. Rather than forcing a flush of
the line buffer or generating vertical space before and after their occurrence, they are
part of the flow of the filling line. The icons you define with them, therefore, can be
entered as ordinary text, and they will appear in-line with text or with other icons.

Icons are most easy to use when they are encapsulated in string variables. For
example, the following specification defines a string variable in terms of a line-
drawing primitive:

`.ds` *xx* `\D´c n´`

where *c* is a drawing instruction type and *n* is a numeric specification.

The following are examples of Hebrew characters in the style of an Israeli newspaper
headline:

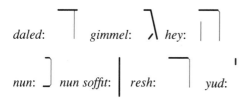

These characters were printed with the

```
  \f2daled\fP:  \*d   \f2gimmel\fP:  \*g   \
  \f2hey\fP:  \*h
  .sp 2
  \f2nun\fP:  \*n    \
5 \f2nun soffit\fP:  \*(nS   \
  \f2resh\fP:  \*r   \f2yud\fP:  \*y
```

instructions, where d, g, h, n, nS, r, and y are string variables containing definitions for the characters *daled, gimmel, hey, nun, nun soffit, resh* and *yud*. The string variables are defined in terms of local motions and lines. Before we discuss these definitions, here is another one — the Hebrew for Reagan:

which was input as

`\*(nS\*g\*y\*y\*r`

Although Hebrew is written from right-to-left, we are still bound to express it in `troff` from left-to-right.

The following is the definition of *daled* :

```
  .ds d \
  \h'.1i'\v'-0.3i'\
  \s(36\D'l 0.2i 0'\s(10\
  \h'-0.03i'\
5 \D'l 0 0.3i'\
  \h'.1i'
```

To provide inter-character spacing, forward horizontal motion must precede and follow each character. Those motions appear in lines 2 and 6 of the *daled* definition. Upward vertical motion precedes each character because the characters are drawn from top to bottom. To preserve the baseline of all characters on a given line, short characters such as the *yud* must be followed by downward vertical motion.

The *daled* itself begins in line 3. Parts of the character are thicker than others, so the top line is drawn using a 36 point font while the rest of the *daled* is drawn using a 10 point font (line 3). Note that changing the point size will not proportionately increase the height (or length) of the character, as it does with fonts, but only the thickness of the line.

The *daled* is constructed by first drawing a horizontal line 0.2 inches to the right (line 3). Next, a left horizontal motion was specified (line 4), so the following instruction will begin 0.03 inches to the left (line 4). This instruction (line 5) draws a vertical line 0.3 inches down.

The definition of *resh* is almost identical to that of *daled*:

```
.ds  r  \
\h'.1i'\v'-0.3i'\
\s(36\D'l 0.2i 0'\s(10\
\D'l 0.02i 0.02i'\
\D'l 0 0.29i'\
\h'.1i'
```

(line 5 marked in left margin)

The only significant difference is that the *resh* is specified with a line having both a horizontal and vertical value (line 4). It therefore slants. Because both are positive values, the line will be drawn downward and to the right. This was done to soften the convergence of that character's top and side lines.

For the sake of simplicity we have specified the characters using constant values. We could have also specified them using variables to parameterize the definitions. The sizes of our Hebrew characters would have been easier to change, but the definitions would have been more complex. The following example illustrates a parameterized definition of *daled*. First, here are the variable definitions representing the *daled* parameters:

```
.nr  a  0.1i
.nr  b  \nau*2u
.nr  c  \nau*3u
.nr  d  \nau/3
```

Now here is the parameterized definition of the *daled*:

```
.ds  d  \
\h'\\nau'\v'-\\ncu'\
\s(36\D'l \\nbu 0'\s(10\
\h'-\\ndu'\
\D'l 0 \\ncu'\
\h'\\nau'
```

(line 5 marked in left margin)

Proportional changes to the size of *daled* are done by changing the value of a.

We include definitions of the remaining characters for the sake of completeness:

Gimmel:

```
  .ds g \
  \h'.1i'\v'-0.3i'\
  \s(36\D'l 0.07i 0'\
  \D'l 0.07i 0.3i'\
5 \v'-0.05i'\h'-0.05i'\
  \D'l -0.04i 0.05i'\s(10\
  \h'.1i'
```

Hey:

```
  .ds h \
  \h'.1i'\v'-0.3i'\
  \s(36\D'l 0.2i 0'\s(10\
  \D'l 0.02i 0.02i'\
5 \D'l 0 0.3i'\
  \h'-0.2i'\
  \D'l 0 -0.2i'\
  \v'.18i'\h'.3i'
```

Nun:

```
  .ds n \
  \h'.07i'\v'-0.3i'\
  \s(36\D'l 0.04i 0'\s(10\
  \D'l 0.02i 0.02i'\
5 \D'l 0 0.26i'\
  \D'l -0.02i 0.02i'\
  \s(36\D'l -0.12 0'\s(10\
  \h'.1i'
```

Nun soffit:

```
\h'.05i'\v'-0.3i'\
\s(36\D'l 0 0.4i'\s(10\
\v'-0.1i'\h'.05i'
```

Yud:

```
.ds y \
\h'.05i'\v'-0.3i'\
\s(36\D'l 0 0.06i'\
\v'.24i'\h'.05i'\s(10
```

27.7 Line Drawing and Macros

In previous examples we have encapsulated line-drawing functions in string variables. We will now use macros instead. The primary advantage of macros over string variables is that macros can be passed arguments. We will illustrate this by defining a macro `Hi` that highlights words with boxes. To draw the box proportionately, the line-drawing functions must be able to measure the strings they enclose. First, here is sample output containing boxed words:

Boxing ‖words‖ gives emphasis to strings ‖beyond‖
that supplied by ‖point size and fonts.‖

This was specified as

```
     .sp
     Boxing
     .Hi words
     gives emphasis to strings
  5  .Hi beyond
     .br
     that supplied by
     .Hi "point size and fonts."
     .sp
```

Because lines are drawn according to the length and width of each string, changes in font and point size to those strings will proportionately change each box:

Boxing ‖*words*‖ *gives emphasis to strings* ‖*beyond*‖ *that supplied by* ‖*point size and fonts.*‖

This was specified as

```
     .ftI
     .ps24
     .vs28
     .sp
5    Boxing
     .Hi words
     gives emphasis to strings
     .Hi beyond
     that supplied by
10   .Hi "point size and fonts."
     .sp
     .ps10
     .vs12
     .ftR
```

Hi is defined as follows:

```
     .de Hi
     .nr aW \\w'\|\\$1\|'u
     .nr aH (\\n(stu+\\n(sbu)u
     \|\\$1\|\
5    \\v'\\n(aHu/5u'\
     \\D'l -\\n(aWu 0i'\
     \\D'l 0i -\\n(aHu'\
     \\D'l +\\n(aWu 0i'\
     \\D'l 0i +\\n(aHu'\
10   \\v'-\\n(aHu/5u'
     ..
```

The width of the argument (line 2), padded with narrow space characters, is calculated using the string-width instruction (line 2). That computed width is stored in the variable aW. The height of the first argument, stored in the variable aH, is determined by evaluating predefined variables whose values are set by the width instruction (line 3). st contains the height of the measured string above the baseline including character ascenders; sb contains the depth of the measured string below the baseline including character descenders. The argument is printed together with narrow space characters (line 4). Lines 6-9 contain the instructions for drawing the box. The arguments of these instructions are specified using the width and height of the argument to Hi (the word to be boxed). Vertical motion is used to center the box on the string (lines 5 and 10). This slight vertical adjustment is equal to one-fifth of the total argument height.

28. The UNIX Environment

`troff`'s considerable power derives in part from its ability to cooperate with other UNIX system tools. `troff` is intended to be used in the context of a larger environment. For example, `troff`, in conjunction with `grap`, `pic`, `tbl` and `eqn` can take input from the file system to display user names, software performance data, entries from a database, or whatever on-line information lends itself to graphical or tabular representation. In addition, other tools usually found in the UNIX environment—such as `awk`, `lex`, `yacc`, the shell language and C—can be used to advantage with `troff`.

`troff` is able both to generate data for other tools to manipulate and to accept input dynamically from other tools.

We will demonstrate `troff`'s compatibility with UNIX system tools using some brief examples and by describing the automatic generation of tables of contents.

28.1 Communicating with the Operating System

`troff` provides two instructions for communicating with the UNIX operating system. The `.sy` instruction is used for executing system commands, and the `.tm` instruction is used for writing output to the standard error file.

28.1.1 Command Execution: The system instruction `.sy` can be used to collect run-time information that can then be read as input to the document being formatted.[1] This instruction has the general form

`.sy` *system_command*

where *system_command* is any UNIX system command (with arguments and file redirection).

For example, the UNIX System V `date` command can supplement `troff`'s predefined variables for month, day and year:

```
.sy date '+%H:%M:%S' > /tmp/\n($$
.so /tmp/\n($$
.sy rm /tmp/\n($$
```

First the `date` command is executed, and its output stored in a /tmp file (line 1), which is named for the current `troff` process (stored in the predefined numeric variable $$). This output is then included in the document using the `.so` instruction (line 2). After it is included, the /tmp file is removed (line 3).

---

1. The `.sy` instruction requires access to the `fork` and `exec` system calls. Consequently, restricted execution environments, such as attached processors, will cause `.sy` to fail.

The date can be stored in a string variable `Ti`, which can then be evaluated for the time in hours, minutes and seconds:

The current time is 22:09:41.

The above line was specified as

```
The current time is \*(Ti.
```

The string variable definition is built dynamically as follows:

```
.sy echo .ds Ti \\\\ >/tmp/\n($$
.sy date '+%H:%M:%S' >>/tmp/\n($$
.so /tmp/\n($$
.sy /bin/rm /tmp/\n($$
```

The initial call to `.sy` (line 1) invokes the UNIX system command `echo` which inserts the line `.ds Ti \` into line 1 of the /tmp file. The `date` command (line 2) inserts the current time into line 2 of the /tmp file. This information is included with the `.so` instruction (line 3), and the file is then removed (line 4) since the data is now stored in the string variable.

The four backslashes in line 1 will result in one backslash in the /tmp file. Given the rule that \\ becomes \ during copy mode, four backslashes will result in two. In addition, the UNIX system shell (the `sh` command) will interpret two backslashes as one leaving a single backslash to escape the new line in our string variable definition. Should escape sequences be passed to multiple macros, as they are in the mm macro package, a number of backslashes are necessary to "protect" a single backslash. A commonly seen example of this is the invocation of the mm macro `.PH` for specifying the page header:

```
.PH "´´´\\\\nP´"
```

This invocation results in a right-adjusted page number being printed at the top of each page.

28.1.2 Debugging with Terminal Messages: The terminal-message instruction `.tm` writes its arguments to the standard error file. This instruction has the general form

```
.tm data
```

where *data* is a string of characters written on the standard error file. Output from `.tm` appears on the controlling terminal by default though it is possible to redirect it to a file as the following UNIX system command illustrates:

```
troff file 2>tm_output | postprocessor
```

The `.tm` instruction is frequently used for trace statements, much as the `printf` function is used to instrument C code. Suppose you receive a message that a diversion is too large for a single page. Instead of executing the `.ex` instruction in a diversion trap (as we did in our discussion of the `.dt` instruction above), follow the diversion `Dv` with debugging instructions, as the following example illustrates:

```
more instructions and text
.di
.Dv
.nr Rs 1i
.nr d> \n(dn/\n(Rs
.nr p> \n(.p/\n(Rs
.tm diversion: \n(d> inches deep
.tm current page: \n(p> inches deep
```

During processing, a message will be printed reporting the depth (in inches) of both the diversion and the page.

28.2 Example of Automatic Generation of Tables of Contents

Information for building tables of contents and indices must be generated by `troff`. Page references, section numbers, incrementing figure legends and the like can only be accessed through `troff` variables though other tools can be used to sort and format these data items once they are collected.

For example, if a given section title were represented by the parameter `\\$1` in a macro definition and its section number were stored in the variable `Sc`, then the

`.tm \\n(Sc \\$1 \\n%`

instruction will write the current section number, title and page number reference to the standard error stream. This information can be collected in a file by redirecting it on the `troff` command line.

Chapter-level tables of contents primarily consist of heading titles, heading numbers and page number references. We will name our heading macro `Hd`, which will be used as follows:

```
.Hd 1 "First Level Heading"
text
.Hd 2 "Second Level Heading"
text
```

Here is the definition of macro `Hd`:

```
   .de Hd
   .sp
   .ne 8
   .if \\$1=1 \{\
5  .      ps 16
   .      vs 18
   \fB\\$2\fP
   \.      tm .head 1: \\$2 \\n%
   .      sp \}
10 .if \\$1=2 \{\
   .      ps 14
   .      vs 16
   \fB\\$2\fP
   \.      tm .head 2: \\$2 \\n%
15 .      sp 0.33 \}
   .vs 12
   .ps 10
   .ti 1.5P
   ..
```

For the sake of simplicity, we will specify the macro Hd to handle only two levels of headings: 1 and 2. Table of contents information, including the heading name and current page number, is written to the standard error (lines 8 and 14) using the .tm instruction. Note that the tag .head *n*: is prepended to the data for later identification.

Interpretation of .tm is delayed with a prepended escape character. As we discussed earlier, information that is true during copy mode is not necessarily true during the final stage of troff processing. For example, the heading number and the title cannot change during processing, but a given page number variable could. Suppose that the contents of a diversion save area unknown during copy mode become available during final evaluation of variables. Should that save area contain a two-page table, all pagination following the point where it is read back into the document would change. Because the sequence \. is interpreted as . during copy mode, interpretation of the .tm instruction is delayed until final processing occurs.

Formatting a document, say *file*, redirecting its standard error output to toc and then using the UNIX stream editor sed

```
troff file 2>toc | postprocessor
sed -n '/^\.head/p' toc >ntoc
```

creates a file ntoc in the current directory containing lines such as

```
.head 1: Introduction 1
.head 2: Further Reading 5
.head 1: Real-Time Processing 6
...
```

This format is a simple one to assist editing or proofreading. It is the programmer's responsibility to write a short program — using `sed`, `awk`, `lex` or `C` — translating this file into `troff` input, which can then be formatted.

Certain instructions when passed to the standard error by `troff` will be interpreted by the shell in unexpected ways. Variables will evaluate normally before being passed, but some `troff` instructions are meaningful to the `sh` command. The zero-width character `\&`, for example, will become an octal 022 when interpreted by `sh`. To translate these interpreted sequences back to sequences that are useful to our table of contents, a program, say `trans`, must filter the output written to the standard error file and used as follows:

```
troff file 2>toc | postprocessor
sed -n '/^\.head /p' toc | trans > ntoc
```

That is, after the standard error has been redirected to the file `toc`, all lines beginning with the tag `.head` are filtered through `trans`. The output `ntoc` will be readable text containing only table of contents information.

Keep in mind that the entire standard error has been redirected, so all error messages from `troff` have been withheld from the user. Once the table of contents information has been extracted, it is possible to send the remaining error messages to the terminal with a command such as

```
sed -n '/^[^.]/p' ntoc >&2
```

which selects all lines from the file `ntoc` that do not begin with a dot and writes them back on the standard error.

Here is the C source code for `trans`:

```
   /*   trans:
    *   filter for translating undesired octals
    */

5  #include <stdio.h>
   #include <ctype.h>

   main()
   {
10     int c;
       while ((c = getchar()) != EOF)
            if (isascii(c) &&
                (isprint(c) ||
                 c == '\n' || c == '\t' || c == ' '))
15               putchar(c);
       /* backslash-ampersand */
            else if (c == '\022')
                    printf("\134\046");
       /* backslash-e */
20          else if (c == '\026')
                    printf("\134e");
       /* backslash-space*/
            else if (c == '\027')
                    printf("\134 ");
25     /* backslash-hyphen */
            else if (c == '\215')
                    printf("\055");
       /* backslash-backward quote */
            else if (c == '\222')
30                  printf("\140");
       /* backslash-forward quote */
            else if (c == '\224')
                    printf("\047");
            else
35                  printf("\\%03o", c);
       return(0);
   }
```

Input to `trans` that is within the range of ASCII characters (line 12) and printable (line 13) is written to the standard output (line 15). Note that new line characters (' \n'), tabs (' \t') and spaces (' ') are not printable characters according to the semantics of C language macro `isprint`.

After processing specific non-ASCII and non-printing characters (lines 16-33), all remaining characters are printed in an octal format using a field width of 3 characters (line 35). These "garbage" characters are printed on the premise that the user will want to see them before discarding them.

Note that `troff` processing for different output devices, as specified by the `troff` option −T, may result in different translations for some characters.

When all the heading entries have been gathered in the file `ntoc`, then they are ready to be manipulated by another UNIX-based program. `troff` instructions must be interleaved with the contents of `ntoc` in order to specify the typesetting characteristics of the tables of contents. Once these instructions for font, point size, indentation and so on have been inserted, the table of contents is ready to be processed by `troff`.

29. Special Characters

The following tables display characters that extend the set found on the conventional keyboard. Specifically, the first table presents the denotation for characters found on the standard fonts; the final two tables display Greek and mathematical characters found on the Special fonts.

29.1 Non-ASCII Characters and Minus on the Standard Fonts

char.	denotation	name	char.	denotation	name
'	´	close quote	fi	\(fi	fi ligature
`	`	open quote	ff	\(ff	ff ligature
′	\(fm	foot mark	fl	\(fl	fl ligature
¢	\(ct	cent sign	ffi	\(Fi	ffi ligature
—	\(em	3/4 em dash	ffl	\(Fl	ffl ligature
−	\-	current font minus	¼	\(14	one-fourth
_	\(ru	rule	½	\(12	one-half
-	\(hy	hyphen	¾	\(34	three-fourths
-	-	literal hyphen	†	\(dg	dagger
°	\(de	degree	‡	\(dd	double dagger
•	\(bu	bullet	®	\(rg	registered
□	\(sq	square	©	\(co	copyright
■	\(bx	box	TM	\(tm	trademark

Note the input `` ` ` `` and `` ´ ´ `` results in the double quote pair `` " `` and `` " ``. Correct placement and spacing for these characters are done by `troff` automatically.

29.2 Greek Characters

lower-case			upper-case		
char.	**denotation**	**name**	**char.**	**denotation**	**name**
α	\ (*a	alpha	A	\ (*A	Alpha†
β	\ (*b	beta	B	\ (*B	Beta†
γ	\ (*g	gamma	Γ	\ (*G	Gamma
δ	\ (*d	delta	Δ	\ (*D	Delta
ε	\ (*e	epsilon	E	\ (*E	Epsilon†
ζ	\ (*z	zeta	Z	\ (*Z	Zeta†
η	\ (*y	eta	H	\ (*Y	Eta†
θ	\ (*h	theta	Θ	\ (*H	Theta
ι	\ (*i	iota	I	\ (*I	Iota†
κ	\ (*k	kappa	K	\ (*K	Kappa†
λ	\ (*l	lambda	Λ	\ (*L	Lambda
μ	\ (*m	mu	M	\ (*M	Mu†
ν	\ (*n	nu	N	\ (*N	Nu†
ξ	\ (*c	xi	Ξ	\ (*C	Xi
ο	\ (*o	omicron	O	\ (*O	Omicron†
π	\ (*p	pi	Π	\ (*P	Pi
ρ	\ (*r	rho	P	\ (*R	Rho†
σ	\ (*s	sigma	Σ	\ (*S	Sigma
ς	\ (ts	terminal sigma	T	\ (*T	Tau†
τ	\ (*t	tau	Y	\ (*U	Upsilon
υ	\ (*u	upsilon	Φ	\ (*F	Phi
φ	\ (*f	phi	X	\ (*X	Chi†
χ	\ (*x	chi	Ψ	\ (*Q	Psi
ψ	\ (*q	psi	Ω	\ (*W	Omega
ω	\ (*w	omega			

Note that characters followed by a dagger (†) are mapped into upper-case English letters in the current font. For example, the input characters \ (*M and M are identical on output.

29.3 Mathematical Characters

char.	denotation	name
+	\ (pl	math plus
−	\ (mi	math minus
×	\ (mu	multiply
÷	\ (di	divide
±	\ (+−	plus-minus
∪	\ (cu	cup (union)
∩	\ (ca	cap (intersection)
∞	\ (if	infinity
⊂	\ (sb	subset of
⊃	\ (sp	superset of
⊆	\ (ib	improper subset
⊇	\ (ip	improper superset
∅	\ (es	empty set
∈	\ (mo	member of
∂	\ (pd	partial derivative
=	\ (eq	math equals
∇	\ (gr	gradient
∗	\ (**	math star
¬	\ (no	not
∝	\ (pt	proportional to
√	\ (sr	square root
	\ (rn	root en extender
≥	\ (>=	greater than or equal to
≤	\ (<=	less than or equal to
≃	\ (~=	approximately equal
≡	\ (==	identically equal
≠	\ (!=	not equal
~	\ (ap	approximates
|	\ (or	or
∫	\ (is	integral sign

29.4 Miscellaneous Characters

character	denotation	name
_	\ (ul	underrule
/	\ (sl	slash
´	\ (aa	acute accent
`	\ (ga	grave accent
|	\ (br	box vertical rule
☞	\ (rh	right hand index
☜	\ (lh	left hand index
○	\ (ci	circle
⎫	\ (rt	right top of big curly bracket
⎬	\ (rk	right center of big curly bracket
⎭	\ (rb	right bottom of big curly bracket
⎧	\ (lt	left top of big curly bracket
⎨	\ (lk	left center of big curly bracket
⎩	\ (lb	left bottom of big curly bracket
⎤	\ (rc	right ceiling (right top of big square bracket)
⎦	\ (rf	right floor (right bottom of big square bracket)
⎡	\ (lc	left ceiling (left top of big square bracket)
⎣	\ (lf	left floor (left bottom of big square bracket)
|	\ (bv	bold vertical
→	\ (->	right arrow
←	\ (<-	left arrow
↑	\ (ua	up arrow
↓	\ (da	down arrow
⌒	\ (cs	control-shift indicator
⊓	\ (vs	visible space indicator
§	\ (sc	section

30. List of Predefined Variables

Predefined numeric variables are in two classes: read-write (whose values and formats can be altered) and read-only.

30.1 Read-write Variables

variable	description
%	current page number
.R	count of numeric variables that remain available for use
.b	emboldening factor of current font
c.	input line-number in the current input file (contains the same value as the read-only .c variable)
ct	character type (set by width function)
dl	width (maximum) of last completed diversion
dn	height (vertical size) of last completed diversion
dw	current day of the week (1-7)
dy	current day of the month (1-31)
ln	output line number
mo	current month (1-12)
nl	vertical position of last printed text base-line
sb	depth of string below base line (generated by width function)
st	height of string above base line (generated by width function)
yr	last two digits of current year

Read-write variables are initialized at the start of document formatting. Their values can change during processing indirectly as a consequence of instruction use or directly as a consequence of explicit alteration (using the .nr instruction). For example, instruction .pn *n* assigns the value of *n* to the variable % following the next page break. Instruction .bd R 3 assigns the value 3 to the variable .b. As discussed earlier, use of the \w´*string*´u instruction will cause assignments of new values to the variables ct, sb and st describing respectively the character type, height above baseline and depth below baseline of *string*.

30.2 Read-only Variables

variable	description
.$	number of arguments available at the current macro level
$$	process id number for current troff (nroff process)
.A	set to 1 in troff if −a option used; always 1 in nroff
.F	*string* that is the name of the current input file
.H	available horizontal resolution in internal units
.L	current line-spacing parameter (see instruction, .ls)
.P	set to 1 if the current page is being printed; else set to 0
.T	set to 1 if −T option used; otherwise set to 0
.V	available vertical resolution in internal units
.a	post-line extra line-space last utilized using \x´N´
.c	number of lines read from current input file
.d	current vertical place in current diversion; equal to nl, if no diversion
.f	current font as numerical position
.h	text base-line high-water mark on current page or diversion
.i	current indentation
.j	current adjustment mode and type. Can be saved and later given to the .ad instruction to restore a previous mode
.k	horizontal size (without indent) of the current partially collected output line, if any, in the current environment
.l	current line length
.n	length of text portion on previous output line
.o	current page offset
.p	current page length
.s	current point size
.t	distance to the next trap
.u	in fill mode 1 and in no-fill mode = 0 (each occurrence of .fi in fill mode will increment .u by 1)
.v	current vertical line spacing
.w	width of previous character
.x	reserved version-dependent variable
.y	reserved version-dependent variable
.z	name of current diversion

Read-only variables are initialized at the start of document formatting. Their values cannot be changed by using the .nr instruction. Their values may be changed by `troff`, however, to reflect the current state of parameters.

For example, as a result of executing the `.nf` instruction, `troff` assigns 0 to the `.u` variable. And execution of `\s`n or `.ps` n leads `troff` to make a corresponding change to the value of `.s`.

30.3 Character Values in Numeric Variables

Two read-only numeric variables, `.F` and `.z`, store non-numeric values. Variable `.F` contains the name of the current input file and variable `.z` contains the name of the current diversion.

30.4 Predefined String Variable

`troff` predefines the string variable `.T` to contain the name of the current output device.

31. Miscellaneous

31.1 Margin Characters

The margin-character instruction `.mc` can be used to identify sections of text by placing an identifying mark in the right margin. This instruction has the general form

`.mc` [c] [n]

where c is the identifying margin character and n specifies its distance from the right margin. The initial value of n is one em. The default scale of n is ems.

As an illustration of the use of the margin character, consider the following example in which text that has been revised is marked with a vertical bar for the reader's attention.

> The Renaissance printer has long been assumed to have influenced the content of the books he prepared. In 1924 Walter Greg completed the first study of an author's manuscript that had passed through the hands of an Elizabethan printer. Contrasting John Harington's holograph of *Orlando Furioso* to the edition Richard Field had printed, Greg concluded that the printer had decided spelling and punctuation.

The above example was specified as

```
The Renaissance printer has long been assumed
to have influenced the content of the books
he prepared.
.mc | 4
In 1924 Walter Greg completed the first study
of an author's manuscript that had passed
through the hands of an Elizabethan printer.
.mc
Contrasting John Harington's holograph of
\fIOrlando Furioso\fP to the edition Richard
Field had printed, Greg concluded that the
printer had decided spelling and punctuation.
```

31.2 Line Numbering

Numbering lines is useful in a wide variety of documents ranging from literary texts to computer program listings. Line numbers facilitate references to specific lines of the document.

Line numbering is initiated with the `.nm` instruction, which has the general form

`.nm` $[[\pm]n]$ $[m]$ $[s]$ $[i]$

where an unsigned n specifies the number of the next line and a signed n specifies that the next line number is $n \pm$ the current line number. Argument m specifies that the line numbers are to be printed only for lines with numbers that are multiples of m. Argument s is the number of digit-width spaces that should separate the line number from the text. The final argument i specifies the number of digit-width spaces by which the numbered text is indented.

Because `.nm` only interprets numbers, individual arguments can be changed without affecting the others by using alphabetical characters as placeholders. Thus the `.nm p p p 8` instruction alters the line indentation to 8 digit spaces without changing the other parameters.

Line numbering is turned off with a `.nm` instruction without any arguments:

`.nm`

A later appearance of the

`.nm +0`

instruction causes line numbering to be resumed.

Line numbering can be suspended with the no-numbering instruction `.nn`, which has the form

`.nn` n

where n is the number of following lines for which line numbering is suspended.

Line numbering is automatically resumed after *n* lines have been printed.

As an example, consider the following text with line numbers [Lally 1987]:

O light of Troy, O Troian hope at nede that neuer failde,
What contre the so long hath kept? what cause hath so preuailde.
That after slaughters great of men, thy town thy people tierd,
With sondry paynes and daungers past, the long (so sore desierd)
5 At last we see: what chaunce vnkynd thy face before so bright
Hath made so foule alas? and why of woundes I see this sight?
He nothing hereto spake, nor me with vaine talke long delayed
But heauy from his brest he fet his depe sigh, than he said.
Flee flee thou goddess sonne (alas) thy self saue from these flames,
10 The walls ar wonne (quoth he) the Grekes of Troy pul down
the frames.

The above text was specified as

```
     .br
     .ps 6
     .ft I
     .nm 1 5 3 1
 5   .ft P
     .ps 10
     .br
     O light of Troy, O Troian hope
     at nede that neuer failde,
10   .br
     What contre the so long hath kept?
     what cause hath so preuailde.
     .br
     more text and instructions
15   .br
     The walls ar wonne (quoth he)
     the Grekes of Troy pul down
     .br
     the frames.
20   .br
     .nm
     .br
```

Line numbers are specified to print in 6-point, Italic font (lines 2-3). The `.br` instructions on lines 1 and 7 ensure that only the line numbers are printed in 6-point, Italic font.

31.3 Changing the Control Character

As discussed, lines beginning with the control characters . and ′ are interpreted as `troff` instructions. These characters can be changed by using the .cc and .c2 instructions. The .cc instruction has the form

```
.cc  c
```

where *c* is the new control character. For example, following the

```
.cc  +
```

instruction, all new instructions must begin with a +:

```
+in
```

The no-break control character is changed by using the .c2 instruction, which has the form

```
.c2  c
```

where *c* is the new no-break control character.

32. Examples

We will now show you some large examples to illustrate the power and versatility of `troff`. Specifically, we will discuss two-dimensional graphics in letterhead, page headings and headers, variable-item lists, bullet lists and creation of new characters.

32.1 Two-dimensional Graphics in Letterhead

TRANSCENDENTAL
TRANSPORTATION

a new physics of tire manufacture —————————————————

June 14, 1990

Dear Customer:

Thank you for your interest in our semi-circular tire.

Experiencing half the friction of a conventional tire, this tire represents a design breakthrough, diminishing the average automobile's fuel requirement by 40%.

Here is a table comparing its efficiency with that of our other tires:

tire	miles/gallon
circular	30.0
square	36.0
elliptical	40.0
semi-circular	42.0

Sincerely,

M. M. Yogi
President

As you can see, Transcendental Transportation has prospered with their line of innovative tires, and they are now producing their own letterhead on a laser printer. To keep the discussion of the raw document reasonably clear, we will discuss the input file in small chunks. The following shows the definition of the paragraph macro Pp:

```
.\"           Paragraph
.de Pp
.sp
.ti +3n
..
```

The next chunk defines the Transcendental Transportation letterhead:

```
     .de Lt
     .in  0.3i
     .nf
     .vs 3p
10   \D'c 0.5i'
     \D'c 0.5i'
     \D'c 0.5i'
     \D'c 0.5i'
     .ft PB
15   .ps 16p
     .vs 16p
     .sp -0.3i
     .in 1i
     \s+4T\s-4RANSCENDENTAL
20   \s+4T\s-4RANSPORTATION
     .in 0.3i
     .ll 4.5i
     .ps 10
     .vs 12
25   .ti 0.2i
     .sp 0.1i
     \f(BIa new physics of tire manufacture\ \
     \v'-2p'\D'l 2i 0'
     .ft R
30   .sp
     .fi
     .ad r
     June \n(dy, 19\n(yr
     ..
```

The \D´c 0.5i´ instruction draws a circle with a diameter of half an inch (lines 10-13). The .vs 3p instruction (line 9) specifies that the vertical distance between output lines be 3 points (about 0.05 inches) enabling the circles to be closely overlapped, in order to typeset the company logo. The company's name is set in 16-point Palatino Bold Italic characters having a vertical spacing of 16 points (lines 14-16). The company's name is vertically aligned with the logo by specifying a negative spacing of 0.3 inches (line 17). The company's name is also indented an inch (line 18) to avoid overprinting the logo. The horizontal line prints out of the side of the company's motto by specifying a negative vertical motion of 2 points (line 28).

Here is the body of the letter:

```
       .\"           Letter start
       .rs
       .sp |2i
       .Lt
40     .sp
       .ad l
       Dear Customer:
       .Pp
       Thank you for your interest in our
45     semi-circular tire.
       .sp
       .ti \n(.lu/2u-3n
       \D'a 3 0 3 0'\D'l -6 0'
       .sp 3n+2v
50     Experiencing half the friction of a conventional
       tire, this tire represents a design breakthrough,
       diminishing the average automobile's fuel
       requirement by 40%.
       .Pp
55     Here is a table comparing its efficiency with
       that of our other tires:
       .sp
       .nf
       .ta 1i 2i
60     .ft B
       ☞tire☞miles\(slgallon
       .sp
       .ft
       .ta 0.75i 2.25i
       ☞circular☞30.0
```

```
☛square☛36.0
☛elliptical☛40.0
☛semi-circular☛42.0
.sp
70 .in \n(.lu/2u
Sincerely,
.sp 4
\fBM. M. Yogi
President
```

The `.Lt` instruction (line 39) invokes the letterhead macro to print the letterhead. After the letterhead, a blank line is printed (line 40) and then the left-adjusted format is restored (line 41). Note that the right-adjusted format was used for printing the date.

The semi-circular tire (lines 46-49) is drawn using line and arc drawing instructions and arithmetic expressions. At line 48 we draw an arc — all arcs are drawn counterclockwise — then follow with a line 6 ens long, drawn from right to left. The temporary indentation (line 47) centers the figure specified to be half the line length minus half the figure width (3 ens).

The drawing completes printing at the upper right corner, so we generate a downward space equal to its depth plus 2 vertical spaces (line 49). (Vertical spaces are measured from baseline to baseline.) Had we not known the depth of the display, we would have placed it in a diversion and requested a downward spacing equal to the depth of the diversion (`dn`) plus 2 vertical spaces.

Lines 57-69 are instructions for building the table; no-fill mode (`.nf`) is used, so input and output will be the same, line-for-line. Tabs (`.ta`) specify columns and are expressed in absolute values, each measured (in inches) from the left margin.

32.2 Page Headers

Headings (titles preceding sections of a document) and headers (information printed at the top of a page) communicate important information to the reader. In this section we will expand the definition of the macro `Hd` to take advantage of this fact.

The header macro `pH`, which we will describe, prints the current first-level heading at the top of all but the first page of each first-level section. In order to pass the first-level section heading to the page header macro `pH`, it is first collected in a string variable. Each heading title is stored in the string variable `sE` in the `Hd` macro definition:

```
.de Hd
.br
.if \\$1=1 \{\
.       rn pH @#
'       bp
.       rs
'       sp 1i
\D\'l \\n(.lu 0\'
'       sp 0.3i
\fB\s(12\\$2\s0\fR
\.      tm .head 1: \\$2 \\n%
.       ds sE "\\$2
.       rn @# pH
.       sp \}
.if \\$1=2 \{\
.       br
.       ne 5
\fB\s(11\\$2\\s0\\fR
\.      tm .head 2: \\$2 \\n%
.       sp 0.75 \}
.if \\$1=3 \{\
.       br
.       ne 5
\fB\s9\\$2\\s0\\fR
\.      tm .head 3 \\$2 \\n%
.       sp 0.5 \}
..
```

Macro Hd takes arguments specifying the desired heading levels (1–n). Each first-level heading begins on a new page and prints under a full-width hair-line rule. In the case of a first-level heading (line 3), the page header macro is temporarily disabled (line 4), the current page is ejected (line 5), and a hair-line rule is printed at the top of the page (lines 6-8). The section heading title is saved in the string variable sE (line 12).

Note that instructions doing the work of the now disabled page header macro (lines 5-12) do not flush the line buffer. Page header and footer macros must not generate any line breaks; otherwise buffers containing text carried from the bottom of one page to top of the next will be flushed unpredictably.

The page header macro pH prints the current section heading title (centered) and the page number (right-adjusted) at the top of each page:

```
.de pH
.rs
'sp 1i
.tl ''\s9\fB\\*(sE'%\fP\s0'
'sp 0.5i
..
```

5

The output

On to New Topics

As I was saying, the involutions of half-remembered points, the crumbling remains of vague assertions, make for more matter of moldy musings.

was specified as

```
.Hd 1 "On to New Topics"
As I was saying, the involutions of
half-remembered points, the crumbling remains
of vague assertions, make for more matter of
moldy musings.
```

The running header on the pages following the beginning of a new section appears as follows:

On to New Topics   **246**

Note that the numeric variable % (line 4) prints as the current page number.

32.3 Variable-item Lists

Variable-item lists, commonly used for glossaries, use a word or phrase as a list tag. The following variable-item list macros accept scaled input from the user for specifying indentations of the tag and list body and establish default values to be applied to unscaled input.

We will now show you definitions of macros for specifying lists similar to the mm macros VL, LI and LE. Macro Vl begins a new list and accepts two arguments understood to be some number of ens by default. Vl also accepts scaled input, overriding ens. Macro Li specifies each new entry accepting the variable item as an argument. Macro Le ends the list.

Here is an example of a variable-item list specified using these macros:

Semi-circular Tire   The Semi-circular Tire® was the model model that
                              put Transcendental Transportation on the map. It
                              changed forever our customers' understanding of
                              tires.

All-air Tire   Unobstructed by rubber, the All-air Tire™ makes
                              you feel as if you've permanently left the well-worn
                              track.

Emperor's New Tire   Only the most discerning eye will appreciate the
                              rare manufacture of the Emperor's New Tire.™ It
                              will permanently change your experience of motor-
                              ized travel.

The preceding list is specified as follows:

```
   .Vl 24 2
   .Li "\fBSemi-circular Tire\fP"
   The Semi-circular Tire\v´-3p´\s-2\(rg\s0\v´3p´\| was
   the model model that put Transcendental
 5 Transportation on the map.
   It changed forever our customers´ understanding
   of tires.
   .Li "\fBAll-air Tire\fP"
   Unobstructed by rubber, the All-air Tire\(tm\|\|
10 makes you feel as if you've permanently left
   the well-worn track.
   .Li "\fBEmperor's New Tire\fP"
   Only the most discerning eye will appreciate
   the rare manufacture of the Emperor's New
15 Tire.\(tm\|\|
   It will permanently change your experience of
   motorized travel.
   .Le
```

The list body indentation is specified to be 24 ens, and the list item tag indentation is
specified to be 2 ens (line 1). Here is an example that illustrates calling `Vl` with
scaled arguments:

```
.Vl 1.6i 0.12i
```

The definition of Vl follows:

```
     .de Vl
     .sp
     .ds bI \\$1
     .ds iI \\$2
5    .nr Bi \\*(bIn
     .nr Ii \\*(iIn
     ..
```

The first parameter, which is mandatory (otherwise the list body and the list item tag would print in the same space) specifies the body indentation, stored in the string variable bI (line 3). The second parameter (optional) specifies the item indentation, stored in the string variable iI (line 4).

Lines 5-6 are the key to the default scaling. The contents of the string variable bI are stored in the numeric variable Bi, and the contents of the string variable iI are stored in the numeric variable Ii. Each string is appended with n, the scale indicator for ens. Because a numeric variable cannot store characters, it will interpret only the first scale indicator it encounters, in effect stripping off all additional scale indicators from the right. If the strings themselves contain scale indicators, their corresponding numeric variables will interpret them first and ignore n. Otherwise, the numeric contents of the strings will be read in ens. Note that if the user does not enter a second argument to Vl, the evaluated numeric variable \\n(Ii will be equivalent to 0n.

The definition of Li then uses the indentations supplied as arguments to the Vl macro call:

```
     .de Li
     .br
10   .hy 14
     .na
     .fi
     .ne 3
     .sp 0.5
15   .in \\n(Biu
     .ti \\n(Iiu
     .ta \\n(.iu-\\n(Iiu
     \\$1☞\c
     ..
```

The indentation for the list body is specified in line 15. The list item itself is not controlled by general indentation, being specified as temporary indentation in line 16. The argument to .ti corresponds to the user's second argument, which ultimately is stored in the numeric variable `Ii`. The first line of the list body appears on the same output line as the list item and therefore is specified with a tab. That tab setting (line 17) is equal to the current indentation. The tab character itself (line 18) appears after the parameter `\\$1`, which is holding a place for the list item text.

Note that the `\c` instruction appears in line 18. The new line following the tab on line 18 will generate a space on output. Attempting to suppress that space by terminating the line with a backslash would interfere with the end-macro instruction `..` (since it would no longer begin in the first column). The *continue* instruction `\c` is used instead; it suppresses the printing of a space until after the first text character is encountered.

The definition of `Le` is straightforward:

```
20  .de Le
    .in 0
    .sp
    ..
```

32.4 Bullet Lists

Bullet lists are used for notices, checklists or any hierarchy of related elements in which sequence is not significant. The following bullet list macros (`bL`, `lI` and `lE`) allow the user to select among two bullet styles, using boxes or circles as list item tags. These macros are similar to the mm macros `BL`, `LI` and `LE`. The bullet list macros select different styles for nested lists. Direction of indentation — either positive or negative — is also decided depending on the value of a counter.

To specify a bullet list with box-like bullets, the bullet-list macro `bL` must be called with the argument b. Here is an example of a list with box-like bullets:

Welcome to Henry Hudson Estates from A. L. Psmith

■ Protect your teeth from cracking in extremes of cold and warmth.

  □ Do not drink warm coffee or cocoa after an extended stroll on the tundra.

    □ We recommend eating cold, raw fish to slowly raise your dental temperature.

    □ Drink ice water (though it will feel warm or even hot to the palate).

  □ Avoid smiling.

■ Do not attempt to tame arctic foxes. They are not dogs.

■ Be careful of ice floe activity (a seasonal concern only).

The raw document for this list is as follows:

```
.ce 1
\fBWelcome to Henry Hudson Estates\
from A. L. Psmith\fP
.bL b
.lI
Protect your teeth from cracking in extremes
of cold and warmth.
.bL b
.lI
Do not drink warm coffee or cocoa after an
extended stroll on the tundra.
.bL b
.lI
We recommend eating cold, raw fish to slowly
raise your dental temperature.
.lI
Drink ice water (though it will feel warm or
even hot to the palate).
.lE
.lI
Avoid smiling.
.lE
.lI
Do not attempt to tame arctic foxes.
They are not dogs.
.lI
Be careful of ice floe activity (a seasonal
concern only).
.lE
```

To specify a bullet list with circular bullets, the bullet-list macro `bL` must be called with the argument `c`. Here is an example of a list with circular bullets:

- Protect your teeth from cracking in extremes of cold and warmth.
  ○ Do not drink warm coffee or cocoa after an extended stroll on the tundra.
  ○ Avoid smiling.

And here is the raw document for this list:

```
   .bL c
   .lI
   Protect your teeth from cracking in extremes
   of cold and warmth.
 5 .bL c
   .lI
   Do not drink warm coffee or cocoa after an extended
   stroll on the tundra.
   .lI
10 Avoid smiling.
   .lE
   .lE
```

We will now show you the bullet-list macro definitions. First, here is the definition of the bL macro:

```
   .de bL
   .br
   .if !\\n(@B \{\
   .      nr @B 0 1
 5 .      nr @l 4.2i
   .      nr @i 0.42i
   .      ps 10
   .      vs 12
   .      ft R
10 .      in 0
   .      ll \\n(@lu \}
   .ie \\n+(@B=1 .in \\n(@iu
   .el .in +0.25i
   .ie ^G\\$1^G^G \{\
15 .      ds Mk \(bx
   .      ds mK \(sq
   .      tm \\n(.F: bullets printing in box style
   '      br \}
   .el \{\
20 .if (^G\\$1^Gb^G) \{\
   .      ds Mk \(bx
   .      ds mK \(sq \}
   .if ^G\\$1^Gc^G \{\
   .      ds Mk \(bu
25 .      ds mK \(ci \} \}
   ..
```

The `.if` instruction (line 3) tests to see if any bullet lists are currently active indicated by the flag `\\n(@B`. If not, it sets that flag (line 4) and specifies default values such as those for line length (line 5) and indentation (line 6) stored in the variables @l and @i respectively. In the first .ie-.el instruction pair (lines 12-13), the flag @B doubles as a counter: \\n+(@B, incrementing or decrementing by 1 as specified in line 4. It is incremented before its value is used. The counter will be equal to 1 only at the primary, or non-nested, list level. That is, if bL is called to initiate the list, the indentation is set to 0.42i. Otherwise, the indentation is incremented by 0.25i starting a new nested level.

The next .ie-.el pair (lines 14-25) tests to see if the user has specified a bullet style: if no argument has been given (line 14), then the box style bullet is selected (lines 15-16), and a terminal message (.tm) is sent to the standard error (line 17). Otherwise, the user input is read (lines 20-23).

Note that the closing *if-else* delimiter \} is not given on the same line as the .tm instruction; otherwise, it would be included in the terminal message printing garbage characters on the terminal screen.

The if instructions (lines 20-25) nested in the *else* part of the .ie-.el instruction pair conduct string comparisons to read the user input. When user input is tested, unlikely characters such as control-G (^G) characters should be used for comparison delimiters reducing the possibility that the string to be tested contains the delimiter, which would corrupt the comparison.

Once the general bullet style is decided in the bL macro definition, a subset of style issues are decided in the lI macro definition: if the level counter is greater than 1 indicating a nested level, then an unfilled bullet (□ or ○) is selected; otherwise, a filled bullet (■ or •) is selected. The corresponding test appears below (lines 33-40):

```
     .de lI
     .br
     .hy 14
30   .fi
     .ne 3
     .sp 0.5
     .ie \\n(@B>1 \{\
     .        nr i1 \\w'\s4\\*(mK\s0\ \ 'u
35   .        ti -\\n(i1u
     \s4\u\\*(mK\d\s0\ \}
     .el \{\
     .        nr i2 \\w'\\*(Mk\ \ 'u
     .        ti -\\n(i2u
40   \\*(Mk\ \}
     .sp -1
     ..
```

For nested lists the temporary indentation instruction (line 35) positions the marker to the left of the current indentation. Note that the value for the temporary indentation is computed (line 34) based on the width of the list item tag and two trailing blanks. Lines 39-40 do the same for the outer-most list level. After printing a list item tag, upward vertical motion is generated (line 41) to align the first line of a list item with the corresponding tag. The local motion escape sequence \u elevates a nested list item tag slightly (line 36) to center it vertically; the escape sequence \d lowers it an equal distance after the marker has been printed.

Each call to bL increments the counter (line 12), and each call to lE decrements it (line 49). It also decrements the indentation a quarter inch (line 44) matching the quarter inch incrementation specified in bL (line 13):

```
      .de lE
      .in -0.25i
45    .ie \\n(@B=1 \{\
      .       in 0
      .       rr @B
      .       sp 0.5 \}
      .el .nr @B -1
      ..
```

Because the counter @B evaluates to 2 or greater in nested levels, calls to lE from a nested list level fail the test in line 45 suppressing execution of lines 46-48. When calls to lE are made from the outer-most level, normal indentation is resumed (line 46), the counter is removed and the flag simultaneously is unset (line 47), and a half space is generated following the list (line 48).

Note that code included in conditional instructions is indented for the sake of readability. Tabs or spaces appearing between the control character and instruction are syntactically legal. Tabs or spaces following an instruction on the same line, however, are not legal and can produce undesirable typesetting behavior.

The conditionally accepted part of an .if or .ie instruction is completely ignored if the test fails.

32.5 Creating New Characters

`troff` fonts and special characters provide a rich variety of characters. In addition, you can supplement this set by constructing new characters using existing characters and local motions. The following display, for example, includes a representation of an early English printer's ornament made only with curly brackets and horizontal motion [Lally 1987]:

THE ARGUMENTES OF
the thirteene bookes of Aeneidos,

expressed in verse.

1. AENEAS, *in the first, to* **Lyby** *land arriueth well.*

2. *The fall of* **Troy,** *and wofull dole,* ẙ *second booke doth tell.*

3. *The thyrd of wandringes speakes, and father dead, and laid full low.*

4. *In fourth Queene* **Dido** *burnes, & flames of raginge loue doth show.*

5. *The fift declareth plaies, and how the fleete with fier was cought.*

6. *The sixt doth speake of ghosts, and howe deepe* **Plutoes** *reygne was sought.*

7. *The seuenth booke,* **Aeneas** *bringes vnto his fatall land.*

8. *The eight prepareth war, and power how foes for to withstand.*

9. *The ninth of battels telles, and yet the captaine is away.*

10. **Aeneas** *greeuous wrath* **Mezentius,** *in the tenth doth slay.*

11. *The eleuenth in vnequall fight* **Camilla** *castes to ground.*

12. *The twelfth with heauenly weapons giues to* **Turnus** *mortall wound.*

13. *The thirteenth weds Æneas wife, and brings him to eternall life.*

The input for the ornament is simply a long row of right and left curly bracket pairs, each pair drawn together with one en of horizontal motion:

```
     .rs
     .sp 4
     .ps 36
     .ds{} }\h´-1n´{\h´-9p´
5    \*({}\*({}\*({}\*({}\*({}\*({}\*({}\*({}\*({}\*({}\
     \*({}\*({}\*({}\*({}\*({}\*({}\*({}\*({}\*({}\*({}\
     \*({}\*({}\*({}\*({}\*({}\*({}\*({}\*({}\*({}\*({}\
     \*({}\*({}\*({}\*({}\*({}\*({}\*({}\*({}\*({}\*({}\
     \*({}\*({}
10   .sp 2
     .ce 3
     \f2\s(22THE ARGUMENTES OF
     .sp
     the thirteene bookes of Aeneidos,
15   .sp 2
     \f3\s(11expressed in verse.
     .sp 3
     .nf
     .ps 10
20   .vs 16
     . . .
```

33. Exercises

1. Define the following terms:

    i.   vertical spacing
    ii. string variable format
    iii. internal unit
    iv. unpaddable space
    v.   diversion save area
    vi. environment
    vii. trap
    viii. font position
    ix. line buffer

2. What is the difference between page offset and line indentation? How are they related to line length.

3. Explain the restrictions on the use of unmounted fonts.

4. What is the difference between the two default control characters that are used to begin the `troff` line-oriented (stand-alone) instructions?

5. Of what use is the rename-macro instruction `.rn`? How is it related to the input-line-count trap?

6.   Given the instruction sequence

```
.ev 1
.ev 2
.ev
```

what is the current environment?

Chapter 5

Example ms Document Templates

We will now show you several ms templates for specifying three kinds of documents: letters, papers and books. To avoid remembering the instructions needed for producing documents, their format and order of appearance, it is a good idea to make templates for commonly used documents. These templates can be modified where necessary or appropriate for producing custom documents.

1. Letters

We will give templates for three different kinds of letters: an intra-company letter template and two inter-company letter templates. The first inter-company letter template is for letters to be printed on stationery preprinted with the company logo and address; the second inter-company letter template is for printing letters on plain paper.

1.1 Intra-Company Letters

The template for intra-company letters is

```
     .IM
     .po  1.0i
     .ND  "m  d,  y"
     .TL
5    title
     .AU
     sender-name
     location  dept
     room  xext
10   .LP
     .DS  L
     .sp  3
     receiver-name
     .DE
15   .sp  1
     .LP
     message ...
     .sp  2
     .ti  3.0i
20   sender-name
     .sp  3
     .nf
     Copy to
     persons getting copies
25   .sp
     Encs.
     enclosures
```

Intra-Company Letter Template

A letter produced using the above intra-company letter template has the form

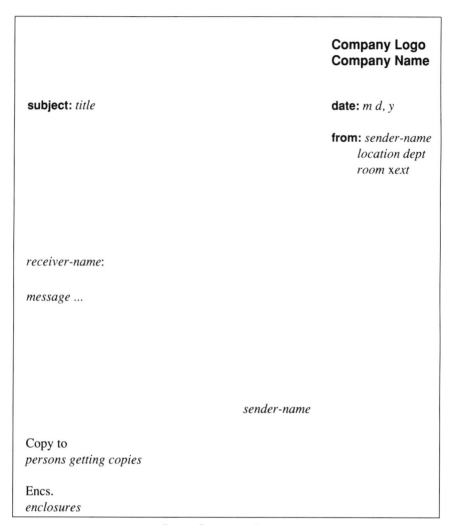

Intra-Company Letter

1.2 Inter-Company Letters On Preprinted Company Stationery

The template for printing inter-company letters on stationery preprinted with the company logo and address is

```
    .LP
    .rs
    .sp |2.25i
    .po 1.0i
5   .ND
    .tl '''m d, y'
    .DS L
    receiver-name
    receiver-address
10  .sp 3
    salutation
    .DE
    .sp 1
    .LP
15  message ...
    .sp 2
    .ti 3.0i
    Sincerely
    .sp 2
20  .ti 3.0i
    sender-name
    .sp 3
    .nf
    Copy to
25  persons getting copies
    .sp
    Encs.
    enclosures
```

Inter-Company Letter (on Preprinted Stationery) Template

A letter produced using the above inter-company letter template has the form

Company Name/Logo
Address/Phone number
(Preprinted stationery)

m d, y

receiver-name
receiver-address

salutation

message ...

Sincerely,

sender-name

Copy to
persons getting copies

Encs.
enclosures

Inter-Company Letter (on Preprinted Stationery)

1.3 Inter-Company Letter On Plain Paper

The template for inter-company letters printed on plain paper is

```
     .LP
     .rs
     .sp |2.25i
     .po 1.0i
  5  .ND
     .tl '''m d, y'
     .DS L
     receiver-name
     receiver-address
 10  .sp 3
     salutation
     .DE
     .sp 1
     .LP
 15  message ...
     .sp 2
     .ti 3.0i
     Sincerely
     .sp 2
 20  .in 3.0i
     .nf
     sender-name
     company name & street
     city, state & zipcode
 25  .in
     .sp 3
     Copy to
     persons getting copies
     .sp
 30  Encs.
     enclosures
```

Inter-Company Letter (on Plain Paper) Template

A letter produced using the above inter-company letter template has the form

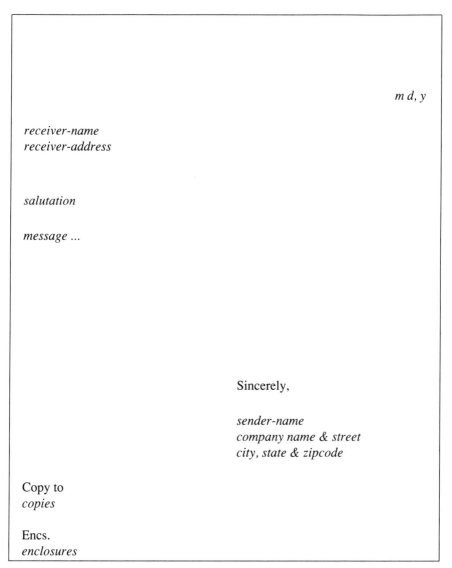

m d, y

receiver-name
receiver-address

salutation

message ...

Sincerely,

sender-name
company name & street
city, state & zipcode

Copy to
copies

Encs.
enclosures

Inter-Company Letter (on Plain Paper)

Alternatively, with some effort, a user can actually print the company logo (provided the printer has some graphic facilities) and the company address on top of a plain paper sheet just as it appears on letterhead.

2. Papers

This template works for both internal and released papers; for internal papers the first instruction must be the .TM instruction while for released papers it must be the .RP instruction:

```
   .RP
   .EQ
   eqn definitions and
   environment specification
 5 .EN
   .ND "month  day,  year"
   .TL
   paper title
   .AU room-no  extension
10 author-name
   .AI
   .MH
   .AU room-no  extension
   author-name
15 .AI
   author-affiliation and
   company-location
   .OK
   keywords
20 .AB
   abstract
   .AE
   .CS
   .NH
25 Introduction
   .LP
   text
   .NH
   Acknowledgement
30 .LP
   acknowledgment
   .bp
   .NH
   References
```

Released Paper Template

A released paper produced using this template has the form

Title of Paper
author-name

author-affiliation
company-location

ABSTRACT

Abstract ...

month day, year

Released Paper Cover Sheet

Title of Paper
author-name

author-affiliation
company-location

1. Introduction
Text ... (including other headings)

m. **Conclusions**
Conclusions ...

n. **Acknowledgment**
Acknowledgment ...

Released Paper Body

```
┌─────────────────────────────────────────────────────────────┐
│                          -page no-                            │
│                                                               │
│                                                               │
│       p. References                                           │
│                                                               │
│                                                               │
└─────────────────────────────────────────────────────────────┘
```

First Page of References

3. Books

Apart from the time spent on content of a book, an author typesetting the book by himself/herself must devote considerable effort to format the book. Fortunately, book formats are fairly standard. In this section, we will give templates for formatting different sections of a book.

A book can be partitioned into three major logical parts [Chicago Manual of Style 1982]:

1. Front or preliminary matter.
2. Chapters.
3. End or reference matter.

Few books have all these parts (e.g., many popular fiction books do not have the end matter part) and some books have additional parts.

Here are the definitions of two terms that we will be using in this section. A *recto* (right-hand) page is an odd-numbered page. A *verso* (left-hand) page is an even-numbered page.

3.1 Front Matter

The front-matter pages are organized as follows:

Organization of the Front-Matter	
Section	*Page Number*
Book half title	i*
Series Title or Blank Page	ii*
Title Page	iii*
Copyright notice, printing history, ISBN number, Library of Congress cataloging data, etc. (sometimes the publisher will insert this material for the author)	iv*
Dedication	v*
Blank Page	vi*
Table of Contents	v or vii (depending on whether or not a dedication has been included)
Foreword	recto**
Preface	recto**
Acknowledgment	recto**

3.2 Chapters

Each chapter starts on a right-hand page.

3.3 End Matter

The end-matter pages are organized as follows:

Organization of the End-Matter	
Section	*Page Number*
Appendix(es)	recto**
Glossary	recto**
Bibliography	recto**
Index	recto**

---

* Page numbers are not printed on these pages; if a book does not have a dedication, then the table of contents begins on page v.

** The page number on the starting page of these sections should be at the bottom of the page.

3.4 Running Heads

A *running head* is information printed on the top of a page; this information indicates the position in the book. The running head we use consists of the page number (*folio*) and the current book section (e.g., chapter) title. A folio is printed on the left side of a verso page and on the right side of a recto page; the folios are printed flush with the outside of a page. The section title is printed on the right side of a verso page and on the left side of recto page.

In the case of an opening page of a new section (e.g, a new chapter), the running head is omitted and the folio is printed at the bottom of the page.

3.5 Templates for Different Parts of a Book

ms does not know about book formats; that is, books are not a predefined document type. Consequently, the format of the various book components has to be specified explicitly. We will give three templates: one each for the front part of a book, for a book chapter and for the end part of a book.

Note that because of their length, the templates have been split into smaller parts.

3.5.1 Template for the Front Part of a Book:

```
   .LP
   .nr !? 1
   .af !? i
   .nr !! 2
5  .af !! i
   .ds CF
   .ds CH
   .am NP
   .ds CF
10 .nr !! +1
   .if e .if \\n%>6 \{\
   .      ds LH \\\\*(cH
   .      ds RH \\\\*(cP
   \}
15 .if o .if \\n%>6 \{\
   .      ds RH \\\\*(cH
```

```
.       ds LH \\\\*(cP \}
..
.rs
.sp 3.0i
.ce
\fB\s+5Book Title\s0\fP
.bp
.rs
.bp
.ce
\fB\s+5Book Title\s0\fP
.sp 15
.ce
\fB\s+5Author\s0\fP
.ce 2
\s+3Organization Name
City, State, Zipcode\s0
.sp 16
.ce 2
Publisher
Address
.bp
.rs
.bp
.rs
.sp 3.0i
.ce number-of-lines-in-dedication
Dedication
.bp
.rs
.nr % 6
.bp
.rs
.sp 4
.nr !? \n%
.ds CF \\n(!?
.ds cH \fB\s-1Contents\s0\fP
.ds cP \\n(!!
```

```
      .ce
      \fB\s+5Contents\s0\fR
      .sp 5
      .TS
60    center;
      l l l.
      Preface☞☞Page Number

      Acknowledgment☞☞Page Number
65
      Chapter 1☞Chapter 1 Title\a☞1
      ☞    1.    Section 1 Title☞Page Number
      ☞    2.    Section 2 Title☞Page Number
      ☞    3.    Section 3 Title☞Page Number
70         ...
      ☞    m.    Section m Title☞Page Number
           .
           .
           .
75    Chapter n☞Chapter n Title\a☞Page Number
      ☞    1.    Section 1 Title☞Page Number
      ☞    2.    Section 2 Title☞Page Number
      ☞    3.    Section 3 Title☞Page Number
           ...
80    ☞    p.    Section p Title☞Page Number

      Appendix 1☞Appendix 1 Title\a☞Page Number
           ...
      Appendix q☞Appendix q Title\a☞Page Number
85    Bibliography☞\&\a☞Page Number
      Index☞\&\a☞Page Number
      .TE
      .ds cH
      .ds cP
90    .bp
      .if e \{\
      .    rs
      .    bp \}
```

```
 95  .nr !? \n%
     .ds CF \\n(!?
     .ds cH \fB\s-1Foreword\s0\fP
     .ds cP \\n(!!
     .ce
100  \fB\s+5Foreword\s0\fR
     .sp 5
     Foreword
     .ds cH
     .ds cP
105  .bp
     .if e \{\
     .      rs
     .      bp \}
     .nr !? \n%
110  .ds CF \\n(!?
     .ds cH \fB\s-1Preface\s0\fP
     .ds cP \\n(!!
     .ce
     \fB\s+5Preface\s0\fR
115  .sp 5
     Preface
     .ds cH
     .ds cP
     .bp
120  .if e \{\
     .      rs
     .      bp \}
     .nr !? \n%
     .ds CF \\n(!?
125  .ds cH \fB\s-1Acknowledgment\s0\fP
     .ds cP \\n(!!
     .ce
     \fB\s+5Acknowledgment\s0\fR
     .sp 5
130  Acknowledgment
```

Front Part of Book Template

3.5.2 Template for a Book Chapter:

```
   .ds CF
   .ds CH
   .nr !! 0 \"have not put out any page number yet
   'br \"Get header ready for even page
5  .ds LH
   .ds RH
   .am NP
   'br\"change footer
   .ie !\\n(!! .if o  \{\
10 .     ds CF \\\\n%
   .     nr !! 1
   '     br \}
   .el  .ds CF
   .if \\n(!! \{\
15 .     ie o \{\
   '         br \"Get header ready for even page
   .         ds LH \\\\n%
   .         ds RH \fB\s-1Chapter Title\s0\fP
   '         br \}
20 .     el \{\
   '         br \"Get header ready for odd page
   .         ds LH \fB\s-1Chapter Title\s0\fP
   .         ds RH \\\\n%
   '         br \}\}
25 ..
   .br   \"make sure we're on a real page
   .if \n%>1 .if !\n(!! .if e \{\
   .     rs
   .     bp
30 '     br \}
   .LP
   .ce
   \s+5Chapter n
   .sp
35 .ce
   \fBChapter Title\fR\s0
   .sp 5
   .LP
   Chapter Contents
```

Book Chapter Template

3.5.3 Templates for a Book Appendix, Glossary, Bibliography or Index:

```
     .ds CF
     .ds CH
     .nr !! 0 \"have not put out any page number yet
     'br\" Get header ready for next page--even
5    .ds LH
     .ds RH
     .am NP
     'br\"change footer
     .ie !\\n(!! .if o  \{\
10   .      ds CF \\\\n%
     .      nr !! 1
     '      br \}
     .el .ds CF
     .if \\n(!! \{\
15   .      ie o \{\
     '         br\" Get header ready for even page
     .         ds LH \\\\n%
     .         ds RH \fB\s-1Title of End Part of a Book\s0\fP
     '         br \}
20   .      el \{\
     '         br\" Get header ready for odd page
     .         ds LH \fB\s-1Title of End Part of a Book\s0\fP
     .         ds RH \\\\n%
     '         br \}\}
25   ..
     .br  \" make sure we're on a real page
     .if \n%>1 .if !\n(!! .if e \{\
     .      rs
     .      bp
30   '      br \}
     .LP
     .ce
     \s+5\fBTitle of End Part of a Book\fR\s0
     .sp 5
35   .LP
     Contents of End Part of a Book
```

End Part of Book Template

3.6 Using the Templates to Produce the Book

These templates for different parts of a book have been designed to typeset each part separately. By default, page numbers start with 1. Consequently, each book part (except the front part and the first chapter) must be typeset with a file containing the starting page number. Suppose that the last page of chapter 1 was page 29. Then chapter 2 should be typeset with the file containing the `troff` instruction

```
.pn 30
```

Each part of the book is typeset separately using the command `book` that is defined as the *shell* script:

```
grap size header $* | pic | tbl | eqn | troff -ms -
```

`grap` input consists of the two files `header` and `size`, and the text files supplied as arguments to the command `book` (denoted by `$*`). File `size` contains the following instructions that specify the document page size:

```
.pl 9.25i
.ll 4.75i
.nr LL 4.75i
```

File `header` contains the definitions that are used in the different parts of the book.

The output of `grap` becomes the input of `pic`, the output of `pic` becomes the input of `tbl`, and so on. To use the special `eqn` characters defined in `/usr/pub/eqnchar`, the command `book` must be modified slightly, as shown below, to include this file:

```
grap ... | eqn /usr/pub/eqnchar - | ...
```

Command `book` is used as

book *page-no-file file-containing-part-of-book >book-part-file*

The output of command `book`, which is stored in the file *book-part-file*, is sent to the printing device as

command-to-send-file-to-printer book-part-file

3.7 Index Generation Macros

Generating a good book index is a difficult task; fortunately, the mechanical aspects of this task can be simplied somewhat. To generate the index, we use a macro called `iX`; this is a `troff` macro defined as

```
.de iX \"index macro
.tm \\$1 \\$2 \\$3 \\$4 \\$5 \\$6 \\$7 \\n%
..
```

Macro `iX` takes as arguments an index entry that can consist of up to seven words; calling `.iX` prints these words along with the current page number (the value of the `troff` predefined page-number variable %) on the UNIX system standard message (error) file. Calls to `iX` must be inserted in the appropriate places in the text.

Some examples of calls to this macro are

```
.iX main program
.iX program, main
.iX & operator
.iX character set, transliteration to the basic
.iX characters, replacements for unavailable
```

When formatting a book, we redirect the standard message (error) output so that we can manipulate the index later, for example,

book *page-no-file raw-book-part-file >finished-book-part-file 2>index-file*

The output of the iX macro calls is collected in *index-file*. Here is some sample output produced by the above .iX macro calls:

```
main program       2
program, main      2
& operator      2
transliteration into the basic character set    4
character set, transliteration to the basic    4
characters, replacements for unavailable    5
```

After the index has been generated, it must be sorted and duplicates eliminated (for example, with the UNIX system sort command), and references to the same item with different page numbers combined. Finally, the index must be massaged to improve its final appearance and readability.

4. Exercise

1. Write an inter-company letter template that also prints information about your company at the top of the sheet so that plain paper can be used instead of letterhead.

Appendix A

Document Formatting Commands and Macros

In this appendix, we will describe the document formatting commands available on AT&T UNIX System V and other UNIX systems, for the facilities described in this book. These descriptions are modified versions of excerpts from the corresponding descriptions in the *UNIX System Reference Manual* [AT&T UNIX 1983] unless stated otherwise. They have been modified to remove non-essential parts of the descriptions. For complete details, please refer to the *UNIX System Reference Manual*.

The commands and macros described in this chapter are summarized in the following table:

command/ macros	use
grap	draw graphs
ms	page-layout macros for use with troff and nroff
mvt	use troff to format viewgraphs specified using the mv macro package
nroff	format text for printing on a typewriter
troff	format text for printing on typesetter, laser printer or viewing on a bitmap display

1. grap (Preprocessor for Drawing Graphs)

grap is a pic preprocessor for drawing graphs. A document containing grap specifications must be processed by pic after it has been processed by grap. The grap command has the form

grap [-T*device*] *files* | pic | ...

By default, grap produces output for Autologic APS-5 typesetter (device name used is aps). The -T option can be used to specify other devices such as the Imagen Imprint 10 (e.g., -Tdi10).

Graph specifications are enclosed within the instructions .G1 and .G2. Graph data is scaled and plotted, with tick marks supplied automatically. Facilities are provided for modifying the frame, specifying labels, overriding the default ticks, changing the plotting style, defining coordinate ranges and transformations, and including data

277

from files. In addition, grap provides loop and conditional statements, and macro facilities; these facilities are similar to the corresponding facilities in pic.

2. ms (Page-Layout Macros)

The ms text formatting macros are invoked by specifying the option −ms with the nroff and troff commands:

nroff −ms [*options*] *files*
troff −ms [*options*] *files*

ms provides facilities for specifying a variety of document types. When producing 2-column output on a terminal or line printer using nroff or when reverse line motions are needed, the output should be filtered through col. Many nroff and troff instructions should not be used in conjunction with ms. However, the first four instructions given below may be used freely after initialization, and the last two may be used even before initialization:

instruction	explanation
.bp	break page (skip to a new page)
.br	break line (skip to a new line)
.sp *n*	insert *n* spacing lines
.ce *n*	center next *n* lines
.ls *n*	line spacing: *n*=1 single, *n*=2 double space
.na	no alignment of right margin

Font and point size changes using the escape sequences \f and \s are also allowed; for example, \fIword\fR will italicize *word*.

3. mvt (Format Viewgraphs and Slides)

The mvt command is used for typesetting viewgraphs and slides. It has the form

mvt *options* *files*

This command is similar to the mmt command except that it typesets its input with the mv macro package for viewgraphs and slides (instead of the mm macro package).

Options specific to mvt are given below.

-e   Invokes the equation preprocessor eqn and reads in the
            file /usr/pub/eqnchar which contains definitions of
            special eqn symbols.

-t   Invokes the table preprocessor tbl.

-p   Invokes the figure preprocessor pic.

$-g$	Invokes the graph preprocessor `grap`.
$-T$*device*	Creates output for the specified printing device; the output is sent to the device via an appropriate postprocessor.
$-z$	Invokes no output filter to process or redirect the output of `troff`. Used to send output to the terminal or a file.
$-o$*list*	Print only the pages listed.
$-$	Read input from the standard input.

Other options are passed to `troff`. Options can occur in any order, but they must be given before the input *files*. If no *options* or *files* are specified, then `mvt` prints a list of its options.

4. `nroff` (Format Text)

The `nroff` command is used to format and print text on typewriter-like devices and line printers. It has the form

`nroff` *options* [*files*]

If no *files* are specified, then `nroff` reads the standard input. An argument consisting of a minus − is taken to be the standard input.

Allowed options, which can be given in any order, are

$-o$*list*	Print only pages whose page numbers appear in the comma-separated *list* of numbers and ranges. A range *n*−*m* means pages *n* through *m*; an initial −*n* means from the beginning to page *n*; and a final *n*− means from *n* to the end.
$-n$*p*	Number first generated page *p*.
$-s$*n*	Stop every *n* pages. `nroff` will halt after every *n* pages (default is 1) to allow paper loading or changing, and will resume upon receipt of a line-feed or new-line (new-lines do not work in pipelines). When `nroff` halts between pages, the *bel* character is sent to the terminal.
$-r$*aN*	Set register *a* (which must have a one-character name) to *n*.
$-i$	Read standard input after *files* are exhausted.
$-q$	Invoke the simultaneous input-output mode of the `.rd` request.
$-z$	Print only messages generated by `.tm` (terminal message) requests.

−m*name*	Prepend to the input *files* the macro file /usr/lib/tmac/tmac.*name*.
−T*name*	Prepare output for the specified terminal.
−e	Produce equally-spaced words in adjusted lines using the full resolution of the terminal.
−h	Use output tabs during horizontal spacing to speed output and reduce output character count. Tab settings are assumed to be every eight nominal character widths.
−u*n*	Set the emboldening factor (number of character overstrikes) for the third font position (bold) to *n* or to zero if *n* is missing.

If the document contains two-column text or tables, then it should be processed with the UNIX system program col before it is printed. col performs the line overlays implied by the reverse line feeds, and by the forward and reverse half-line feeds produced by nroff and tbl in the above documents.

5. troff (Format Text)

The troff command is used for formatting documents that will be typeset and printed on a sophisticated device such as a phototypesetter or a laser printer. The troff command has the form

troff *options* [*files*]

If no *files* are specified then standard input is read. An argument consisting of a single minus − is taken to be the standard input.

Allowed options, which can be given in any order, are:

−o*list*	Print only pages whose page numbers appear in the comma-separated *list* of numbers and ranges. A range *n−m* means pages *n* through *m*; an initial *−n* means from the beginning to page *n*; and a final *n−* means from *n* to the end.
−n*p*	Number first generated page *p*.
−s*n*	Generate output that makes the printing device stop every *n* pages.
−m*n*	Prepend macro file /usr/lib/tmac/tmac.*n* to the input *files* (−ms prepends the ms macros).
−r*aN*	Set register *a* (one character name) to *n*.
−i	Read standard input after the input files are exhausted.

-q	Invoke the simultaneous input-output mode of the `.rd` request.
-z	Print only messages generated by `.tm` requests.
-a	Send a printable ASCII approximation of the results to the standard output.
-T*name*	Prepare output for typesetter *name*.

Bibliography

Anderson, M. D. 1971. *Book Indexing. Cambridge Author's and Printer's Guide*— Volume 6, The University Press, Cambridge.

AT&T UNIX 1983a. *UNIX System V User Reference Manual.* AT&T Technologies.

AT&T UNIX 1983b. *UNIX System V Programmer Reference Manual.* AT&T Technologies.

AT&T UNIX 1983c. *UNIX Programmer's Manual (Seventh Edition), Volume 2.* AT&T Bell Telephone Laboratories, published by Holt, Rinehart and Winston. Contains papers describing the document preparation facilities on the UNIX system.

Bentley, J. L. and B. W. Kernighan 1984. `grap`—A Language for Typesetting Graphs: Tutorial and User Manual. Computing Science Technical Report No. 114, AT&T Bell Laboratories.

Bentley, J. L. and B. W. Kernighan 1986. `grap`—A Language for Typesetting Graphs. *CACM*, v29, no. 8, pp. 782-792.

Berg, N. E. 1978. *Electronic Composition.* Graphics Arts Technical Foundation, Pittsburgh, 1978.

Bourne, S. R. 1982. *The UNIX System.* Addison-Wesley. A detailed and comprehensive guide to the UNIX operating system and the facilities available on it. One chapter is devoted to the document preparation facilities on the UNIX system.

Business Week 1984. Compugraphic: Trying to Move Typesetting From the Shop to the Office (in the July 2 issue).

Cherry, L. 1981. Computer Aids for Writers. *Proceedings of the ACM SIGPLAN SIGOA Symposium on Text Manipulation* (June), pp. 62-67, Portland, Oregon.

Cherry, L. 1982. Writing Tools. Special Issue of the *IEEE Transactions on Communications* on *Communications in the Automated Office*, pp. 100-105, vCOM-30, no. 1 (January).

Chicago Manual of Style 1982. *A Manual of Style* (Thirteenth Edition, Revised). The University of Chicago Press. This excellent book deals with all aspects of writing and making a book. The first part deals with the fundamentals of book making: the logical organization of a book, preparation of the manuscript and the legal aspects of publishing such as copyrights and getting permission to republish copyrighted material. Part two deals with writing style; items covered include punctuation, spelling, tables, mathematical equations, footnotes, bibliographies and indexes. Part three deals with book design and typography, and contains a glossary of technical terms.

Christian, K. 1983. *The UNIX Operating System*. John Wiley.

Corbett, C. and I. H. Witten 1982. On the Inclusion and Placement of Documentation Graphics in Computer Typesetting. *Computer Journal*, v25, no. 2, pp. 272-3.

DWB 1986a. *UNIX System V DOCUMENTER'S WORKBENCH Software Release 2.0: User's Guide*. Select Code 310-004, AT&T.

DWB 1986b. *UNIX System DOCUMENTER'S WORKBENCH Software Release 2.0: Technical Discussion and Reference Manual*. Select Code 310-005, AT&T.

Frase, L. T. 1983. The UNIX Writer's Workbench Software: Philosophy. *BSTJ*, pp. 1883-1890, v62, no. 6, part 3, July-August 1983.

Freund, J. E. 1981. *Statistics: A First Course*. Prentice-Hall.

Furuta, R., J. Scofield, A. Shaw 1982. Document Formatting Systems: Survey, Concepts and Issues. *ACM Computing Surveys*, v14, no. 3 (September), pp. 417-472. Extensive survey of document formatting systems. Characterizes document formatting, describes and evaluates many document formatting systems, for example, UNIX document formatting facilities, $T_E X$ and SCRIBE.

Gehani, N. H. and W. D. Roome 1984. Concurrent C. AT&T Bell Laboratories.

Gehani, Narain 1989. *C: An Advanced Introduction (ANSI C Edition)*. Computer Science Press.

Gehani, Narain 1987. *Document Formatting and Typesetting on the UNIX System (2nd Ed.)*. Silicon Press, 25 Beverly Road, Summit, NJ 07901. Describes the basic formatting concepts and discusses in detail mm (for specifying the document format), tbl (for specifying tables), pic (for drawing graphs) and eqn (for specifying equations). The formatter troff and the Writer's Workbench facilities are also delved into. The book contains a glossary of typesetting terms and several example templates for specifying a variety of documents.

Gingrich, P. S. 1983. The UNIX Writer's Workbench Software: Results of a Field Study. *BSTJ*, pp. 1909-1921, v62, no. 6, part 3, July-August 1983.

Goren, C. H. 1984. *Goren's Modern Backgammon Complete*. Cornerstone Library.

Kernighan, B. W. 1978. A troff Tutorial. In *UNIX Programmer's Manual (Seventh Edition, Volume 2)* [AT&T UNIX 1983c]. A must for those who insist on programming in troff.

Kernighan, B. W. 1981. `pic`—A Crude Graphics Language for Typesetting: User Manual. Computing Science Technical Report no. 85, AT&T Bell Laboratories.

Kernighan, B. W. 1982a. `pic`—A Language for Typesetting Graphics. *Software— Practice and Experience*, v12, no. 1 (January), pp. 1-21.

Kernighan, B. W. 1982b. A Typesetter-Independent `troff`. Computing Science Technical Report no. 97, AT&T Bell Laboratories. The original `troff` was designed for the CAT typesetter. Early `troff` "compilers" produced output for the CAT, that is, device-dependent code. Kernighan has modified `troff` to improve it and changed the `troff` compiler to make it produce device-independent output (this book is based on the new `troff`). Using appropriate postprocessors, the output of the device-independent `troff` can be printed or viewed on a variety of devices.

Kernighan, B. W. 1984. `pic`—A Graphics Language for Typesetting: Revised User Manual. Computing Science Technical Report No. 116, AT&T Bell Laboratories. This manual describes the latest version of `pic`. Unlike the previous version [Kernighan 1982a], the new version of `pic` provides facilities such as trigonometric functions, a random number generator, loop and conditional statements; text strings are now treated as first class citizens.

Kernighan, B. W. and L. L. Cherry 1975. A System for Typesetting Mathematics. *CACM*, v18, no. 3 (March), pp. 151-157. Also in *UNIX Programmer's Manual (Seventh Edition, Volume 2)* [AT&T UNIX 1983c]. Describes the eqn preprocessor for typesetting equations—an important contribution that has had significant impact on mathematical typesetting.

Kernighan, B. W. and M. E. Lesk 1982. UNIX Document Preparation. In *Document Preparation Systems* [Nievergelt, Coray, Nicoud and Shaw 1982].

Kernighan, B. W., M. E. Lesk, and J. F. Ossanna, Jr. 1978. UNIX Time-Sharing System: Document Preparation. *Bell System Technical Journal*, Part 2, v57, no. 6 (July-August), pp. 2115-2135.

Kernighan, B. W. and R. Pike 1984. *The UNIX Programming Environment*. Prentice-Hall. One chapter is devoted to the document formatting facilities on the UNIX system.

Kernighan, B. W. 1986. Recent Work in UNIX Document Preparation Tools. *Proceedings of EUUG Conference*, Copenhagen, Denmark.

Kimble, G. A. 1978. *How to Use (and Misuse) Statistics*. Prentice-Hall.

Knuth, D. E. 1979. T_EX *and METAFONT: New Directions in Typesetting*. Digital Press and American Mathematical Society.

Knuth, D. E. 1984. *The $T_EX$book*. Addison-Wesley.

Lally, S. 1987. *The Aeneid of Thomas Phaer and Thomas Twyne: A Critical Edition Introducing Renaissance Metrical Typography*. Garland Publishing.

Lear, E. 1964. *The Nonsense Books of Edward Lear*. The New American Library.

Lesk, M. E. 1976. tbl—A Program To Format Tables. Computing Science Technical Report no. 49, AT&T Bell Laboratories. Also in *UNIX Programmer's Manual (Seventh Edition, Volume 2)* [AT&T UNIX 1983c].

Lesk, M. E. 1978a. Typing Documents on the UNIX System—Using the -ms Macros with troff and nroff. In *UNIX Programmer's Manual (Seventh Edition, Volume 2)* [AT&T UNIX 1983c]. Contains a description of the ms macros.

Lesk, M. E. 1978b. Some Applications of Inverted Indices on the UNIX system. Computing Science Technical Report no. 69, AT&T Bell Laboratories. Contains a description of refer, the troff preprocessor that finds and inserts literature references in documents.

Lesk, M. E. and, B. W. Kernighan 1977. Computer Typesetting of Technical Journals on UNIX. *AFIPS National Comput. Conf. Expo. Proceedings*, v46, pp.879-888. Computer typesetting is faster and more cost effective than typewriter composition. This assertion is supported by experimental results.

Lowenstein, D. 1979. *Graphs*. Franklin Watts.

Macdonald, A. H., L. T. Frase, P. S. Gingrich and S. A. Keenan 1982. The Writer's Workbench: Computer Aids for Text Analysis. *IEEE Transactions on Communication*, v30, no. 1 (January), part 1, pp. 105-110.

Macdonald, A. H. 1983. The UNIX Writer's Workbench Software: Rationale and Design. *BSTJ*, v62, no. 6 (July-August), part 3, pp. 1891-1908.

Marx, G. 1983. *The Groucho Marx Letters*. Sphere Books Limited, London.

McIlroy, M. D. 1982. Development of a Spelling List. *IEEE Transactions on Communication*, v30, no. 1 (January), part 1, pp. 91-99.

Milton, John 1667. *Paradise Lost*, edited by Alastair Fowler. Longman, London, 1971.

Morison, S. 1967. *First Principles of Typography. Cambridge Author's and Printer's Guide* (Volume 1). Cambridge University Press.

Meyers, C. H. 1970. *Handbook of Basic Graphs: A Modern Approach*. Dickenson Publishing Co.

Nievergelt, J., G. Coray, J. D. Nicoud, and A. C. Shaw (Editors) 1982. *Document Preparation Systems: A Collection of Survey Articles*. North-Holland, Amsterdam, Netherlands, 1982.

Ossanna, Jr., J. F. 1977. `nroff/troff` User's Manual. Computing Science Technical Report no. 54, AT&T Bell Laboratories. Also in *UNIX Programmer's Manual (Seventh Edition, Volume 2)* [AT&T UNIX 1983].

Poe, Edgar Allan, 1975. "The Cask of Amontillado" in *Complete Tales and Poems of Edgar Allan Poe*. Random House.

Reid, B. K. 1980. Scribe: A High-Level Approach to Computer Document Formatting. *Seventh Symposium on Principles of Programming Languages* (January), Las Vegas. Scribe is a high-level document formatting tool which provides the user with standard types of documents. Detailed information about these documents is contained in a database freeing the user from specifying low-level details such as margins, indenting, fonts and spacing.

Ritchie, D. M. 1979. The Evolution of the UNIX Time-Sharing System. *Proceedings of the Symposium on Language Design and Programming Methodology*, pp. 25-35, *Lecture Notes in Computer Science*, no. 79, Springer-Verlag.

Seybold, J. W. 1979. *Fundamentals of Modern Photocomposition*. Seybold Publications Inc, Box 644, Media, Pennsylvania.

Scrocca (L'Hommedieu), C. 1978. New Graphic Symbols for `eqn` and `neqn`. AT&T Bell Laboratories.

Selby, P. H. 1979. *Using Graphs and Tables*. John Wiley.

Snyder, G. 1982. *Riprap & Cold Mountain Poems*. Grey Fox Press.

Spivak, M. 1982. *Joy of T$_E$X: A Gourmet Guide to Typesetting Technical Text by Computer*. American Mathematical Society.

Tufte, E. R. 1983. *The Visual Display of Quantitative Information*. Graphics Press, Chesire, Connecticut.

van Leunen, M. 1978. *A Handbook for Scholars*. Knopf, New York., N.Y. A guide to scholarly writing; discusses document format and style, and how to write citations, references, footnotes and bibliographies, etc.

Van Uchelen, R. 1980. *Word Processing: A Guide to Typography, Taste, and In-House Graphics*. Van Nostrand Reinhold.

Van Wyk, C. J. 1981a. A Graphics Typesetting Language. *Proceedings of the ACM SIGPLAN SIGOA Symposium on Text Manipulation* (June), pp. 99-107, Portland, Oregon. Describes `ideal` which, like `pic` is a `troff` preprocessor for specifying figures in documents; also see [Van Wyk 1981b].

Van Wyk, C. J. 1981b. `ideal` User's Manual. Computing Science Technical Report no. 103, AT&T Bell Laboratories.

Webster's Dictionary 1977. *Webster's New Collegiate Dictionary.* G. & C. Merriam Company, Springfield, MA.

Wiseman, N. E., C. I. O. Campbell and J. Harradine 1978. On Making Graphics Quality Output by Computer. *Computer Journal*, v21, no. 1 (Feb.), pp. 2-6.

WWB 1982. *UNIX Writer's Workbench Software—User's Manual.* AT&T Bell Laboratories. Detailed explanation of the analysis done by the Writer's Workbench programs, a tutorial introduction to using these programs, and a reference manual for the Writer's Workbench programs.

Index

289

A

M